高等院校"十三五"规划教材

营销英语

主 编 张 竞 张 强 李 妍
副主编 杨雯惠

哈尔滨工业大学出版社

内容简介

本书涵盖营销基本知识、市场调查、营销战略、4P 理论、公共关系、广告、人员推销、网络营销、营销管理等内容。每章配有基本单词释义、课外阅读,以便学生和教师系统地学习和巩固相关知识。本书旨在帮助学生掌握营销专业基础英语,培养其在今后工作中运用英语进行实际营销活动的能力。本书既注重理论创新,又很好地将理论知识与实践运用紧密地结合起来,全书深入浅出,具有较强的可读性。

本书既可作为普通高等院校经济管理专业的教材和教辅用书,也可用作培训及自学参考书。

图书在版编目(CIP)数据

营销英语/张竞,张强,李妍主编.—哈尔滨:哈尔滨工业大学出版社,2016.5
ISBN 978 - 7 - 5603 - 6050 - 8

Ⅰ.①营⋯ Ⅱ.张⋯ ②张⋯ ③李⋯ Ⅲ.①市场营销学-英语-教材 Ⅳ.①H31

中国版本图书馆 CIP 数据核字(2016)第 119766 号

策划编辑	杨秀华
责任编辑	丁桂焱
封面设计	刘长友
出版发行	哈尔滨工业大学出版社
社　　址	哈尔滨市南岗区复华四道街 10 号　邮编 150006
传　　真	0451-86414749
网　　址	http://hitpress.hit.edu.cn
印　　刷	哈尔滨工业大学印刷厂
开　　本	787mm×960mm　1/16　印张 14.75　字数 278 千字
版　　次	2016 年 6 月第 1 版　2016 年 6 月第 1 次印刷
书　　号	ISBN 978 - 7 - 5603 - 6050 - 8
定　　价	36.00 元

(如因印装质量问题影响阅读,我社负责调换)

前　言

随着全球经济一体化进程的不断深入,社会对"外语+专业"复合实用型人才的需求不断上升。跨国经营对营销人才,尤其是懂双语的国际营销人才的需求十分旺盛。提高课堂专业英语教学质量,优化学生知识结构,提升学生专业外语应用能力,对于培养国际型专业人才具有重要意义。

本书面向高校营销专业学生,内容涵盖营销基本知识、市场调查、营销战略、4P 理论、公共关系、广告、人员推销、网络营销、营销管理等市场营销学知识。本书旨在帮助学生掌握营销专业基础英语,培养运用英语进行实际营销活动的能力。本书参考了大量的文献资料,既注重理论创新,又很好地将理论知识与实践紧密结合,全书深入浅出,具有较强的可读性。本书既可作为普通高等院校经济管理专业的教材和教辅用书,又可用作培训及自学参考书。每章编排了单词释义和课外阅读,以便学生和教师系统地学习和巩固每一章的知识。

本书由张竞、张强、李妍担任主编,杨雯惠担任副主编。具体编写分工如下:张竞(北华大学)编写第 1～4 章;李妍(哈尔滨理工大学)编写第 5～8 章;张强(北华大学)编写第 9～12 章;杨雯惠(北华大学)编写第 13～14 章。《营销英语》在编写和出版过程中,得到哈尔滨工业大学出版社的大力支持和帮助,在此表示衷心的感谢!

本书在编写过程中,吸收和借鉴了国内外市场营销研究及其应用的基本理论和研究成果,在此对相关人员表示感谢。由于编者水平有限,书中难免存在不足之处,敬请读者批评指正。

编　者

2016 年 1 月

Contents

Chapter 1: Introduction of Marketing 1

    Part One: Text 1
    Part Two: Questions 10
    Part Three: Words and Phrases 10
    Part Four: Further Reading 11

Chapter 2: Nature of Marketing 13

    Part One: Text 13
    Part Two: Questions 25
    Part Three: Words and Phrases 25
    Part Four: Further Reading 25

Chapter 3: Marketing Environment 27

    Part One: Text 27
    Part Two: Questions 44
    Part Three: Words and Phrases 45
    Part Four: Further Reading 45

Chapter 4: Buyer Behavior and Consumer Decision Making Process 47

    Part One: Text 47
    Part Two: Questions 60
    Part Three: Words and Phrases 60
    Part Four: Further Reading 61

Chapter 5: Marketing Research 63

    Part One: Text 63

    Part Two: Questions ·· 81
    Part Three: Words and Phrases ·· 81
    Part Four: Further Reading ·· 82

Chapter 6: Market Segmentation ·· 83

    Part One: Text ·· 83
    Part Two: Questions ·· 93
    Part Three: Words and Phrases ·· 93
    Part Four: Further Reading ·· 94

Chapter 7: New Product Development ··· 96

    Part One: Text ·· 96
    Part Two: Questions ·· 106
    Part Three: Words and Phrases ·· 106
    Part Four: Further Reading ·· 107

Chapter 8: Managing the Marketing Mix ···································· 109

    Part One: Text ·· 109
    Part Two: Questions ·· 122
    Part Three: Words and Phrases ·· 123
    Part Four: Further Reading ·· 123

Chapter 9: Pricing ·· 126

    Part One: Text ·· 126
    Part Two: Questions ·· 141
    Part Three: Words and Phrases ·· 141
    Part Four: Further Reading ·· 141

Chapter 10: Distribution Channel Management ························ 145

    Part One: Text ·· 145
    Part Two: Questions ·· 164
    Part Three: Words and Phrases ·· 165
    Part Four: Further Reading ·· 165

Chapter 11: Promotion Mix 167

Part One: Text 167
Part Two: Questions 175
Part Three: Words and Phrases 175
Part Four: Further Reading 176

Chapter 12: The Marketing of Services 178

Part One: Text 178
Part Two: Questions 187
Part Three: Words and Phrases 187
Part Four: Further Reading 188

Chapter 13: E-Marketing 191

Part One: Text 191
Part Two: Questions 203
Part Three: Words and Phrases 203
Part Four: Further Reading 204

Chapter 14: International Marketing 207

Part One: Text 207
Part Two: Questions 224
Part Three: Words and Phrases 224
Part Four: Further Reading 225

References 227

Chapter 1: Introduction of Marketing

Part One: Text

Most of the people define marketing as selling or advertising. It is true that these are parts of the marketing. But marketing is much more than advertising and selling. In fact marketing comprises of a number of activities which are interlinked and the decision in one area affects the decision in other areas.

Marketing is everywhere and it affects our day-to-day life in every possible manner. Formally or informally people and organizations engage in a vast number of activities that could be called as marketing. Good marketing is not accident, but a result of careful planning and execution. It is both an art and science. Let's discuss various concepts and issues in marketing.

1.1 Definition

Marketing management is the art and science of choosing target markets and getting, keeping and growing customers through creating, delivering and communicating superior customer value.

In short "Meeting needs profitably". Marketing has been defined by different authors in different ways which can be broadly classified into three:

1.1.1 Product-oriented definition

The emphasis is given on products. In 1985 AMA redefined marketing as "Marketing is the process of planning and executing the conception, pricing, promotion and distribution of ideas, goods and services to create exchanges that satisfy individual and organizational goals."

1.1.2 Customer-oriented definition

Here the emphasis is on customers and their satisfaction. In the words of Philip Kotler: "Marketing is the human activity directed at satisfying needs and wants through an exchange process."

1.1.3 Value-oriented definition

In 2004 the American Marketing Association defined "Marketing is an organizational function and a set of processes for creating, communicating and delivering value to customers and for managing customer relationships in ways that benefit the organization and its stakeholders."

To illustrate the number of activities that are included in marketing, think about all the bicycles being peddled with varying degree of energy by bicycle riders in India. Most bicycles are intended to do the same thing—get the rider from one place to another. But a bicyclist can choose from a wide assortment of models. They are designed in different sizes, with different frames for men and women and with or without gears. Trekking cycles have large knobby tyres, and the tyres of racing cycles are narrow. Kids want more wheels to make balancing easier; clowns want only one wheel, to make balancing more interesting.

The variety of styles and features complicates the production and sale of bicycles. The following list shows some of the many things a firm like Atlas Cycles or Hero Cycles should do before and after it decides to produce a bicycle.

First, analyze the needs of people who might buy a bicycle and decide if they want more or different models.

Second, predict what types of bicycles like handle bar styles, type of wheels, weights and materials different customers will want and decide to which firm will try to satisfy their need.

Third, estimate how many of these people will be riding bicycles over the next several years and how many bicycles they will buy.

Fourth, predict exactly when these people will want to buy bicycles.

Fifth, determine where in the India these bicyclists will be and how to get the company's bicycles to them.

Sixth, estimate the price they are willing to pay for their bicycles and if the firm can make a profit selling at that price.

Seventh, decide which kinds of promotion should be used to tell potential customers about the company's bicycles.

Eighth, estimate how many competing companies will be making bicycles, how many bicycles they will produce, what kind, and at what prices.

Ninth, figure out how to provide warranty service if a customer has a problem after buying the bicycle.

The above activities are not the part of production—actually making goods or performing services. Rather, they are part of a larger process—called marketing—that provide needed direction for production and helps make sure that the right goods and services are produced and find their way to consumers. In order to understand the concept of marketing, firstly you must understand what is "market".

1.2 Market

The term "market" originates from the Latin word "Marcatus" which means "a place where business is conducted". A layman regards market as a place where buyers and sellers personally interact and finalist deals.

According to Perreault and McCarthy, market is defined as a group of potential customers with similar needs or wants who are willing to exchange something of value with sellers offering various goods and/or services to satisfy those needs or wants. Of course, some negotiation will be needed. This can be done face-to-face at some physical location (for example, a farmer's market). Or it can be done indirectly through a complex network that links middlemen, buyers and sellers living far apart. Depending upon what is involved, there are different types of markets which deal with products and/or services such as:

1.2.1 Consumer market

In this market the consumers obtain what they need or want for their personal or family consumption. This market can be subdivided into two parts—fast moving consumer goods market from where the consumers buy the products like toothpaste, biscuits, facial cream etc. and services like internet, transportation etc; another is durables market from where the consumers buy the products of longer life like motorcycles, cars, washing machines, etc. And services like insurance cover, fixed deposits in the banks and non-banking financial companies, etc.

1.2.2　Industrial/Business market

In this market, the industrial or business buyers purchase products like raw materials (iron ore, coke, crude oil, etc.), components (wind-screen, tyres, picture tubes, micro-processors, etc.), finished products (packaging machine, generators, etc.), office supplies (computers, pens, paper, etc.) and maintenance and repair items (grease, lubricating oil, broom, etc.). Apart from products, now-a-days due to outsourcing the industrial buyers also require a number of services like accounting services, security services, advertising, legal services, etc. from the providers of these services.

1.2.3　Government market

In most of the countries central/federal, state or local governing bodies are the largest buyers requiring a number of products and services. Government is also the biggest provider of services to the people, especially in a developing country like India where army, railways, post and telegraph, etc. services are provided by the Central Government and State Govt. and local municipality provides services like roadways, police, sewage, disposal, water supply respectively.

1.2.4　Global market

The world is rapidly moving towards border less society thanks to information revolution and the efforts of WTO to lower the tariff and non-tariff barriers. The product manufacturers and service providers are moving in different countries to sustain and increase their sales and profits. Although the global companies from the developed countries are more in number, the companies from developing countries are also making their presence felt in foreign countries. The ultimate winners are the consumers who are getting world class quality products and services at an affordable price.

1.2.5　Non profit market

On one hand the society is making progress in every field, on the other hand the number of problems that it is facing are also increasing. Most of the people don't care for these problems due to variety of reasons such as-lack of awareness, lack of time, selfish nature, etc. So in order to fill the void, the non profit organizations came into being. These organizations support a particular issue or a charity and create awareness among the general public towards these issues and try to obtain financial and non-financial support. For example, there are NGOs who are working towards the conservation of flora and fauna, Narmada Bachao Andolan, Chipko Andolan (to conserve the trees in Himalayan region), etc. These non profit organizations basically need monetary support from the individuals, institutions and governments to promote a cause or a charity like old age home, free dispensary, free education, home for destitutes, etc.

These are the major markets which exist in country. These can also be different markets which deal in a particular product or service such as grain market, vegetable and fruit market, fish market, political market, etc. which serve a specific need or want of the consumers and marketers.

The concept of exchange leads to the concept of market. A market consists of all the potential customers sharing a particular need or want who might be willing and able to engage in exchange to satisfy that need or want. The size of market depends upon the number of persons who exhibit the need, have resources that interest others, and are willing to offer these resources in exchange for what they want.

Originally the term market stood for the place where buyers and sellers gathered to exchange their goods, such as a village square. Economists use the term market to refer to a collection of buyers and sellers who transact over a particular product or product class, the housing market, the grain market, and so on. Marketers, however, see the sellers as constituting the industry and the buyers as constituting the market.

Business people use the term markets colloquially to cover various groupings of customers. They talk need markets, product markets, demographic markets (such as the youth market), and geographic markets (such as the Indian market). The concept is extended to cover non-customer groupings as well, such as voter markets, labor markets, and donor.

1.3 Who does marketing

The short answer to the question of who does marketing is "everybody"! But that answer is a bit glib and not too useful. Let's take a moment and consider how different types of organizations engage in marketing.

1.3.1 For profit companies

The obvious answer to the question, "Who does marketing?" is for profit companies like McDonald's, Procter&Gamble (the makers of Tide detergent and Crest toothpaste, P&G for short), and Wal-Mart. For example, McDonald's creates a new breakfast chicken sandwich for $1.99 (the offering), launches a television campaign (communicating), makes the sandwiches available on certain dates (delivering), and then sells them in its stores (exchanging). When Procter&Gamble creates new Crest tartar control toothpaste, it launches a direct mail campaign in which it sends information and samples to dentists to offer to their patients. P&G then sells the toothpaste through retailers like Wal-Mart, which has a panel of consumers sample the product and provide feedback through an online community. These are all examples of marketing activities.

For profit companies can be defined by the nature of their customers. A B2C (business-to-consumer) company like P&G sells products to be used by consumers like you, while a B2B (business-to-business) company sells products to be used within another company's operations, as well as by government agencies and entities. To be sure, P&G sells toothpaste to other companies like Wal-Mart (and probably to the army and prisons and other government agencies), but the end user is an individual person.

Other ways to categorize companies that engage in marketing is by the functions they fulfill. P&G is a manufacturer, Wal-Mart is a retailer, and Grocery Supply Company is a wholesaler of grocery items and buys from companies like P&G in order to sell to small convenience store chains. Though they have different functions, all these types of for profit companies engage in marketing activities. Wal-Mart, for example, advertises to consumers. Grocery Supply Company salespeople will call on convenience store owners and take orders, as well as build in-store displays. P&G might help Wal-Mart or Grocery Supply Company with templates for advertising or special cartons to use in an in-store display, but all the companies are using marketing to help sell P&G's toothpaste.

Similarly, all the companies engage in dialogs with their customers in order to understand what to sell. For Wal-Mart and Grocery Supply, the dialog may result in changing what they buy and sell; for P&G, such customer feedback may yield a new product or a change in pricing strategy.

1.3.2 Non profit organizations

Non profit organizations also engage in marketing. When the American Heart Association(AHA) created a heart-healthy diet for people with high blood pressure, it bound the diet into a small book, along with access to a special web site that people can use to plan their meals and record their health-related activities. The AHA then sent copies of the diet to doctors to give to patients. When does an exchange take place, you might be wondering? And what does the AHA get out of the transaction?

From a monetary standpoint, the AHA does not directly benefit. Nonetheless, the organization is meeting its mission, or purpose, of getting people to live heart-healthy lives and considers the campaign a success when doctors give the books to their patients. The point is that the AHA is engaged in the marketing activities of creating, communicating, delivering, and exchanging. This won't involve the same kind of exchange as a for profit company, but it is marketing. When a non profit organization engages in marketing activities, this is called non profit marketing. Some schools offer specific courses in non profit marketing, and many marketing majors begin their careers with non profit organizations.

Government entities also engage in marketing activities. For example, when the U.S. Army advertises to parents of prospective recruits, sends brochures to high schools, or brings a Bradley Fighting Vehicle to a state fair, the army is engaging in marketing. The U.S. Army also listens to its constituencies, as evidenced by recent research aimed at understanding how to serve military families more effectively. One result was advertising aimed at parents and improving their response to their children's interest in joining the army; another was a program aimed at encouraging spouses of military personnel to access counseling services when their spouse is serving overseas.

Similarly, the Environmental Protection Agency (EPA) runs a number of advertising campaigns designed to promote environmentally friendly activities. One such campaign promoted the responsible disposal of motor oil instead of simply pouring it on the ground or into a storm sewer.

There is a difference between these two types of activities. When the army is promoting the benefits of enlisting, it hopes young men and women will join the army. By contrast, when the EPA runs commercials about how to properly dispose of motor oil, it hopes to change people's attitudes and behaviors so that social change occurs. Marketing conducted in an effort to achieve certain social objectives can be done by government agencies, non profit institutions, religious organizations, and others and is called social marketing. Convincing people that global warming is a real threat via advertisements and commercials is social marketing, as is the example regarding the EPA's campaign to promote responsible disposal of motor oil.

1.3.3 Individuals

If you create a resume, are you using marketing to communicate the value you have to offer prospective employers? If you sell yourself in an interview, is that marketing? When you work for a wage, you are delivering value in exchange for pay. Is this marketing, too?

Some people argue that these are not marketing activities and that individuals do not necessarily engage in marketing (Some people also argue that social marketing really isn't marketing either). Can individuals market themselves and their ideas?

In some respects, the question is a rhetorical one, designed for academics to argue about in class. Our point is that in the end, it may not matter. If, as a result of completing this book, you can learn how to more effectively create value, communicate and deliver that value to the receiver, and receive something in exchange, then we've achieved our purpose.

1.4 Why study marketing

1.4.1 Marketing enables profitable transactions to occur

Products don't, contrary to popular belief, sell themselves. Generally, the "build it and they will come" philosophy doesn't work. Good marketing educates customers so that they can find the products they want, make better choices about those products, and extract the most value from them. In this way, marketing helps facilitate exchanges between buyers and sellers for the mutual benefit of both parties. Likewise, good social marketing provides people with information and helps them make healthier decisions for themselves and for others.

Of course, all business students should understand all functional areas of the firm, including marketing. There more to marketing, however, than simply understands its role in the business. Marketing has tremendous impact on society.

1.4.2 Marketing delivers value

Not only does marketing deliver value to customers, but also that value translates into the value of the firm as it develops a reliable customer base and increases its sales and profitability. So when we say that marketing delivers value, marketing delivers value to both the customer and the company. Franklin D. Roosevelt, the U. S. president with perhaps the greatest influence on our economic system, once said, "If I were starting life over again, I am inclined to think that I would go into the advertising business in preference to almost any other. The general raising of the standards of modern civilization among all groups of people during the past half century would have been impossible without the spreading of the knowledge of higher standards means of advertising." Roosevelt referred to advertising, but advertising alone is insufficient for delivering value. Marketing finishes the job by ensuring that what is delivered is valuable.

1.4.3 Marketing benefits society

Marketing benefits society in general by improving people's lives in two ways. First, as we mentioned, it facilitates trade. As you have learned, or will learn, in economics, being able to trade makes people's lives better. Otherwise people wouldn't do it. In addition, because better marketing means more successful companies, jobs are created. This generates wealth for people, who are then able to make purchases, which, in turn, creates more jobs.

The second way in which marketing improves the quality of life is based on the value delivery function of marketing, but in a broader sense. When you add all the marketers together who are trying to deliver offerings of greater value to consumers and are effectively communicating that value, consumers are able to make more informed decisions about a wider array of choices. From an economic perspective, more choices and smarter consumers are indicative of a higher quality of life.

1.4.4 Marketing costs money

Marketing can sometimes be the largest expense associated with producing a product. In the soft drink business, marketing expenses account for about one-third of a product's price—about the same as the ingredients used to make the soft drink itself. At the bottling and retailing level, the expenses involved in marketing a drink to consumers like you and me make up the largest cost of the product.

Some people argue that society does not benefit from marketing when it represents such a huge chunk of a product's final price. In some cases, that argument is justified. Yet, when marketing results in more informed consumers receiving a greater amount of value, then the cost is justified.

Marketing is the interface between producers and consumers. In other words, it is the one function in the organization in which the entire business comes together. Being responsible for both making money for your company and delivering satisfaction to your customers makes marketing a great career. In addition, because marketing can be such an expensive part of a business and is so critical to its success, companies actively seek good marketing people.

A career in marketing can begin in a number of different ways. Entry-level positions for new college graduates are available in many of the positions mentioned above. A growing number of CEOs are people with marketing backgrounds. Some legendary CEOs like Ross Perot and Mary Kay Ash got their start in marketing. More recently, CEOs like MarkHurd, who runs Hewlett-Packard, and Jeffrey Immelt at General Electric Co. (GE) are showing how marketing careers can lead to the highest pinnacles of the organization.

Part Two: Questions

1. What are the marketing practices in daily life?
2. Do you know any successful marketing cases?

Part Three: Words and Phrases

1. day-to-day life	日常生活
2. target markets	目标市场
3. emphasis	强调
4. customer-oriented	消费者导向的
5. product-oriented	生产导向的
6. estimate	评估
7. negotiation	谈判

8.	global market	全球市场
9.	dynamic	动态的
10.	integrated	整合
11.	concepts	概念
12.	facilitate	促进,使容易
13.	pinnacle	顶峰
14.	motor oil	机油
15.	interface	接口
16.	array	数组
17.	categorize	分类
18.	retailing level	零售水平
19.	rhetorical	夸张的
20.	mutual benefit	互惠互利

Part Four: Further Reading

Who is Philip Kotler?

(菲利普·科特勒) Philip Kotler, the S. C. Johnson & Son Distinguished **Professor** of International Marketing at Northwestern University's Kellogg School of **Management**, is widely regarded as the Father of Modern Marketing. He trained as an economist at the University of Chicago, learning from the legendary Milton Friedman. He later did his PhD at MIT under the guidance of Nobel Prize winning economist Paul Samuelson.

Kotler rose to the forefront in the field of marketing in 1967 when he authored the seminal textbook Marketing Management. The book cut through the clutter by introducing rigor and mathematical analysis to the field of marketing. Ever since, the book became the marketing Bible for MBA students. More than four decades have gone by, and 14 editions of the book have been published and Kotler's popularity has grown.

One of Kotler's biggest contributions to the field of marketing was popularizing the idea of the Marketing Mix, also known as the Four Ps of Marketing, an idea first proposed by an academic Jerome McCarthy in 1960. The Four Ps stand for "product" "price" " place" (i. e., distribution) and "promotion" (i. e., advertising). According to Kotler, "(The) Marketing Mix is the set of controllable variables that the firm can use to influence the buyer's response." These four variables help a company develop a unique selling point as well as a brand image.

With the rise of the internet and the advent of new concepts like social media, e-commerce and digital marketing, critics started questioning the relevance of the classic Four Ps model of marketing. Some proclaimed that the Four Ps model is dead. Take "promotion". Many brands like Google, for instance, never really advertised, yet they became so popular. The rise of social media itself started to bring into question the classic notion of "promotion". Similarly with the rise of e-commerce, the idea of "place" doesn't have the same relevance as before.

Yet Kotler chooses to staunchly defend the concept. In this interview he explains why the Four Ps are still relevant, how the marketing landscape has evolved and the impact of digital media.

Chapter 2: Nature of Marketing

Part One: Text

2.1 Nature of marketing

2.1.1 Marketing is both consumer-oriented and competitor-oriented

The consumer and competitor orientations can be easily understood by the following diagram, see Figure 2.1.

	Competitor Emphasis		
	Minor	Major	
Customer Emphasis	Self-Centered	Competitor Oriented	Minor
	Customer Oriented	Market Driven	Major

Figure 2.1 Consumer and competitors emphasis

Self-centered companies do not give any concern to the consumers and competitors. This type of company can exist in the situation of monopoly. In the competitive economy, these companies cannot remain in the business for long.

Competitor-oriented companies mainly focus on competitor's activities, what the competitors are doing and what they are likely to do in the near future are the major areas of concern. The companies can be either reactive or proactive. The reactive company will follow the moves of competitors. For example, if the competitor reduce price of its product or service then the reactive competitor-oriented company will also reduce its prices. Whereas the proactive competitor-oriented company will try to identify what its major competitor is going to do.

Customer-oriented companies believes in satisfying the customers at any cost. These companies obtain inputs from the customers and then develop their product or service as per customers requirements and then earn profit through customer satisfaction. The biggest problem is that they don't consider what their competitors are doing and in the long run it might prove counter productive.

Market driven companies are concerned about customers as well as competitors. These companies regularly interact with the customers to know about their satisfaction levels and their future requirements and then try to develop the product or service which is better than their competitors. In the era of cut throat competition, these companies are more likely to be successful than the other companies.

2.1.2 Marketing is a dynamic activity because a number of variables keep changing

For example, marketing environment, customer's requirements, competitor's actions, etc., keep changing thereby necessitating the changes in the company's offer. The companies may have to modify product, price, place or promotion due to changes in any of the numerous variables. For example, Indian manufacturers either have to improve the quality or reduce the cost to meet the competition from foreign companies.

2.1.3 Long term objective of marketing is profit maximization through customer satisfaction

This is so because a satisfied customer will come back again for the same or different need to the company. Apart from this, the satisfied customer is the company's best advertisement because word of mouth communication by the customer has more credibility than any other form of marketing communication and he'll recommend the companies products/services to his friends and relatives.

2.1.4 Marketing is an integrated function and all the marketing decisions are linked with each other

One decision will automatically lead to another decision. For example, if a company has decided to launch a product for limited number of customers then its price will be high and that product will be available through exclusive distribution system and the promotion strategy will depend on the media preferred by the target market. So, if a company decides the first step then decisions regarding the remaining steps will follow automatically.

2.1.5 Marketing is the core functional area of modern day organizations and is the driving force behind every organization

Marketing provides the vital input for corporate planning which in turn dictates the plans for other functional areas.

2.1.6 Marketing is interlinked with other functional areas of the organization

Marketing people collects the information regarding (customer's requirements and pass it to) the research and development and engineering people who will turn the customer requirements into the product or service features. The finance and accounts people help in obtaining the money for the development of new product and also help in arriving at the final price decision. The human resource department provides the necessary manpower for carrying out various activities not only in the marketing area but also in the other functional areas.

2.2 Scope of marketing

Marketing is typically seen as the task of creating, promoting and delivering goods and services to consumers and businesses. In fact, marketing people are involved in marketing 10 types of entities: goods, services, experiences, events, persons, places, properties, organizations, information and ideas. **Marketing** concepts can be used effectively to market these entities.

2.2.1　Goods

Good is defined as something tangible that can be offered to market to satisfy a need or want. Physical goods constitute the bulk of most countries production and marketing effort. In a developing country like India fast moving consumer goods and consumer durable are produced and consumed in large quantities every year.

2.2.2　Services

As economies advance, the share of service in Gross Domestic Product (GDP) increases. For example, in the USA, service jobs account for 79% of all jobs and 74% of GDP. A service can be defined as any performance that one party can offer to another that is essentially intangible and does not result in the ownership of anything.

Its production may or may not be tied to a physical product. Services include the work of hotels, airlines, banks, insurance companies, transportation corporations, etc. as well as professionals like lawyers, doctors, teachers, etc. Many market offerings consist of a variable mix of goods and services. At the pure service end would be psychiatrist listening to a patient or watching movie in a cinema hall; at another level would be the landline or mobile phone call that is supported by a huge investment in plant and equipment; and at a more tangible level would be a fast food establishment where the consumer consume both a good and a service.

2.2.3　Experiences

By mixing several services and goods, one can create, stage and market experiences. Such as water parks, zoos, museums, etc. provide the experiences which are not the part of routine life. There is a market for different experiences such as climbing Mount Everest, traveling in Palace on Wheels, river rafting, a trip to moon, traveling in Trans Siberian Railways across five time zones, etc.

2.2.4　Events

Marketers promote time-based, theme-based or special events such as Olympics, company anniversaries, sports events (Samsung Cup India-Pakistan Cricket Series), artistic performances, trade shows, award ceremonies, beauty contests. There is a whole profession of event planners who work out the details of an event and stage it. In India event management companies are growing, for example, organizing Miss

World at Bangalore and World Cricket Cup (Hero Cup), so that they won the acclaim from all over the world. Other notable example is organizing of Ardh Kumbh and Maha Kumbh at Hardward, Ujjain, Nasik, etc. during different years.

2.2.5 Persons

Celebrity marketing has become a major business. Years ago, someone seeking fame would hire a press agent to plant stories in newspapers and magazines. Today most of cricket players like Sachin Tendulkar, Saurav Ganguly, Rahul Dravid, etc. are drawing help from celebrity marketers to get the maximum benefit. Even Star Plus TV channel focused more on Amitabh Bachhan to promote their programme Kaun Banega Crorepati and this programme turned around fortunes of both Star Plus and Amitabh Bachhan. Even in the 14th Lok Sabha election BJP's election strategy revolves around Mr. Atal Bihari Vajpayee, that's power of personality. Mr Shiv Khera is busy in building his business empire and is busy telling others how to achieve this or that through books and lectures.

2.2.6 Places

Places—cities, states, regions and whole nations—compete actively to attract tourists, factories, company headquarters and new residents. India and China are competing actively to attract foreign companies to make their production hub. Cities like Bangalore, Hyderabad and Gurgaon are promoted as center for development of software. Bangalore is regarded as software capital of India and Hyderabad is emerging as the hub of biotechnology industry. Gurgaon and Noida are competing for call centers to open their offices. Kerala, Himachal Pradesh, Uttranchal Pradesh and Raj Asthan are aggressively promoting themselves to attract local as well as foreign tourists. Due to its cost effectiveness and competitive ability of Indian doctors coupled with ancient therapies, India is fast emerging as country that can provide excellent medical treatment at minimum costs. If developed properly, Bihar has strong potential to emerge as ultimate destination for Buddhists.

2.2.7 Properties

Properties are intangible rights of ownership of either real property (real estate) or financial property (share and debt instruments). Properties are bought and sold, and this requires marketing effort. Property dealers in India work for property owners or seekers to sell or buy plots, residential or commercial real estate. In India some builders like Ansal, Sahara Group, both build and market their residential and commercial real estates. Brokers and sub-brokers buy and sell securities on behalf of individual and institutional buyers.

2.2.8 Organizations

Organizations actively work to build a strong, favorable image in the mind of their publics. We see ads of Reliance Infocomm Ltd. which is trying to provide communication at lower rates, Dhirubhai Ambani Entrepreneur programme to promote entrepreneurship among the Indians. Companies can gain immensely by associating themselves with the social causes. Universities and colleges are trying to boost their image to compete successfully for attracting the students by mentioning their NAAC grades in the advertisements and information brochures.

2.2.9 Information

Information can be produced and marketed as a product. This is essentially what schools, colleges and universities produce and distribute at a price to parents, students and communities. Encyclopedia and most non-fiction books market information. Magazines such as Fitness and Muscle provide information about staying healthy. Business India, Business Today and Business World provide information about business activities which is taking place in various organizations. Outlook Traveler provides information about various national and international tourist destinations. There are number of magazines which are focused an automobiles, architecture and interior designing, computers, audio system, television programmes, etc. which cater to the information needs of the customers. We buy CDs and visit internet sites to obtain information. In fact, production, packaging and distribution of information are one of the society's major industries. More and more companies are using professional research agencies to obtained information they need.

2.2.10 Ideas

Film makers, marketing executives and advertising continuously look for a creative spark or an idea that can immortalize them and their work. Idea here means the social cause or an issue that can change the life of many. Narmada Bachao Andolan was triggered to bring the plight of displaced people and to get them justice.

Endorsement by Amitabh Bachhan to Pulse Polio Immunization drive and pledge by Aishwarya Rai to donate her eyes after her death gave immense boost to these. Various government and non-government organizations are trying to promote a cause or issue which can directly and indirectly alter the life of many. For example, traffic police urges to not to mix drinks and drive, central and state government urging not to use polyethylene as carrying bag for groceries.

2.3 Importance of marketing

2.3.1 To the society

It is instrumental in improving the living standards. Marketing continuously identifies the needs and wants satisfying products or services which can propel the people to do an extra to earn money which can be exchanged for the desired products or services. The people are likely to spend the additional income over and above the disposable income on the products or services which helps in minimizing the physical efforts. Thus marketing by indirectly increasing the earning ability will help in improving the standard of living of the customers.

Marketing generates gainful employment opportunities both directly and indirectly. Directly, marketing provides employment to the people in various areas like in advertising agency, in the company sales force, in the distributor's sales force, in public relation firms, etc. Indirectly, marketing is responsible for selling the offerings of the organization. If the organization's products or services are able to satisfy the customers, then customers will demand organization's products or services again and again, thereby sustaining the production activities. Thus marketing indirectly provides employment in other functional areas like finance, production, research and development, human resource management, etc.

Marketing helps instabilizing economic condition in the sense that marketing helps in selling the products or services, which keeps the various organizations functioning and gainful employment is available to the people. With the earnings from the employment, the people will purchase the products and/or services, thus sustaining the demand. This will happen in all the industries, then gainful employment will be available throughout the time period and economy will remain stable, healthy and vibrant.

2.3.2　To the firms

Marketing sustains the company by bringing in profits. Marketing is the only activity that brings revenue to the firm, whereas other activities incur expenditure. If the company's products or services satisfy the customer's requirements, then the satisfied customers will keep the company in business by repeat orders and recommending other profitable customers. Thus marketing is the driving force behind a successful company.

Marketing is the source of new ideas. New product or service ideas usually come from the research laboratories, employees or from marketplace. It's the marketing people who are in continuous touch with the consumers and marketing intermediaries. Interaction with them helps in identifying strong and weak points of company's product or services as well as competitor's products or services. This interaction can also help in identifying unmet needs or wants of the consumers and the features, consumers are looking into the products or services which can satisfy those unmet needs or wants. Thus marketing can help immensely in identifying new product or service ideas which can help in sustaining the firm's operations. Successful companies are those which identify customer's requirements early and provide the solution earlier than the competitors.

Marketing provides direction for the future course. The marketing-oriented company continuously brings out new product and service ideas which provide the direction for corporate strategic planning for longer time horizon.

2.3.3　To the consumers

Meeting the unmet needs or wants. Marketing identifies those needs or wants which were not satisfied and helps in developing the product or service which can satisfy those unmet needs or wants of the people. For example, a number of drugs were invented to treat various physical problems of the people. Again the low cost formulations were developed to treat the people who are unable to afford the expensive drugs.

Reducing the price of products or services. Marketing helps inpopularizing the product or service which attracts the customers as well as competitors towards that product or service categories. Due to increase in demand, the manufacturing capacity increase which brings down per unit fixed costs of the product or service. Furthermore increase in competition led to decrease in the prices charged by the firm. Thus the growing demand and increasing competition both help in bringing down the price of the product or service. For example, price of both mobile phone handset and mobile phone service are showing a continuous downward trend thereby making the mobile phone service affordable to more and more people.

2.4 Evolution of marketing concept

Marketing concept has undergone a drastic change over years. Earlier it was production or later selling which was key to marketing idea but moving ahead now these have given way to customer satisfaction rather delight developing a modern marketing concept. Let's review the evolution of earlier marketing ideas.

2.4.1 The production concept

It is one of the oldest concepts in business. It holds that consumers will prefer products that are widely available and inexpensive. Managers of production-oriented business concentrate on achieving high production efficiency, low costs, and mass distribution.

2.4.2 The product concept

It proposes that consumers favor products that feature. Managers in these organizations focus overtime. On offer the most quality, performance, or innovative making superior products and improving them.

2.4.3 The selling concept

It holds that consumers and businesses, if left alone, won't buy enough of the organization's product. The organization must therefore undertake an aggressive selling and promotion effort.

The marketing concept emerged in mid-1950s, instead of a product-centered, make-and-sell philosophy, business shifted to a customer-centered, sense-and-respond philosophy.

The marketing concept holds that the key to achieving organizational goals is being effective than competitors in creating, delivering, and communicating superior customer value to your chosen target markets.

Theodore Levitt of Harward drew a perceptive contrast between the selling and marketing concepts. Selling focuses on the needs of the seller, marketing on the needs of the buyer. Selling is preoccupied with the seller's need to convert his product into cash, marketing with the idea of satisfying the needs of the customer by means of the product and the whole cluster of things associated with creating, delivering, and finally consuming it.

Several scholars have found that companies that embrace the marketing concept achieve superior performance. This was first demonstrated by companies practicing a reactive market orientation—understanding and meeting customer' expressed needs.

2.5 Core concepts of marketing

Marketing can be further understood by defining several of its core concepts, see Figure 2.2.

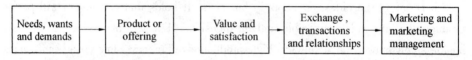

Figure 2.2　The core concepts of marketing

2.5.1　Needs, wants and demands

The marketer must try to understand the target market's needs, wants, and demands. Needs describe basic human requirements. People need food, air, water, clothing and shelter to survive. People also have strong needs for recreation, education, and entertainment. These needs become wants when they are directed to specific object that might satisfy the need. An American needs food but want a hamburger, French fries, and a soft drink. A person in Mauritius needs food but wants a mango, rice, lentils and beans. Wants are shaped by one's society.

Demands are wants for specific products backed by an ability to pay. Many people want a big&beautiful house; only a few are able and willing to buy one. Companies must measure not only how many people want their product but also how many would actually be willing and able to buy it.

These distinctions shed light on the frequent criticism that "marketers create needs" or " marketers get people to buy things they don't want." Marketers do not create needs. Needs preexist marketers. Marketers, along with other societal influences, influence wants. Marketers might promote the idea that a Mercedes would satisfy a person's need for social status. They do not, however, create the need for social status.

2.5.2 Product or offering

People satisfy their needs and wants with products. A product is any offering that can satisfy a need or want. We mentioned earlier the major types of basic offerings: goods, services, experiences, events, persons, places, properties, organizations, information, and ideas.

A brand is an offering from a known source. A brand name such as McDonald's carries many associations in the minds of people: hamburgers, fun, children, fast food, Golden Arches. These associations make up the brand image. All companies strive to build brand strength—that is, a strong, favorable brand image.

2.5.3 Value and satisfaction

The product or offering will be successful if it delivers value and satisfaction to the target buyer. The buyer chooses between different offerings on the basis of which is perceived to deliver the most value. We define value as a ratio between what the customer gets and what he gives. The customer gets benefits and assumes costs. The benefits include functional benefits and emotional benefits. The costs include monetary costs, time costs, energy costs, and psychic costs. Thus value is given by:

$$\text{Value} = \frac{\text{Benefits}}{\text{Costs}} = \frac{\text{Functional Benefits} + \text{Emotional Benefits}}{\text{Monetary Costs} + \text{Time Costs} + \text{Energy Costs} + \text{Psychic Costs}}$$

2.5.4 Exchange, transactions and relationships

The fact that people have needs and wants and can place value on products does not fully explain the concept of marketing. Marketing emerges when people decide to satisfy needs and wants through exchange. Exchange is one of the four ways people can obtain products they want. The first way is self production. People can relieve hunger through hunting, fishing, or fruit gathering. In this case there is no market or marketing. The second way is coercion. Hungry people can steal food from others. The third way is begging. Hungry people can approach others and beg for food. They have nothing tangible to offer except gratitude. The fourth way is exchange. Hungry people can approach others and offer some resource in exchange, such as money, another food, or service.

Marketing arises from this last approach to acquire products. Exchange is the act of obtaining a desired product from someone by offering something in return. For exchange to take place, five conditions must be satisfied:

First, there are at least two parties.

Second, each party has something that might be of value to the other party.

Third, each party is capable of communication and delivery.

Forth, each party is free to accept or reject the offer.

Fifth, each party believes it is appropriate or desirable to deal with the other party.

If the above conditions exist, there is a potential for exchange. Exchange is described as a value creating process and normally leaves both the parties better off than before the exchange. Two parties are said to be engaged exchange if they are negotiating and moving towards an agreement. The process of trying to arrive at naturally agreeable terms is called negotiation. If an agreement is reached, we say that a transaction takes place. Transactions are the basic unit of exchange. A transaction consists of a trade of values between two parties. A transaction involves several dimensions: at least two things of value, agreed upon conditions a time of agreement, and a place of agreement. Usually a legal system arises to support and enforce compliance on the part of the transaction.

A transaction differs from a transfer. In a transfer A gives X to B but does not receive anything tangible in return. When A gives B a gift, a subsidy, or a charitable contribution, we call this a transfer.

Transaction marketing is a part of longer idea, that of relationship marketing. Smart marketers try to build up long term, trusting, "win-win" relationships with customers, distributors, dealers and suppliers. This is accomplished by promising and delivering high quality, good service and fair prices to the other party over time. It is accomplished by strengthening the economic, technical, and social ties between members of the two organizations. The two parties grow more trusting, more knowledgeable, and more interested in helping each other. Relationship marketing cuts down on transaction costs and time. The ultimate outcome of relationship marketing is the building of a unique company asset called a marketing network. A marketing network consists of the company and the firms with which it has built solid, dependable business relationships.

Part Two: Questions

1. How do you understand the meaning of marketing?
2. Does new product development involve very high cost and risks of failure?

Part Three: Words and Phrases

1. dynamic	动态	
2. counter-productive	产生相反效果的；逆效	
3. interact	互相作用	
4. variables	变量	
5. integrated function	集成功能	
6. beauty contests	选美比赛	
7. horizon	地平线	
8. brochure	小册子	
9. service categories	服务类别	
10. security	证券	
11. insurance	保险	
12. biotechnology	生物技术	
13. revenue	收益	
14. coercion	强制	
15. functional benefits	功能性利益	
16. emotional benefits	情感性利益	
17. subsidy	补贴	
18. transaction	交易	
19. distributor	经销商	
20. ultimate	极限	

Part Four: Further Reading

Non Profit Organization in Canada

Canada allows nonprofits to be incorporated or unincorporated. Nonprofits may incorporate either federally, under Part II of the Canada Business Corporations Act or under provincial legislation. Many of the governing acts for Canadian nonprofits date to the early 1900s, meaning that nonprofit legislation has not kept pace with legislation that governs for profit corporations; particularly with regards to corporate governance. Federal, and in some provinces (such as Ontario), incorporation is by way of Letters Patent, and any change to the Letters Patent (even a simple name change) requires formal approval by the appropriate government, as do by-law changes. Other provinces (such as Alberta) permit incorporation as of right, by the filing of Articles of Incorporation or Articles of Association.

During 2009, the federal government enacted new legislation repealing the Canada Corporations Act, Part II—the Canada Not-for-Profit Corporations Act. This act was last amended on 10 October 2011 and the act was current till 4 March 2013. It allows for incorporation as of right, by Articles of Incorporation; does away with the ultra vires doctrine for nonprofits; establishes them as legal persons; and substantially updates the governance provisions for nonprofits. Ontario also overhauled its legislation, adopting the Ontario Not-for-Profit Corporations Act during 2010; pending the outcome of an anticipated election during October 2011, the new act is expected to be in effect as of 1 July 2013.

Canada also permits a variety of charities (including public and private foundations). Charitable status is granted by the Canada Revenue Agency (CRA) upon application by a nonprofit; charities are allowed to issue income tax receipts to donors, must spend a certain percentage of their assets (including cash, investments and fixed assets) and file annual reports in order to maintain their charitable status. In determining whether an organization can become a charity, CRA applies a common law test to its stated objects and activities. These must be:

The relief of poverty;

The advancement of education;

The advancement of religion; or certain other purposes that benefit the community in a way the courts have said is charitable.

Charities are not permitted to engage in partisan political activity; doing so may result in the revocation of charitable status. However, a charity can carry out a small number of political activities that are non-partisan, help further the charities' purposes, and subordinate to the charity's charitable purposes.

Chapter 3: Marketing Environment

Part One: Text

Marketing management rests squarely on the knowledge of the marketing environment. Environment plays a crucial role in marketing and that securing the right fit between the environment and the firm, using the marketing mix as the tool, is the crux of marketing. The firm has to know where the environment is heading, what trends are emerging therein and what should be its response to the environmental changes. Only by analyzing the environment, can the firm grapple with these issues.

Facilitating the corporation's strategic response to the changes taking place in environmental factors is the ultimate purpose of environment analysis. The firm has to come up with alternative programmes and strategies in line with environmental realities.

This is possible only with proper environment analysis. It helps strategic response by highlighting opportunities, the pursuit of which will help the firm attain its objectives. It helps assess the attractiveness and profitability position of these opportunities, and helps prepare a shortlist of those which are relevant to the firm and which can be pursued by it. See Table 3.1 and Table 3.2.

Table 3.1　Purpose of marketing environment analysis

To know where the environment is heading; to observe and size up the relevant events and trends in the environment
To discern which events and trends are favourable from the standpoint of the firm, and which are unfavourable; to figure out the opportunities and threats hidden in the environmental events and trends
To project how the environment—each factor of the environment—will be at a future point of time
To assess the scope of various opportunities and shortlist those that can favourably impact the business
To help secure the right fit between the environment and the business unit, which is the crux of marketing; to help the business unit respond with matching product—market strategies; to facilitate formulation of a marketing strategy in the right way—in line with the trends in the environment and the opportunities emerging therein

Table 3.2　Presents in a nutshell the purpose of environment analysis

Spotting the Opportunities and Threats
Spotting the opportunities and threats is the central purpose here. It is in the environment that the firm finds its opportunities; it is in the environment that it finds the threats it has to encounter; and, it is by tapping the opportunities present and countering the threats embedded there in that the firm achieves its growth objective. The starting point is thus to spot the opportunities and threats.
The Task Involved in Marketing Environment Analysis
Marketing environment analysis is the process of gathering, filtering and analysing information relating to the marketing environment. Involved in the process are the tasks of monitoring the changes taking place in the environment and forecasting the future position in respect of each of the factors. The analysis spots the opportunities and threats in the environment, and pinpoints the ones that are specifically relevant to the firm.

The marketing environment can be divided into two parts:

The macro-environment: broad societal forces that shape the activities of every business and non profit marketer. The physical environment, social-cultural forces, demographic factors, economic factors, scientific and technical knowledge, and political and legal factors are components of the micro-environment: Environmental forces, such as customers, that directly and regularly influence a marketer's activity.

3.1 The macro-environment

Whether it is the domestic environment, a foreign environment, or the world environment that is under consideration, the environment can be divided into two categories: the macro-environment and the micro-environment. The broad societal forces that influence every business and non profit marketer comprise the macro-environment. Every company, however, is more directly influenced by a micro-environment consisting of its customers and the economic institutions that shape its marketing practices. The macro-environment consists of the physical environment, social-cultural forces and so on, see Figure 3.1.

Macroenvironment Influences on the Marketing Mix

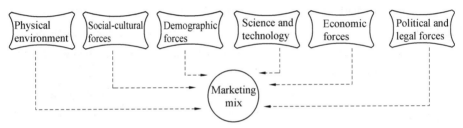

Figure 3.1 Macro-environment influences on the marketing mix

3.1.1 The physical environment

The analysis of the mega environment must also cover aspects like extent of endowment of natural resources in the country, climate, ecology, etc. These constitute the natural environment.

1. Natural resources. Business firms depend on natural resources. The extent to which the country/region under reference is endowed with these resources has an impact on the functioning of the firms. Raw material is one major part of these resources and firms are concerned with their availability; they need to know whether there will be a shortage in any of the critical raw materials; they also need to know the trends governing their costs. Besides raw materials, they are also concerned about energy, its availability as well as cost. Escalation in energy cost is of particular concern to any business firm. The availability of natural resources may have a direct and far-reaching impact on marketing activities in a geographic region. Areas rich in

petroleum, for example, may concentrate on the production and marketing of fuel oil, kerosene, benzene naphtha, paraffin, and other products derived from this natural resource.

2. Climate is another aspect of the natural environment that is of interest to a business firm. Firms with products whose demand depends on climate, and firms depending on climate-dependent raw materials will be particularly concerned with this factor. These firms have to study the climate in-depth and decide their production locations and marketing territories appropriately.

Marketing is influenced by many aspects of the natural environment as well. Climate is one example. It is not difficult to understand why umbrella sales are greater in rainy Meghalaya than in desert-like Rajasthan or why more winter clothing is sold in Himachal Pradesh than in Tamil Nadu.

Climate also greatly influences the timing of marketing activities. In India, more than 65 percent of all soft drinks are sold during the blazing hot months of June through September, for instance. Marketers adapt their strategies to such environmental differences.

3. Ecology. Firms are also concerned with ecology. In modern times, all societies are very much concerned about ecology, especially about issues like environmental pollution, protection of wild life and ocean wealth. And, governments are becoming active bargainers in environmental issues. Business firms will have to know the nature and dimensions of environmental regulations and to what extent these factors will affect their business prospects. They also need to know the role of environmental activists in the region. Finally, consideration of the physical environment of marketing must include an awareness of activities or substances harmful to the earth's ecology. Smog, acid rain, and pollution of the ocean are among the many issues in this category. Such issues are highly interrelated with aspects of the social-cultural environment.

In the case of India, the country is rich in natural resources like iron, coal, rare minerals, ocean wealth, etc. The country also receives good rainfall and has a strong network of rivers. As regards climate, the tropical climate in the country generally favors agriculture and industry. In the matter of energy, in recent years, costs are constantly on the rise.

3.1.2 Social-cultural forces

Every society has a culture that guides everyday life. In the environment of marketing, the word culture refers not to classical music, art and literature but to social institutions, values, beliefs, and behaviors. Culture includes everything people learn as members of a society, but does not include the basic drives with which people are born.

Culture is shaped by mankind. It is learned rather than innate. For example, people are born with a need to eat—but what, when, and where they eat, and whether they season their food with ketchup or curdled goat's is learned from a particular culture. Similarly, the fact that many European women are free from traditional restraints, whereas few Saudi women are, is a cultural phenomenon. Material artifacts and the symbolic meanings associated with them also vary by culture.

3.1.3 Values and beliefs

A social value embodies the goals a society views as important and expresses a culture's shared ideas of preferred ways of acting. Social values reflect abstract ideas about what is good, right, and desirable (and bad, wrong, and undesirable). For example, we learn from those around us that it is wrong to lie or steal.

The achievement of wealth and prestige through honest efforts is highly valued. Such achievement leads to a higher standard of living and improves the quality of life.

1. Work ethic. The importance of working on a regular basis is strongly emphasized. Those who are idle are considered lazy equality. Most Americans profess a high regard for human equality, especially equal opportunity, and generally relate to one another as equals.

2. Patriotism/nationalism. Americans take pride in living in the "best country in the world". They are proud of their country's democratic heritage and its achievements.

3. Individual responsibility and self-fulfillment. Americans are oriented towards developing themselves as individuals they value being responsible for their achievements. The U. S. Army's slogan "Be all that you can be" captures the essence of the desirability of personal growth.

A belief is a conviction concerning the existence or the characteristics of physical and social phenomena. A person may believe, for example, that a high-fat diet causes cancer or that chocolate causes. Whether a belief is correct or not is particularly important in terms of a person's actions. Even totally foolish beliefs may affect how people behave and what they buy.

3.1.4 Values and beliefs vary from culture to culture

Social class is one important concept in social-cultural environment. Any society is composed of different social classes. A social class is determined by income, occupation location of residence, etc., of its members. Each class has its own standards with respect to lifestyle, behavior, etc.; they are known as the class values or class norms. These values have a strong bearing on the consumption pattern and buying behavior of the members of the class. Shifts in class values do take place over time owing to several factors. And, the study of social-cultural aspects should include the study of such shifts as well.

Some facts on social-cultural environment of India: for a better understanding of the dimensions of the social-cultural environment, let us continue with our earlier reference to India. India is a land of many religions. Almost all the major religions of the world are present here. As many as seven different religious groups—Hindus, Muslims, Sikhs, Christians, Zorastrians, Buddhists and Jains live in India sizable numbers, the people of India also speak different languages. With 17 major languages, the language scenario is, in fact, even more diverse than the religious one. India is also a land of many cultures. We have seen that religion and language are two elements of a culture. There are other elements such as education and upbringing. People have the freedom to profess the religion, language and culture of their choice. Many religions, languages and cultures actually co-exist and prosper in this large country.

As a general rule, it can be said that the people of the land are tradition bound. And, these traditions also differ from region to region and segment to segment. This is reflected in matters like marriage, family life, rituals, etc. When we speak of cultural factors in Indian society, we must highlight in particular, the significance given to the institution of family. In recent times, some changes are taking place in the culture arena, owing to increased exposure to different lifestyles, impact of the media, increasing industrialization and consequent mobility of population, and the process of globalization.

The changing position of women in the society is a case in point. In India, the position of women, especially in the growing middle-class segment of the population, is indeed changing fast. From the role of a simple housewife, she is now being transformed into an educated employed member, sharing the responsibilities of the home with the man.

In an environmental survey, therefore, one actually looks for such shifts takingplace, since they can end up as opportunities or threats for the firm.

Demographics. The terms demographics and demographics come from the Greek word demos, meaning "people" (as does the word democracy). Demography may be defined as the study of the size, composition (for example, by age or racial group), and distribution of the human population in relation to social factors such as geographic boundaries. The size, composition and distribution of the population in any geographic market will clearly influence marketing. Demographic factors are of great concern to marketing managers.

The world population exceeds 6 billion people. Because markets consist of people willing and able to exchange something of value for goods and services, this total is of great marketing significance. However, the exponential growth of population, particular in less developed countries, puts a heavy burden on marketing.

Science and technology. Although the two terms are sometimes used interchangeably, science is the accumulation of knowledge about human beings and the environment, and technology is the application of such knowledge for practical purposes. Thus, the discovery that certain diseases can be prevented by immunization is a scientific discovery, but how and when immunization is administered is a technological issue.

Like other changes in the macro-environment, scientific and technological advances can revolutionize an industry or destroy one. Examples of organizations that suffered because they did not adapt to changing technology are easy to find. Remington manual typewriter and electronic typewriters were made obsolete by the computers.

The internet is a worldwide network of computers that gives users access to information and documents from distant sources. People using the internet may be viewing information stored on a host computer halfway around the world. The World Wide Web (WWW) refers to a system of internet servers, computers supporting a retrieval system that organizes information into Hypertext documents called Web pages. [Hypertext is a computer language that allows the linking and sharing of information in different formats. HTTP (Hyper Text Transfer Protocol) is the most commonly used method for transferring and displaying information formatted in HTML (Hyper Text Markup Language) on the internet]

The internet is transforming society. Time is collapsing. Distance is no longer an obstacle. "Instantaneous" has a new meaning. The internet is the most important communication medium to come along since television. The internet, as a new medium for our new era, is a macro-environmental force that is having a profound impact.

The internet is changing everything—especially commerce. E-commerce is the business model for the millennium and that marketing's role has been changed forever by the internet. This does not mean that the familiar neighborhood brick-and-mortar stores and all traditional marketing institutions like shopping centers will disappear, but it does mean that they will adapt and change as new forms of internet marketing become more prevalent.

Today, technology is a major force which industry and business have to reckon with. Technology leads practically all the forces that shape people's lives. For a business firm, technology affect not only its final products but also its raw materials, processes and operations as well as its customer segments. And in the present times, rapid changes are taking place in the realm of technology. The IT industry is one example. Telecom is another.

Government's approach in respect of technology. Regulations by the government in matters relating to technology often restrict the freedom of operation of business firms. There may be areas where the governments may support the use of modern technology; there may be areas where they may ban technologies that are potentially unsafe. All such factors demand careful investigation. In modern times, much of the business opportunities are embedded in technology and firms desiring growth have to harness technologies, of course with necessary adaptations.

Technology selection. It is possible that several levels of technologies are floating at the same time in an industry. Firms have to scan the technology environment and select technologies that will be appropriate for the firm and the given product-market situation. They have to forecast technological trends, assess current and emerging technologies, and develop the inputs for right technology choice. The policy of the government on technology import is also a concern in this regard. India is adopting a fairly liberal approach to technology import. It also supports, at the same time, efforts at internal technology development.

A society's economic system determines how it will allocate its scarce resources. Traditionally, capitalism, socialism, and communism have been considered the world's major economic systems. In general, the western world's economies can be classified as modified capitalist systems. Under such systems, competition, both foreign and domestic, influences the interaction of supply and demand. Competition is often discussed in this context in terms of competitive market structures.

The competitive structure of a market is defined by the number of competing firms in some segment of an economy and the proportion of the market held by each competitor. Market structure influences pricing strategies and creates barriers to competitors wishing to enter a market. The four basic types of competitive market structure are pure competition, monopolistic competition, oligopoly and monopoly.

Pure competition exists when there are no barriers to competition. The market consists of many small, competing firms and many buyers. This means that there is a steady supply of the product and a steady demand for it. Therefore, the price cannot be controlled by either the buyers or the sellers. The product itself is homogeneous—that is, one seller's offering is identical to all the others' offerings. The markets for basic food commodities, such as rice and banana, approximate pure competition. Petrol and diesel now marketed by different companies will also fall in this category.

The principal characteristic monopolistic competition is product differentiation—a large number of sellers offering similar products differentiated by only minor differences in, for example, product design, style, or technology. Firms engaged in monopolistic competition have enough influence on the marketplace to exert some control over their own prices. The fast-food industry provides a good example of monopolistic competition.

Oligopoly, the third type of market structure, exists where a small number of sellers dominate the market. Oligopoly is exemplified by the commercial aircraft industry, which is controlled by two large firms: Boeing and Airbus Industries. Getting established in an oligopoly like the commercial aircraft industry often requires a huge capital investment, which presents a barrier to new firms wishing to enter the industry. The distinguishing characteristic of an oligopoly, however, is not the size of the companies involved, as measured by assets or sales volume, but their control over the marketplace, as measured by market share. Each of the companies in an oligopoly has a strong influence on product offering, price, and market structure within the industry. The companies do not, however, generally compete on price.

Economic conditions around the world are obviously of interest to marketers. The most significant long-term trend in the U.S. economy has been the transition to a service economy. There has been a continuing shift of workers away from manufacturing and into services, where almost 80 percent of U.S. jobs are to be found. This shift has greatly affected economic conditions as well as marketing activity.

The business cycle. Because marketing activity, such as the successful introduction of new products is strongly influenced by the business cycle, marketing managers watch the economic environment closely. Unfortunately, the business cycle is not always easy to forecast.

The phases of the cycle need not be equal in intensity or duration, and the contractions and expansions of the economy do not always follow a predictable pattern. Furthermore, not all economies of the world are in the same stage of the business cycle. So a single global forecast may not accurately predict activity in certain countries. Marketing strategies in a period of prosperity differ substantially from strategies in a period of depression.

For example, products with "frills" and "extras" sell better during periods of prosperity than in periods when the economy is stagnant or declining. During periods of depression or recession, when consumers have less spending power, lower prices become more prominent considerations in spending decisions.

3.1.5 Political environment

Political environment is a major component of the mega environment for an industrial/ business firm. In fact, economic environment is often a by-product of the political environment, since economic and industrial policies followed by a nation greatly depend on its political environment. Moreover, developments on the political front keep affecting the economy all the time: industrial growth depends to a great extent on the political environment; legislation regulating business are also often a product of the political configuration.

Political environment has several aspects. Form of government adopted by the country is the first. Political stability as such is another, for, whatever is the form of government adopted, and stability of government is an essential requisite of economic growth. Elements like social and religious organizations, media and pressure groups, and lobbies of various kinds are also part of the political environment.

Some features of India's political environment. The fact that the democratic form of government has endured ever since the country became independent, is one major feature of the political environment of India. Another important feature is that while in the first 40-odd years since independence, the country had a single party government at the center; in recent times, an experiment with coalition governments has been going on. And, it is also significant that the country has been enjoying a fair amount of political stability despite the absence of a single-party government at the center. Another significant fact is that a political consensus has emerged to the effect that the country must set and achieve a much higher rate of economic growth. A political consensus of sorts also seems to have emerged on the need for economic reforms. The country has also started moving towards a market economy from the earlier socialist moorings and public sector dominated economy.

The political environment. The practices and policies of governments, and the legal environment-laws and regulations and their interpretation, affect marketing activity in several ways. First, they can limit the actions marketers are allowed to take. For example, by barring certain goods from leaving a country, as when Congress passed the *Export Administration Act*, which prohibited the export of strategic high-technology products to nations such as Iran and Libya. Second, they may require marketers to take certain actions. For instance, cookies called "chocolate chips cookies" are required to contain chips made of real chocolate, and the surgeon general's warning must appear on all cigarette packages. Last policies and laws may absolutely prohibit certain actions by marketers—for example, the sale of products such as nuclear weapons—except under the strictest of controls. Political processes in other countries may have a dramatic impact on international marketers. For example, the dissolution of the former Soviet Union was a historic political action that totally changed the business climate and opened new markets in newly independent states such as Russia, Lithuania and Ukraine. It remains to be seen how this major political change will affect marketers who do business in Hong Kong in the 21st century. Laws, in particular, tend to have stable, long-term influence on marketing strategy. For example, almost all countries with commercial airlines have long-standing bans on foreign ownership of these businesses.

Companies operating their businesses in global markets must pay attention to international laws and the laws of foreign lands. Laws and legal systems that govern the marketing of products in foreign countries vary tremendously. For example, in Brazil, advertisers found guilty of harming or misleading consumers may be fined up to $500 000 or given a prison sentence of up to 5 years. This is a harsh punishment by U. S. standards. The rules of competition, trademark rights, price controls, product quality laws, and a number of other legal issues in individual countries may be of immense importance to a global marketer, such as Coca-Cola, Pepsi, TaTa Group, AVB Group, Wipro, Infernos, etc.

Furthermore, not only individual countries, but also multinational bodies, have legal systems to deal with international commerce, multinational marketing groups are groups of countries aligned to form a unified market with minimal trade and tariff barriers among participating member countries. An example is the European Union (formerly called the Common Market). The European Parliament and the Court of Justice deal with legal issues for the European Union.

Environmental interactions. Before concluding this discussion of the macro-environment, we should emphasize that the parts of the macro-environment interact with each other. Therefore, effective marketers must consider the whole of the marketing macro-environment, not just its parts. For example, natural phenomena such as the eruption of volcanoes can affect tourism, agriculture, weather patterns, and radio and television transmission; can heighten public interest in "disaster" movies and books; and can even inspire race-track customers to bet on horses whose names suggest volcanic explosions.

There are many examples of interactions between changes in the economic, technological and social environments. When the U. S. economy is in a period of decline, the divorce rate also declines, because fewer couples can afford the expense of divorce. When medical science reduces the infant mortality rate in a country, that country's birth rate eventually declines, because parents realize that their children can be expected to survive to adulthood. These kinds of interactions make the job of environmental analysis a complex one. Nonetheless, marketing success cannot be achieved without a careful consideration of environmental constraints and opportunities.

3.2 The micro-environment—The Four Cs

The macro-environment, the broad societal forces that affect every business and non profit marketer, was discussed. Marketers, however, are more directly influenced by their individual micro-environments. A micro-environment consists of a company, its customers, and the other economic institutions that regularly influence its marketing practices.

To explain the dramatic impact of the micro-environment, it is useful to organize all micro-environmental forces into four basic categories—companies, customers, competitors and collaborators. Each of these represents a participant that performs essential business activities. We will call these the Four Cs.

3.2.1 Company

The first of the Four Cs is the company, the business or organization itself. Marketing, although very important, is only one functional activity of an organization. Every marketer must work with people in the organization who perform non-marketing tasks. For example, in a large manufacturing company, manufacturing, engineering, purchasing, accounting, finance, and personnel are all part of the internal company environment. These functional activities, the level of technology, and the people who perform them have an impact on marketing. Marketers, for example, work within the framework of the corporate mission set by top managers who are responsible for the company's operations. Companies like 3M, Sony, and Disney have several divisions and market providing many different goods and services. The way one product is marketed often affects the marketing of other company products. See Figure 3.2.

Owners and managers in today's companies must strive to be flexible to keep up with dynamically changing business environments. In doing so, they often take an entrepreneurial approach to running the business. An entrepreneur is someone willing to undertake a venture to create something new. In the traditional view, an entrepreneur is a single individual who sees an opportunity and is willing to work long and hard to turn an idea into a business. Entrepreneurs are typically creative, optimistic, and hard-working individuals who risk their own money to start small companies to make something happen. The story of the entrepreneurial development

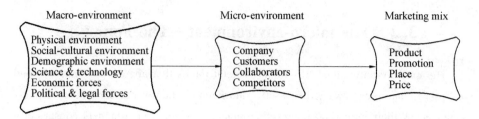

Figure 3.2 The macro-environment and the micro-environment:
forces that shape the marketing mix

of the personal computer is well known. Starting out in a garage, two risk-taking individuals with a vision built the first personal computers and then developed Apple Computer into a multinational corporation. Entrepreneurs who assume all the risks associated with their innovative ideas have always been in the forefront of new product development.

The top managers of many large organizations try to instill an entrepreneurial spirit in their employees. To avoid confusion with the traditional definition of entrepreneur, we define an entrepreneurship organization as a large organization that encourages individuals to take risks and gives them the autonomy to develop new products as they see fit.

Managers of entrepreneurial companies try to create company cultures that encourage employees to be proactive. That is, these companies favor organizational structures that allow employees to initiate marketing action swiftly rather than forcing them to follow rigid bureaucratic procedures before taking action.

3.2.2 Customers

Customers are the lifeblood of every company. A company that does not satisfy its customers' needs will not stay in business over the long run. It is difficult to think of a more direct influence on marketing than the gaining or losing of customers.

In convening raw materials into finished goods, an organization's production department alters the materials' form. It creates form utility. However, transforming leather and thread into a purse does not create form utility unless the new shape formed by the materials satisfies a consumer need. Marketing helps production create form utility by interpreting consumers' needs for products of various configurations and formulations.

Bridging the physical separation between buyers and sellers is where marketing's roots lie. Products available at the right place—that is, where buyers want them—have place utility. A bottle of Pepsi-Cola at a bottling plant far from a consumer's hometown has considerably less place utility than does a Pepsi in a consumer's refrigerator.

Making products or services available when consumers need them creates time utility. A bank may close at 6:00 p.m., but by maintaining a 24-hour automatic teller machine, it produces additional time utility for its customers.

The fourth type of utility is created at the conclusion of a sale, when the transfer of ownership occurs. House owners enjoy greater freedom to alter their homes, such as the right to paint walls bright orange, than do house renters; they have possession utility. Possession utility satisfies the consumer's need to own the product and to have control over its use or consumption. These economic utilities serve as the underlying bases of competition, discussed in the following section.

3.2.3 Competitors

Hero Honda and Yamaha are competitors. So are two general stores in your neighborhood. Competitors are rival companies engaged in the same business. Your competitors are interested in selling their products and services to your company's customers and potential customers. One of the fundamental marketing tasks is identifying and understanding the competition. The marketer does this by analyzing product classes, product categories, and brands.

Product categories are subsets of a product class. For example, household cleaners, taken together, constitute a product class, but the subdivisions of powders and sprays are product categories. Similarly, car is a product class. There are a number of product categories within that class, including expensive cars, mid price cars and economy cars.

To complete their view of competition, marketing managers must consider matter of brand. Brands identify and distinguish one marketer's product from those of its competitors. You are familiar with hundreds of brands of products. For example, the bathing soap category includes brands such as Lux, Liril, Rexona, Fa, Lifebuoy and many more.

All three grouping product class, product category, and brand must be considered in answering the question "Who is the competitor?" A liquid cleaner like Top Job can be used to clean floors. So can a powdered cleaner like Spic Span.

Liquid Lysol can do anything that spray Lysol can do, except provide the convenience of the spray can itself.

In a sense, any bathing soap, car, or hotel can compete against any other members of its product class. However, brands of products compete primarily within product categories. A marketer must of course be aware of the entire class of goods or services being marketed, but it is the product category that contains the most competitors, because the category reflects a specific consumer's wants, needs and desires.

The four types of competition. There are four general types of competition price, quality, time and location. These types of competition are related to the utilities described earlier. To obtain possession utility, consumers must pay a price. That is, they must exchange something of value, called a price, for the good or service they desire. Economists have spent a great deal of time investigating price competition, in general, a price that is lower than competitors' prices will attract customers. However, note that economic price theory is based on the ceteris paribus assumption. That is, all things other than price are assumed to remain the same.

Form utility increases as product quality improves. Many businesses choose to compete on the basis of product quality rather than on the basis of price. Quality-based competition is more complex than price competition because consumers define quality in many different ways. Durability and reliability are traditionally associated with quality. So are design, colors, style and many other attributes that determine the physical nature of products. Prompt, polite, and friendly service is also associated with consumers' perception of quality. If all other things, including price, are equal, the higher the perceived quality, the more likely consumers are to buy a product.

Time-based competition is directly associated with time utility. To put it simply, buyers prefer to take possession of their goods exactly when they need them, which is often as soon as possible. Time-based competition is very important in many industries, especially those in which customers view competing products as virtually identical.

Moreover, time is becoming more important as a competitive weapon in a world of ever-faster global communications. A marketing manager in today's competitive environment "has to think like a fighter pilot". When things move so fast, you can't always make the right decision, so you have to learn to adjust to correct more quickly. Insurance claims representatives once used ballpoint pens, paper, and stacks of huge manuals in their offices to estimate damage from fires and other disasters. Today, they use IBM ThinkPad computers to review building data and calculate and print estimates right at the site of the damage. Using modern information technology has reduced processing time for claims from weeks to hours.

Location-based competition is the effort to provide more place utility than competitors do. Location is extremely important for retail businesses. The soft-drink shop conveniently located at a high-traffic intersection will sell more soft drinks than a general store located on a little-traveled road. A small store inside a shopping mall has many drop-in customers who came to the mall to shop at the large department stores. Today, the internet allows marketers, even small businesses, to connect instantly with customers all over the globe. In traditional business situations, bridging the physical separation between buyers and sellers meant having a better geographical location, but today barriers caused by distance are easier to overcome than they once were.

A company strives to obtain an edge, or competitive advantage, over industry competitors. To establish and maintain a competitive advantage means to be superior to or different from competitors in some way. More specifically, it means to be superior in terms of price, quality, time, or location. A company may achieve superiority by operating a more efficient factory, by selling its products at a lower price, by designing better-quality products, by being the first on the market with an innovation, or by satisfying customers in other ways. In other words, market-oriented organizations can use many alternative strategies to outperform competitors in terms of price, quality, time or location.

3.2.4 Collaborators

For an organization, buying materials and supplies, hiring an advertising agency, or getting a loan from a bank requires that one company work with another company. These companies are collaborators. A collaborator is a person or a company that works with your company. Collaborators help a company run its business but they are not part of the company. They are often specialists who provide particular services or supply raw materials, component parts, or production equipment.

Collaborators that provide materials, equipment, and the like are called suppliers. Hyatt Hotel Corporation believes that establishing long-term relationships with a supplier benefits both companies. Whether it's sheets and linens, emergency fire exit signs, or wine, Hyatt buyers circle the globe looking for the highest-quality products. After Hyatt settles on a supplier, the company works hard at maintaining that relationship.

The terms alliances, networks and informal partnerships, as well as others, have been used to describe the kinds of relationships just mentioned. However, the term collaborator works well because it implies that two companies are engaged in an ongoing relationship. In today's business climate, companies must be flexible and able to change quickly. Working with collaborators helps companies enhance their flexibility, especially in global marketing activities and e-commerce activities.

The number of collaborative relationships has grown significantly in recent years, and organizational collaborations are expected to be increasingly important during the 21st century. Contemporaryorganizations no longer perform all business activities internally. Managers recognize that collaborators may have special competencies that allow them to excel at certain tasks. Managers in today's companies believe that there is value in making joint commitments and sharing resources.

Some companies' marketing strategies are highly dependent on collaborations. In fact, business thinkers have created a name for organizations that use collaboration extensively: virtual corporations. The word virtual is derived from terminology used in the early days of the computer industry. The term virtual memory described a way of making a computer act as if it had more storage capacity than it really possessed. Thus, the so-called virtual corporation, which appears to be a single enterprise with vast capabilities, is the result of numerous collaborations with companies whose resources are called on only when they are needed.

Part Two: Questions

1. What is the relationship between the macro-environment and the micro-environment?

2. How to formulate the corresponding marketing strategy according to different environment?

Part Three: Words and Phrases

1. crux   难题,症结
2. grapple   格斗
3. corporation's strategy   企业战略
4. macro-environment   宏观环境
5. micro-environment   微观环境
6. demography   人口统计,人口统计学
7. endowment   捐赠
8. Benzene Naphtha   苯
9. kerosene   煤油
10. paraffin   石蜡
11. in-depth   深入
12. region   区域
13. abstract   摘要
14. consumption pattern   消费模式
15. category   类别
16. fundamental aspect   基本面
17. rituals   仪式
18. marketing significance   营销意义
19. monopoly   垄断
20. technology selection   技术选择

Part Four: Further Reading

Micro-economics and Institutions

Imaging that you are an executive of a large firm, You wake up one morning and, stumbling out of bed, realize that the day is going to be an unpleasant one. You rush to get a head start on the commuter traffic, but by 7 a.m. your car is caught in a massive traffic jam on the expressway. As your car sits idling on the right side of the road, you watch the barely moving vehicles ahead of you and contemplate the rest of your day.

At 9 a.m. you have an appointment with a representative of your firm's insurance company to find out whether that company will renew your firm's product liability insurance with the same deductible as before. At 10 a. m. you are scheduled to meet with a representative of the local utility company to discuss some proposals for cutting energy usage that might decrease your firm's high utility costs. Because the utility company, your firm cannot simply purchase its utility company, your firm cannot simply purchase its electricity from another company with lower rates. At 2 p. m. a committee that you head will be meeting to vote on some difficult issues. The committee members are deeply divided, and you hope that a majority will emerge on each issue. At 4 p. m. your firm will inform its executives about their yearly bonuses. This event always creates tension because the bonuses are based on top management's assessment of the performance of each executive during the past year.

After work, you will go to your health club. You need the exercise, but the main reason for your visit is that you paid a large annual membership fee and feel guilty about not using the club enough. On your way home, you will stop at a supermarket and buy your favorite fruit-Washington State apples, which, ironically, are not available to the residents of Washington.

This story, as simple as it is, illustrates the wide variety of institutions that shape our economic, social, and political lives. Let us now investigate the subject of institutions more closely.

Chapter 4: Buyer Behavior and Consumer Decision Making Process

Part One: Text

The aim of marketing is to meet and satisfy target customers' needs and wants. The field of consumer behavior studies how individuals, groups, and organizations select, buy, use, and dispose of goods, services, ideas, or experiences to satisfy their needs and desires. Understanding consumer behavior is never simple, because customers may say one thing but do another. They may not be in touch with their deeper motivations, and they may respond to influences and change their minds at the last minute.

Still, all marketers can profit from understanding how and why consumers buy. For example, Whirlpool's staffs anthropologists go into people's homes, observe how they use appliances, and talk with household members. Whirlpool has found that in busy families, women are not the only ones doing the laundry. Knowing this, the company's engineers developed color-coded washer and dryer controls to make it easier for kids and men to pitch in.

In fact, not understanding your customer's motivations, needs, and preferences can lead to major mistakes. This is what happened when Kodak introduced its Advanta camera—a costly bust. The company proudly touted it as a high-tech product, but the marketplace was dominated by middle-aged baby-boomers. In midlife, fancy new technology generally loses its appeal, and simplicity begins to edge out complexity in consumer preferences, so Advanta sales did not skyrocket.

Such examples show why successful marketers use both rigorous scientific procedures and more intuitive methods to study customers and uncover clues for developing new products, product features, prices, channels, messages, and other marketing-mix elements. This chapter explores individual consumers' buying dynamics.

The starting point for understanding buyer behavior is the stimulus-response model shown in Figure 4.1. Marketing and environmental stimuli enter the buyer's consciousness. The buyer's characteristics and decision process lead to certain purchasing decisions. The marketer's task is to understand what happens in the buyer's consciousness between the arrival of outside stimuli and the buyer's purchase decision.

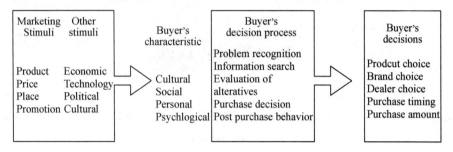

Figure 4.1   Stimulus response model

4.1   The major factors influencing buying behavior

Consumer's buying behavior is influenced by cultural, social, personal, and psychological factors. Cultural factors exert the broadest and deepest influence.

4.1.1   Cultural factors

Culture, subculture, and social class are particularly important in buying behavior.

1. Culture is the most fundamental determinant of a person's wants and behaviors. The growing child acquires a set of values, perceptions, preferences, and behaviors through his or her family and other key institutions. A child growing up in the United States is exposed to the following values: achievement and success, activity, efficiency and practicality, progress, material comfort, individualism, freedom, external comfort, humanitarianism, and youthfulness.

2. Subculture. Each culture consists of smaller subcultures that provide more specific identification and socialization for their members. Subcultures include

nationalities, religions, racial groups, and geographic regions. Many subcultures make up important market segments, and marketers often design products and marketing programs tailored to their needs.

3. Social class. Virtually all human societies exhibit social stratification. Stratification sometimes takes the form of a caste system where the members of different castes are reared for certain roles and cannot change their caste membership. More frequently, stratification takes the form of social classes.

Social classes do not reflect income alone, but also other indicators such as occupation, education, and area of residence. Social classes differ in dress, speech patterns, recreational preferences, and many other characteristics.

Social classes have several characteristics. First, those within each social class tend to behave more alike than persons from two different social classes. Second, persons are perceived as occupying inferior or superior positions according to social class. Third, social class is indicated by a cluster of variables—rather than by any single variable. Fourth, individuals can move from one social class to another—up or down—during their lifetime. The extent of this mobility varies according to the rigidity of social stratification in a given society.

Social classes show distinct product and brand preferences in many areas, including clothing, home furnishings, leisure activities, and automobiles. Some marketers focus their efforts on one social class.

4.1.2 Social factors

In addition to cultural factors, a consumer's behavior is influenced by such social factors as reference group, family, and social roles and statuses. Some membership groups are primary groups, such as family, friends, neighbors, and co-workers, with whom the person interact continuously and informally.

People also belong to secondary groups, such religious, professional, and trade union groups, which tend to be more formal and require less continuous interaction. People are significantly influenced by their reference groups in at least three ways. Reference groups expose an individual to new behaviors and lifestyles. They influence attitudes and self-concept. And they create pressures for conformity that may affect actual product and brand choices.

People are also influenced by groups to which they do not belong. Inspirational groups are those the person hopes to join; dissociative groups are those whose values or behavior an individual rejects.

Marketers try to identify target customers' reference groups. However, the level of reference group influence varies among products and brands. Reference groups appear to influence both product and brand choice strongly only in the case of automobiles and color televisions, mainly brand choice in such items as furniture and clothing, and mainly product choice in such items as beer and cigarettes.

Manufacturers of products and brand where group influence is strong must determine how to reach and influence the opinion leaders in these reference groups. An opinion leader is the person in informal product-related communications who offers advice or information about a specific product or product category, such as which of several brand is best or how a particular product or product category, such as which of several brands is best or how a particular product may be used. Opinion leaders are found in all strata of society, and person can be an opinion leader in certain product areas and an opinion follower in other areas.

Marketers try to reach opinion leaders by identifying demographic and psychographic characteristics associated with opinion leadership, identifying the media read by opinion leaders, and directing messages at the opinion leaders. The hottest trends in teenage music, language, and fashion start in America's inner cities, then quickly spread to more mainstream youth in the suburbs. Clothing companies that hope to appeal to the fickle and fashion-conscious youth market are making a concerted effort to monitor urban opinion leaders' style and behavior.

The family is the most important consumer-buying organization in society, and it has been researched extensively. Family members constitute the most influential primary reference group. We can distinguish between two families in the buyer's life. The family of orientation consists of one's parents and siblings. From parents a person acquires an orientation toward religion, politics, and economics and sense of personal ambition, self-worth, and love. Even if the buyer no longer interacts very much with his or her parents, their influence on the buyer's behavior can be significant. In countries where parents live with their grown children, their influence can be substantial. A more direct influence on everyday buying behavior is one's family of procreation—namely, one's spouse and children.

Marketers are interested in the roles and relative influence of the husband, wife, and children in the purchase of a large variety of products and services. These roles vary widely in different countries and social classes. Vietnamese Americans, for example, are more likely to adhere to the traditional model in which the man makes the decisions for any large purchase. Similarly, successful ads for Korean Americans usually will feature a man in his thirties or forties unless the ad is for a specifically female product, such as jewelry.

In the United States, husband-wife involvement has traditionally varied widely by product category. The wife has traditionally acted as the family's main purchasing agent, especially for food, sundries, and staple-clothing items. In the case of expensive products and services like vacations or housing, husbands and wives have engaged in more joint decision making. Marketers need to determine which member normally has the greater influence in choosing various products. Often it is a matter of who has more power or expertise.

4.1.3 Personal factors

A buyer's decisions are also influenced by personal characteristics. These include the buyer's age and stage in the life cycle, occupation, economic circumstances, lifestyle, and personality and self-concept.

1. Age and stage in the lifecycle. People buy different goods and service over a lifetime. They eat baby food in the early years, most foods in the growing and mature years, and special diets in the later years. Taste in clothes, furniture, and recreation is also age related. Consumption is shaped by the family life cycle. Nine stages of the family life cycle are listed in Table 4.1. along with the financial situation and typical product interests of each group. Marketers often choose life-cycle groups as their target market. Yet target households are not always family based: There are also single households, gay households, and cohabiter households.

Some recent work has identified psychological life-cycle stages. Adults experience certain "passages" or "transformations" as they go through life. Marketers pay close attention to changing life circumstances—divorce, widowhood, remarriage—and their effect on consumption behavior.

Table 4.1 Stage in family life cycle buying or behavioral pattern

1. Bachelor stage: young, single, not living at home	Few financial burdens, fashion leaders. Recreation oriented. Buy: basic home equipment, furniture, cars, equipment for the mating game, vacations
2. Newly married couples: young, no children	Highest purchase rate and highest average purchase of durables: cars, appliances, furniture, vacations
3. Full nest I: youngest child under six	Home purchasing at peak. Liquid assest low. Interested in new products, advertiscd products. Buy: washers, dryers, TV, baby food, chest rubs and cough medicines, vitamins, dolls, wagons, sleds, skates
4. Full nest II: youngest child six or over	Financial position better, less infuluenced by advertising. Buy larger-size packages, multiple-unit deals; many foods, cleaning materials, bicycles, music lessons, pianos
5. Full nest III: older married couples with dependent chileren	Financial position still better. Some chileren get jobs. Hard to influence with advertising. High average purchase of durables: new, more tasterful furniture, auto travel, unnecessary appliances, boats, dental services, magazines
6. Empty nest I: older married couples, no children living with them, head of house-hold in labour force	Home ownership at peak. Most satisfied with financial position and money saved. Interested in travel, recreation, self-education. Make gifts and contributions. Not interested in new products. Buy: vacations, luxuries, home improvements
7. Empty nest II: older married, children living at home, head of house-hold retired	Drastic cut in income, keep home. Buy: medical appliances and medical-care products
8. Solitary survivor, in labour force	Income still good but likely to sell home

2. Occupation and economic circumstances. Occupation also influences a person's consumption pattern. A blue-collar worker will buy work clothes, work shoes, and lunchboxes. A company president will buy expensive suits, air travel, country club membership, and a large sailboat. Marketers try to identify the occupational groups that have above-average interest in their product and services. A

company can even specialize its products for certain occupational groups: Computer software companies design different products for brand managers, engineers, lawyers, and physicians.

Product choice is greatly affected by economic circumstances: spendable income (level, stability, and time pattern), savings and assets (including the percentage that is liquid), debts, borrowing power, and attitude toward spending versus saving. Marketers of income-sensitive goods pay constant attention to trends in personal income savings, and interest rates. If economic indicators point to a recession, marketers can take steps to redesign, reposition, and reprice their products so they continue to offer value to target customers.

3. Lifestyle. People from the same subculture, social class, and occupation may lead quite different lifestyles. Marketers search for relationships between their products and lifestyle groups. For example, computer manufacturers might find that most computer buyers are achievement-oriented. The marketer may then aim the brand more clearly at the achiever lifestyle.

4. Personality and self-concept. Each person has a distinct personality that influences behavior. Personality is usually described in terms of such traits as self-confidence, dominance, autonomy, defensiveness, and adaptability. Personality can be a useful variable in analyzing consumer behavior, provided that personality types can be classified accurately and that strong correlations exist between certain personality types and product or brand choices. For example, a computer company might discover that many prospects show high, self-confidence, dominance and autonomy. These suggest designing computer advertisements to appeal to these traits.

Related to personality is self-concept (or self-image). Marketers try to develop brand images that match the target market's self-image. It is possible that a person's actual self-concept (how she views herself) differs from her ideal self-concept (how she would like to view herself differs from her other self-concept (how she thinks others see her).

Which self will she try to satisfy in making a purchase? Because it is difficult to answer this question, self-concept theory has had a mixed record of success in predicting consumer responses to brand images.

4.1.4 Psychological factors

A person's buying choices are influenced by four major psychological factors—

motivation, perception, learning, and beliefs and attitudes.

1. Motivation. A person has many needs at any given time. Some needs are biogenic; they arise from physiological states of tension such as hunger, thirst, discomfort. Other needs are psychogenic; they arise from psychological states of tension such as the need for recognition, esteem, or belonging. See Table 4.2. A need becomes a motive when it is aroused to a sufficient level of intensity. A motive is a need that is sufficiently pressing to drive the person to act.

Table 4.2 Motives and marketing actions that motivate

Motives	Marketing Actions That Motivate
Hunger reduction	Television and radio ads for fast-food restaurants
Safety	Smoke detector demonstration in stores
Sociability	Perfume ads showing social success due to products
Achievement	Use of consumer endorsements in ads specifying how much knowledge can be gained from and encyclopedia
Economy	Newspaper coupons advertising sales
Social responsibility	Package labels that emphasize how easy it is to recycle products

Each person has distinct motives for purchases, and these change by situation and over time. Consumers often combine economic (price, durability) and emotional (social acceptance, self-esteem) motives when making purchases.

Psychologists have developed theories of human motivation. Three of the best known—the theories of Sigmund Freud, Abraham Maslow, and Frederik Herzberg carry quite different implications for consumer analysis and marketing strategy.

Freud's Theory. Sigmund Freud assumed that the psychological forces shaping people's behavior are largely unconscious, and that a person cannot fully understand his or her own motivations. A technique called laddering can be used to trace a person's motivations from the stated instrumental ones to the more terminal ones. Then the marketer can decide at what level to develop the message and appeal.

When a person examines specific brands, he or she will react not only to their stated capabilities but also to other, less conscious cues. Shape, size, weight, material, color, and brand name can all trigger certain associations and emotions. Motivation researchers often collect "in-depth interviews" with a few dozen consumers to uncover deeper motives triggered by a product. They use various "projective techniques" such as word association, sentence completion, picture interpretation, and role playing.

More recent research holds that each product is capable of arousing a unique set of motives in consumers. For example, whiskey can attract someone who seeks social relaxation, status, or fun. Therefore, different brands have specialized in one of these three different appeals. Jan Callebaut calls this approach "motivational positioning".

Maslow's theory. Abraham Maslow sought to explain why people are driven by particular needs at particular times. Why does one person spend considerable time and energy on personal safety and another on pursuing the high opinion of others? Maslow's answer is that human needs are arranged in a hierarchy, from the most pressing to the least pressing. In their order of importance, they are physiological needs, safety needs, social needs, esteem needs, and self-actualization needs, see Figure 4.2. People will try to satisfy their most important needs first. When a person succeeds in satisfying an important need, that need will cease being a current motivator, and the person will try to satisfy the next-most-important need. For example, a starving man (need 1) will not take an interest in the latest happenings in the art world (need 5), nor in how he is viewed by others (need 3 or 4), not even in whether he is breathing clean air (need 2). But when he has enough food and water, the next-most-important need will become salient.

Maslow's theory helps marketers understand how various products fit into the plans, goals, and lives of consumers.

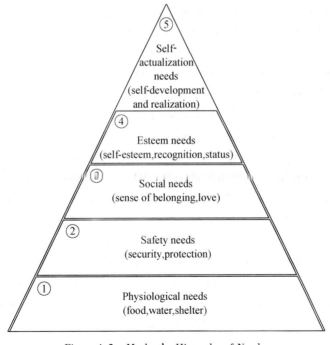

Figure 4.2 Maslow's Hierarchy of Needs

Herzberg's theory. Frederick Herzberg developed a two-factor theory that distinguishes dissatisfies (factors that cause dissatisfaction) and satisfies (factors that cause satisfaction). The absence of dissatisfies is not enough; satisfies must be actively present to motivate a purchase. For example, a computer that does not come with a warranty would be a dissatisfier. Yet the presence of a product warranty would not act as a dissatisfier or motivator of a purchase, because it is not a source of intrinsic satisfaction with the computer. Ease of use would be a dissatisfier.

Herzberg's theory has two implications. First, sellers should do their best to avoid dissatisfiers (for example, a poor training manual or a poor service policy). Although these things will not sell a product, they might easily unsell it. Second, the manufacturer should identify the major dissatisfier or motivators of purchase in the market and then supply them. These dissatisfier will make the major difference as to which brand the customer buys.

2. Perception. A motivated person is ready to act. How the motivated person actually acts is influenced by his or her perception of the situation. Perception depends not only on the physical stimuli but also on stimulates relation to the surrounding field and on conditions within the individual. The key word in the definition of perception is individual. One person might perceive a fast-talking salesperson as aggressive and insincere; another, as intelligent and helpful. People can emerge with different perceptions of the same object because of three perceptual processes: selective attention, selective distortion, and selective retention.

Selective attention. People are exposed to a tremendous amount of daily stimuli. The average person may be exposed to over 1 500 ads a day. Because a person cannot possibly attend to all of these, most stimuli will be screened out a process called selective attention. Selective attention means that marketers have to work hard to attract consumers' notice. The real challenge is to explain which stimuli people will notice.

Selective distortion. Even noticed stimuli do not always come across in the way the senders intended. Selective distortion is the tendency to twist information into personal meanings and interpret information in a way that will fit our preconceptions. Unfortunately, there is not much that marketers can do about selective distortion.

Selective retention. People will forget much that they learn but will tend to retain information that supports their attitudes and beliefs. Because of selective retention, we are likely to remember good points mentioned about a product we like and forget good points mentioned about competing products. Selective retention explains why marketers use drama and repetition in sending messages to their target market.

3. Learning. Most human behavior is learned. Learning theorists believe that learning is produced through the interplay of drives, stimuli, cues, responses, and reinforcement. A drive is a strong internal stimulus impelling action. Cues are minor stimuli that determine when, where, and how a person responds.

Suppose you buy an IBM computer. If your experience is rewarding, your response to computers and IBM will be positively reinforced. Later on, when you want to buy a printer, you may assume that because IBM makes good computers, IBM also makes good printers. In other words you generalize your response to similar stimuli. A counter tendency to generalization is discrimination. Discrimination means that the person has learned to recognize differences in sets of similar stimuli and can adjust responses accordingly.

Learning theory teaches marketers that they can build up demand for a product by associating it with strong drives, using motivating cues, and providing positive reinforcement. A new company can enter the market by appealing to the same drives that competitors use and providing similar cue configurations because buyers are more likely to transfer loyalty to similar brands (generalization). Or the company might design its brand to appeal to a different set of drives and offer strong cue inducements to switch (discrimination).

4. Beliefs and attitudes. Through doing and learning, people acquire beliefs and attitudes. These in turn influence buying behavior. Beliefs may be based on knowledge, opinion, or faith. They may or may not carry an emotional charge. Of course, manufacturers are very interested in the beliefs people carry in their heads about their products and services. These beliefs make up product and brand images, and people act on their images. If some beliefs are wrong and inhibit purchase, the manufacturer will want to launch a campaign to correct these beliefs. Particularly important to global marketers is the fact that buyers often hold distinct belief about brands or products based on their country of origin.

People have attitudes toward almost everything—religion, politics, clothes music, and food. Attitudes put them into a frame of mind of liking or disliking an object, moving toward or away from it. Attitudes lead people to behave in a fairly consistent way toward similar object. People do not have to interpret and react to every object in a fresh way. Because attitudes economize on energy and thought, they are very difficult to change. A person's attitudes settle into a consistent pattern: to change a single attitude may require major adjustments in other attitudes.

Thus a company would be well advised to fit its product into existing attitudes rather than to try to change people's attitudes. Of course, there are exceptions where the cost of trying to change attitudes might pay off.

4.2 The buying decision process

Marketers have to go beyond the various influences on buyers and develop an understanding of how consumers actually make their buying decisions. Specifically, marketers must identify who makes the buying decision, the types of buying decisions, and the steps in the buying process.

4.2.1 Buying roles

It is easy to identify the buyer for many products. In the United States, men normally choose their shaving equipment, and women choose their personal products. But even here marketers must be careful in making their targeting decisions, because buying roles change. ICI, the giant British chemical company, discovered to its surprise that women made 60 percent of the decisions on the brand of household paint; ICI therefore decided to advertise its DeLux brand to women.

4.2.2 Buying behavior

Consumer decision making varies with the type of buying decision. The decisions to buy toothpaste, a tennis racket, a personal computer, and a new car are all very different. Complex and expensive purchases are likely to involve more buyer deliberation and more participants. Assael distinguished four types of consumer buying behavior based on the degree of buyer involvement and the degree of differences among brands

4.2.3 Complex buying behavior

Complex buying behavior involves a three-step process. First, the buyer develops beliefs about the product. Second, he or she develops attitudes about the product. Third, he or she makes a thoughtful choice. Consumers engage in complex buying behavior when they are highly involved in a purchase and aware of significant differences among brands. This is usually the case when the product is expensive, bought infrequently, risky, and highly self-expressive. Typically the consumer does not know much about the product category. For example, a person buying a personal computer may not know what attributes to look for. Many product features carry no meaning unless the buyer has done some research.

The marketer of a high-involvement product must understand consumer's information-gathering and evaluation behavior. The marketer needs to develop strategies that assist the buyer in learning about the product's attributes and their relative importance, and that call attention to the high standing of the company's brand on the more important attributes. The marketer needs to differentiate store sales personnel and the buyer's acquaintances to influence the final brand choice.

4.2.4 Dissonance-reducing buyer behavior

Sometimes the consumer is highly involved in a purchase but sees little difference in brands. The high involvement is based on the fact that the purchase is expensive, in frequent, and risky. In this case, the buyer will shop around to learn what is available but will buy fairly quickly, perhaps responding primarily to a good price or to purchase convenience. For example, carpet buying is a high-involvement decision because carpeting is expensive and self-expressive, yet the buyer may consider most carpet brands in a given price range to be the same.

After the purchase, the consumer might experience dissonance that stems from noticing certain disquieting features or hearing favorable things about other brands. The consumer will be alert to information that supports his or her decision. In this example, the consumer first acted, then acquired new beliefs, then ended up with a set of attitudes. Marketing communications should supply beliefs and evaluations that help the consumer feel good about his or her brand choice.

4.2.5 Variety-seeking buying behavior

Some buying situations are characterized by low involvement but significant brand differences. Here consumers often do a lot of brand switching. Think about cookies. The consumer has some beliefs about cookies, chooses a brand of cookies without much evaluation, and evaluates the product during consumption. Next time, the consumer may reach for another brand out of a wish for a different taste. Brand switching occurs for the sake of variety rather than dissatisfaction.

The market leader and the minor brands in this product category have different marketing strategies. The market leader will try to encourage habitual buying behavior by dominating the shelf space, avoiding out-of-stock conditions, and sponsoring frequent reminder advertising. Challenger firms will encourage variety seeking by offering lower prices, deals, coupons, free samples, and advertising that presents reason for trying something new.

Part Two: Questions

1. What are the solutions to unprofitable customers?
2. Please identify which group of consumers the manufacturer should target, and explain why.

Part Three: Words and Phrases

1. stimulus-response   刺激反应
2. perceptions   感知
3. individualism   个人主义
4. occupation   职位
5. reference   参考
6. humanitarianism   人道主义
7. self-concept   自我概念
8. psychographic   心理
9. distortion   失真
10. rigidity   刚度
11. perception   知觉
12. participant   参与者
13. motivation   动机
14. discrimination   歧视
15. hierarchy   层次结构
16. purchase   购买
17. generalization   泛化
18. coupon   优惠券
19. evaluation   评价
20. dissonance   失调

Part Four: Further Reading

Consumer Behavior Changing

Slowing economic growth and changing consumer behavior are reshaping the strategies pursued by multinational companies in the Chinese market, as innovation and marketing are becoming more important than geographic expansion, a report by consultants Booz&Co said.

"Chinese consumers are increasingly opting for quality goods at higher prices and adopting online shopping and social media to gather product information, which are the two key trends driving company strategy in China," according to a report by the United States-based consulting firm.

The report's findings were based on an annual survey of 89 companies, mostly multinationals, conducted jointly by Booz and the American Chamber of Commerce in Shanghai.

The yearly survey began in 2011, and some of this edition's findings were already seen in China in previous years, said Steven Veldhoen, a partner with Booz.

For the second year, companies ranked the evolution of consumers—from price-driven purchasers to value-driven consumers—as the top trend driving their China market strategy.

Chinese consumers, particularly in first and second-tier cities, are seeking greater reliability, consistency and integrity in consumer products.

"There is no revolutionary trend we see in the Chinese market this year, as was the case during the past decade. This is a signal that the market has started to stabilize," Veldhoen said.

"In the past, it was all about looking for new opportunities. But now, as the market stabilizes, it's more about developing your core competitiveness, and do what you do the best to establish yourself among consumers with an increasing desire for value," he said.

"There are companies that used to adapt to market change very quickly but didn't build their internal strength. These companies are really being hurt by current trends," said Adam Xu, who is with the consultancy's consumer and retail practice.

He quoted a senior executive from a leading international beverage company as saying: "When it comes to the beverage business, it was always about expansion.

Now it's a mixed strategy of grasping new markets, but at the same time emphasizing per-store sales."

Xu said: "China is still a growth market, but it's shifting from a mode of extensive growth to a mode of intensive growth."

"In a way, it's consistent with the macro-economic trend the Chinese economy is undergoing," he added.

The world's second-largest economy expanded 7.5 percent in the second quarter of this year, the second quarterly deceleration in a row. However, the situation is widely seen as a "controlled" slowdown, with the new government giving more importance to the quality of growth.

According to the survey, product development and marketing were the most important steps companies had taken to address the impact of consumer trends. Seeking geographic expansion and overseas markets were seen as less important among the interviewees.

Product innovation and development of marketing channels are the areas where company leaders are most likely to invest in over the next 12 months.

"China's rising middle class has high expectations of consumer products", said Robert Theleen, chair of AmCham Shanghai.

"With the rise of e-commerce and social media, online marketing channels and internet forums offer a platform for consumers to gather the intelligence they need to make informed purchasing decisions," Theleen said.

"In China, consumers are sophisticated in using social networking platforms to form alliances with like-minded consumers... Companies must be alert to the power of online activities, with opportunities for online engagement to enhance or harm a brand," he continued.

"The success of China-basedsmart phone maker Xiaomi Inc is a good example of a company capable of integrating intelligence gleaned online into its business process," Xu said.

For product development, Xiaomi solicits suggestions for new features and improvements from an online community of brand followers. Most of its products are also sold online through preorders, giving it manufacturing and marketing edges.

Chapter 5: Marketing Research

Part One: Text

5.1 Definition of marketing research

Any discussion of the importance of information to the marketer must include a discussion of marketing research. Marketing research allows managers to make decisions based on objective data, gathered systematically, rather than on intuition.

What is the distinction between marketing research and other forms of marketing information? Even without a formal research program, a manager will have some information about what is going on in the world. Simply by reading the newspaper or watching TV, he or she may discover that a competitor has announced a new production, that the inflation rate is stabilizing, or that a new highway will be built and a shopping mall erected north of town. All of these things may affect the marketer's business, and this information is certainly handy to have, but is it the result of marketing research?

The answer to this question is no. Marketing research is the systematic and objective process of generating information for use in making marketing decision. This process includes defining the problem and identifying what information is required to solve the problem, designing a method for collecting information, managing and implementing the collection of data, analyzing the result, and communicating the findings and their implications.

Marketing research: the systematic and objective process of generating information for use in marketing decision making.

This definition suggests that marketing research is a special effort rather than a haphazard attempt at gathering information. Thus, glancing at a news magazine on an airplane or overhearing a rumor is not conducting marketing research. Even if a rumor or a fact casually overheard becomes the foundation of a marketing strategy, that strategy is not a product of marketing research because it was not based on information that was systematically and objectively gathered and recorded. The term marketing research suggests a specific, serious effort to generate new information. The term research suggests a patient, objective, and accurate search.

Although marketing managers may perform the research task themselves, they often seek the help of specialists known as marketing researchers. The researcher's role requires detachment from the question under study. If researchers cannot remain impartial, they may try to prove something rather than to generate objective data. If bias of any type enters into the investigative process, the value of the findings must be questioned. Yet this sort of thing can happen relatively easily. For example, a developer who owned a large parcel of land on which she wanted to build a high-price, high-prestige shopping center conducted a survey of customers' buying habits to demonstrate to prospective mall occupants that there was an attractive market for such a center. By conducting the survey only in elite neighborhoods, she generated "proof" that areas residents wanted a high-prestige shopping center.

Misleading "research" of this kind must be avoided. Unfortunately, business people with no knowledge of proper marketing research methods may inadvertently conduct poorly designed, biased studies or may be sold such work by marketing research firms. All business people should understand marketing research well enough to avoid these mistakes.

5.2 Scope of marketing research

The scope of marketing research is very wide and it provides useful information about all the aspects of marketing, for instance:

5.2.1 Product or service features desired by the customers

This information can be collected from the customers through a well defined research instrument.

Furthermore the relative importance of various features can also be obtained.

5.2.2 Pricing

The information regarding the prices charged by the competitors for the same and nearly same products or services can be obtained by market survey.

5.2.3 Consumer behavior

The research can be conducted to know about buying habits of the consumers. Information can be obtained regarding why consumers buy something; when do they buy it; from where they buy; how much do they buy; who accompanies them during the shopping, etc. Information to these key questions will help the marketer in improving his offering.

5.2.4 Distribution

The information can be obtained about the effectiveness of channel member, their motivation level and what needs to be done to improve their motivation level, in identifying the training needs, etc.

5.2.5 Promotion

Vital information can be obtained regarding the media habits of consumers which can provide vital inputs for the media planning. Advertising effectiveness can also be measured by post testing techniques which can help in identifying the best advertisement and its impact on the consumers. The consumers' response both qualitative and quantitative can help in identifying the best sales promotion technique for ones product or service.

5.3 The stages in the research process

Marketing is not an exact science like physics, but that does not mean that marketers and marketing researchers should not try to approach their jobs in a scientific manner. Marketing research is a systematic inquiry into the characteristics of the marketplace, just as astronomy is a systematic investigation of the stars and planets. Both use step-by-step approaches to gain knowledge.

The steps in the research process are highly interrelated and one step leads to the next. Moreover, the stages in the research process often overlap.

Disappointments encountered at one stage may necessitate returning to previous stages or even starting all over again. Thus, it is something of an oversimplification to present marketing research as a neatly ordered sequence of activities. Still, marketing research often follows a generalized pattern of seven stages. These stages are: stage 1, defining the problem; stage 2, planning the research design; stage 3, selecting a sample; stage 4, collecting data; stage 5, analyzing data; stage 6, drawing conclusions and preparing a report. ; stage 7, following up.

Again, these stages overlap and affect one another. For example, the research objectives outlined as part of the problem definition stage will have an impact on sample selection and data collection. In some cases, the "later" stages may be completed before the "early" ones. A decision to sample people of low educational levels (stage 3) will affect the wording of the questions posed to these people (stage 2). The research process, in fact, often becomes cyclical and ongoing, with the conclusions of one study generating new ideas and suggesting problems requiring further investigation. Within each stage of the research process, the researcher faces a number of alternative methods, or paths, from which to choose. In this regard, the research process can be compared to a journey. On any map, some paths are more clearly charted than others. Some roads are direct; others are roundabout. Some paths are free; others require the traveler to pay a toll. The point to remember is that there is no "right" or "best" path. The road taken depends on where the traveler wants to go and the amounts of time, money, ability and other resources available for the trip.

Although there is no "right" path, the researcher must choose an appropriate one—that is, one that addresses the problem at hand. In some situations, where time is short, the quickest path is best. In other circumstances, where money, time, and personnel are plentiful, the chosen path may be long and demanding.

Exploring the various paths marketing researchers encounter is the main purpose of this section, which describes the seven stages of the research process. Figure 5.1 illustrates some choices researchers face at each stage.

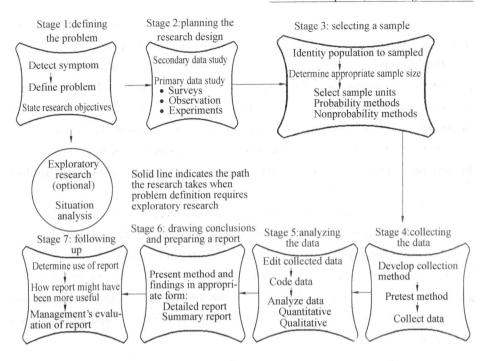

Figure 5.1   Research process

5.3.1   Stage 1: defining the problem

The idea that problem definition is central to the marketing research process is so obvious that its importance is easily overlooked. Albert Einstein noted that "The formulation of a problem is often more essential than its solution." This is valuable advice for marketing managers and researchers who, in their haste to find the right answer, may fail to ask the right question. Too often, data are collected before the nature of the problem has been carefully established. Except in cases of coincidence or good luck, such data will not help resolve the marketer's difficulties. Researchers are well advised to remember the adage "a problem well defined is a problem half solved".

Problems can be opportunities: on many occasions, the research process is not focused on a problem but on an opportunity. For example, a toy maker who has developed a fabulous new item might face the "problem" of determining what age groups will most likely want the toy or which advertising media are the best to use. In this happy circumstance, the problem definition stage of the research might well be called the "opportunity definition" stage. The point is that the problems addressed by marketing research are frequently "good" problems and not disasters.

Don't confuse symptoms with the real problem: there is a difference between a problem and the symptoms of that problem. Pain, for example, is the symptom of a problem. The cause of the pain, perhaps a broken leg, is the problem. In marketing, falling sales are symptoms that some aspect of the marketing mix is not working properly. Sales may be falling because price competition has intensified or because buyer preferences have changed. Defining the general nature of the problem provides a direction for the research.

As Figure 5.2 shows, defining the problem begins with the detection of symptoms. If managers are uncertain about the exact nature of the problem, they may spend time analyzing and learning about the situation. For example, they may discuss the situation with others, such as sales representatives, who are close to the customers. They may conduct exploratory research to shed more light on the situation and reveal more details about the problem. Exploratory research is optional and is not used in all research projects.

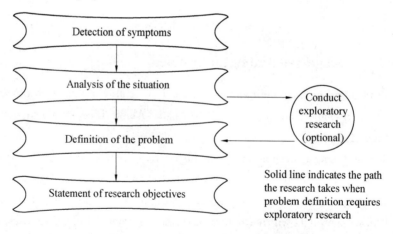

Figure 5.2   Clear-cut research objectives

Finally, as Figure 5.2 shows, the problem is defined, and a series of research objectives related to the problem are stated. No decisions about the remaining stages of the marketing research process should be made until managers and researchers clearly understand the objectives of the research about to be undertaken.

Exploratory research. Exploratory research is sometimes needed to clarify the nature of a marketing problem. Management may know, from noting a symptom such as declining sales, that some kind of problem is "out there" and may undertake exploratory research to try to identify the problem. Or, management may know what the problem is but not how big or how far-reaching it is. Here too, managers may need research to help them analyze the situation.

Providing conclusions is not the purpose of exploratory research. Its purpose is simply to investigate and explore. Usually, exploratory research is undertaken with the expectation that other types of research will follow and that the subsequent research will be directed at finding possible solutions.

In any research situation, it is generally best to check available secondary data before beginning extensive data collection. Some work at a library, on the internet, or with an internal database may save time and money. However, there isn't any set formula that outlines exactly how to analyze a situation.

Sometimes checking secondary sources may not be the appropriate first step. Instead, a short series of interviews with a few customers may be in order. Exploratory research in this case could serve to identify problem areas or points to a need for additional information.

Although there are many techniques for exploratory research, our discussion will highlight one popular method—the focus group interview—to illustrate the nature of exploratory techniques.

Focus group interviews are loosely structured interviews with groups of 6 to 10 people who "focus" on a product or some aspect of buying behavior. During a group session, individuals are asked to comment on and react to new product ideas or explain why they buy (or do not buy) certain products. Researchers later analyze those comments for useful ideas, such as that a product is "too high priced" or "looks like it would break easily." Focus group research is extremely flexible and may be used for many purposes—for example, to learn what problems consumers have with products. During one of Rubbermaid Inc.'s focus groups on housewares, a woman accused the industry of sexism. "Why do companies continue to treat brooms and mops like they were 'women's tools'?" she complained, "They're poorly designed and second class to hammers and saws, which are balanced and molded to fit men's hands. Brooms and mops make housework more miserable, not easier." At the time, Rubbermaid did not make cleaning products, but the woman's remarks eventually convinced the company that an opportunity awaited. After five years of research and development, Rubbermaid introduced a line of about 50 cleaning products and brushes designed to make cleaning easier, with handles that fit comfortably in consumers' hands and bristles angled to reach tight spaces.

What is "good" research objectives? Marketers contemplating a research project must decide exactly what they are looking for. The end of stage 1 of the research process must be a formal statement of the problems and the research objective(s). These provide the framework for the study.

The best way to express a research objective is as a well-constructed, testable hypothesis. A hypothesis is an unproven proposition or a possible solution to a problem, a statement that can be supported or refuted by empirical data. In its simplest form, it is a guess. In times of inflation or economic recession, an auto manufacturer might hypothesize that lower-income families were cutting back on car purchases more than wealthy families were. This is a hypothesis that can be tested.

5.3.2 Stage 2: planning the research design

After researchers have clearly identified the research problem and formulated a hypothesis, the next step is to develop a formal research design. The research design is master plan that identifies the specific techniques and procedures that will be used to collect and analyze data about a problem. The research design must be carefully compared to the objectives developed in stage 1 to assure that the sources of data, the data collected, the scheduling and costs involved, etc. are consistent with the researchers' goals.

At the outset, the researchers should determine if the data they need have already been generated by others or if primary research is required. In other words, researchers planning a researcher design must first choose between using secondary data and using primary data.

Research design using secondary data. As we have mentioned, data already in the researcher's decision support system or in the library may provide an adequate basis for a formal research effort. For example, a marketer of mobile phones might know that sales of this products showing regular increase in the numbers. A comparison of past sales record will verify it. In this case, the research design involves the analysis of secondary data only.

Meaningful secondary data may come from internal sources, such as company databases, or external sources, such as government agencies, trade associations, and companies that specialize in supplying specific types of data. Figure 5.3 shows some

Chapter 5 : Marketing Research

examples of the types of secondary data that are available.

The biggest advantages of secondary data are that first, they are always less expensive to collect than primary data and second, they can be obtained rapidly. Secondary sources must be used with care however as they have certain disadvantages.

Secondary data are "old" and possibly outdated, so the prediction for the future on the basis of past rather than present can turn out to be off the mark. Some data are collected only periodically. For examples, the population census is taken only once a decade. Comparatively up-to-data estimates if available in such cases must be used to predict the consumption of child related products.

Data may not have been collected in the form preferred. Sales figures may be available for a country but not for a particular town within that country. Similarly total sales data may be available but the product or brand wise sales data may not be available.

Users of secondary data may not be able to assess the data's accuracy. For example, previous researchers may have "bent" the data to "prove" some point or theory. So there will be in-built error in the research that used the secondary data.

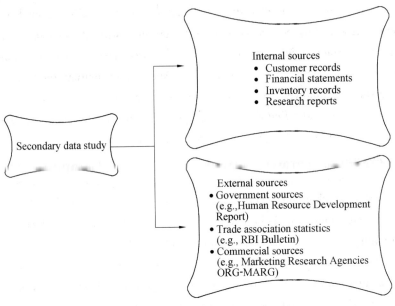

Figure 5.3   Secondary data sources

In general, a basic disadvantage of secondary data is that they were not collected specifically to meet the researcher's needs. The manager's task is to determine if the secondary data are pertinent and accurate.

The internet as a source of secondary data. The internet is a worldwide network of computers that gives users access to information and documents from distant sources. Many managers see the internet as the world's largest public library, because both noncommercial and commercial organizations post secondary data there. A wealth of data from reliable sources is available. For example, most of the companies provide complete details about their products and services which are accurate.

The internet is very user-friendly; information can be viewed using a mouse and menu-based software system called a web browser. Netscape and Microsoft Explorer are two popular web browsers that allow the user to enter a uniform resource locator, or URL.

A search engine is a computerized directory that allows users to search the internet for information indexed in a particular way. Most portals, such as Yahoo, Rediff, and Google, etc. contain comprehensive and accurate internet search engine. All a researcher has to do is type the search term in plain English or click on key words and phrases. Anyone can access most web sites without previous approval. However, many commercial sites require that the user have a valid accounts and password to access a site. For example, the Dalal Street Journal Interactive is a valuable resource; however, only subscribes who pay a fee can read it via the internet. Researchers who find that no appropriate secondary data are available can choose from three basic techniques for collecting primary data: surveys, observation, and experiments.

Survey. Primary data are commonly generated by survey research. Survey results on one topic or another are reported almost daily by the news media. Most adult Indian have been stopped by interviewers at shopping centers or voting places or have received mailings or phone calls from survey takers. In general, a survey is any research effort in which data are gathered systematically from a sample of people by means of a questionnaire. Researchers using surveys may collect data by means of telephone interviews, mailed questionnaires, personal interviews (either door-to-door or in shopping malls or some other public place), or some other communication method such as fax or the internet.

Survey research has several advantages. For one thing, surveys involve direct communication. How better to provide buyers with what they want is to first ask them what they want. For example, U. S. automobile makers operate style research clinics to appraise consumer reactions to car designs. First, mock-ups of proposed designs are constructed; then consumers, or respondents, are recruited through short telephone interviews. These respondents are brought in to a showrooms and shown a carbon mock-up along with competing autos from around the world. As the "buyers" look over the cars, professional interviewers ask for their reactions to virtually every detail. The survey results are then given to designers.

When surveys are properly planned and executed, they are quick, efficient, and accurate means of gathering data. Survey research can involve problems, however. Careless researchers may design or conduct surveys improperly and thus produce incorrect and worthless results—that is results marked by systematic bias. The survey questions might be poorly worded, respondents might be reluctant to provide truthful answers, the sample may not be representative, or mistakes might be made entering data into the computer.

Tables 5. 1 summarizes the advantages and disadvantages of the most popular types of surveys. You can see from this exhibit that choosing one method over another involves trade-offs. For instance, a low-cost mail survey takes more time and is less versatile than a highest-cost personal interview at the consumer's doorstep.

How does the researchers choose the appropriate survey technique? The marketing problem itself generally suggests which technique is most appropriate. A manufacturer of industrial equipment might choose a mail survey because the executives it wishes to question are hard to reach by phone. A political party might prefer to employ a door to door personal survey so that voters can formulate and voice their opinions on current issues. In these examples, the cost, time, and perhaps accuracy involved vary. It is the researcher's job to weigh the advantages and disadvantages of each method and find the most appropriate way to collect the needed data.

Table 5.1 Characters of survey methods

	Personal Interview		Mail-in questionnaire	Telephone interview	Internet survey
	Door-to door	Shopping mall			
Speed of data collection	Moderate to fast	Fast	Researcher has no control over return of questionnaire	Very fast	Instantaneous
Respondent cooperation	Good	Moderate	Moderate—poorly designed questionnaire will have low response rate	Good	Varies depending on web site
Flexibility of questioning	Very flexible	Very flexible	Highly standardized format is very inflexible	Moderately flexible	Extremely flexible
Questionnaire length	Long	Moderate to long	Varies depending on purpose	Moderate	Modest
Possibility for respondent misunderstanding	Low	Low	Highest—no interviewer to clarify questions	Moderate	High
Influence of interviewer on answers	High	High	None	Moderate	None
Cost	Highest	Moderate to high	Low	Low to moderate	Lowest

Wording survey questions appropriately is a skill that must be learned. The questionnaire writer's goals are to avoid complexity and use simple, accurate, conversational language that does not confuse or bias the respondent. The wording of questions should be simple and unambiguous so that the questions are readily understandable to all respondents.

Consider, for example, the following question: should the limited continue its excellent gift-wrapping program?

Yes or No.

The gift-wrapping program may not be excellent at all. By answering "yes," a respondent is implying that things are just fine as they are. But by answering "no," it implies that the limited should discontinue the gift wrapping. Question should be worded so that the respondent is not put in this sort of bind.

Many respondents are susceptible to leading questions, such as "You do agree that U. S. automobiles are a better value than Japanese automobiles, don't you?" Leading questions should be avoided.

Observation. If the purpose of a research effort is to note actions that are mechanically or visually recordable, observation techniques can form the basis of that effort. Observation research involves the systematic recording of behavior, objects, or events as they are witnessed. Companies that sell space on outdoor hoardings are interested in traffic patterns—specifically, the numbers of cars and people passing the hoarding installations each day. Mass transit organizations may want to know how many people ride each bus and where most of them get on or off. In both cases, the information could be recorded either by human observers or by mechanized counters.

Observation can be more complicated than these simple head-counting examples might suggest. For example, Fisher-Price's Play Laboratory is a well-stocked day-care center where toy designers and marketing researchers sit behind a one way mirrors to observe children who are trying out new toys. They observe how long children play with various toys and evaluate whether prototype toys catch children's interest.

"Mystery shoppers" can be used to check on salespeople's courtesy or product knowledge. Researchers disguised as customers, store employees, or product demonstrators might subtly observe consumer reactions to prices, products, package designs, or display cases, leaving the consumers unaware that their behavior was being observed.

The greatest strength of observation is that it permits the recording of what actually occurs in a particular situation. Its biggest weakness is that the observer cannot be sure why the observed behavior occurred. Still, in some cases, it is enough to know that something happened.

Experiments have long been used by scientists attempting to discover cause-and-effect relationships. Almost every day, you can read news stories about experimental groups of white mice that were exposed to some substance and then developed more cancers than mice in groups not exposed. The assumption, of course, is that the substance involved the chance of developing cancer. A properly run experiment allows an investigator to change one variable, such as price, and then observe the effects of the change on another variable, such as sales. Ideally, the experimenter holds all factors steady except the one being manipulated, thus showing that changes are caused by the factor being studied.

Marketing researchers use experimental techniques both in the marketplace ("in the field") in controlled, or laboratory, situations. For example, McDonald's conducted experiments in the marketplace to determine if it should add a single-slice McPizza to its menu. The company sold the product in test markets-cities where a test product is sold just as it would be if it were marketed nationwide. Test markets provide a trial run to determine consumers' reaction and actual sales volume. For McDonald's, sales of the pizza slices were disappointing, and the company discontinued its plans to market pizza to adults. The company test marketed pizza in children's Happy Meals, finding the response favorable, it was introduced nationwide.

In contrast, advertisers often use laboratory settings to test advertising copy. One group of subjects is shown a television program that includes one version of an advertisement. A second group views the same program with a different version of advertisement. Researchers compare the group's responses. Research like this is conducted in a controlled setting, rather than a natural setting, to increase researchers' control of environmental variables. Such an experiment is known as laboratory experiment.

Selecting the research design. After considering research alternatives, a marketing researcher must pick one. Because there are many ways to tackle a problem, there is no one "best" research design. Certain techniques are simply more appropriate than others.

For example, what technique should the "Gwalior's Museum of Royal Scindia Family" use to determine which of its exhibits is the most popular? Survey? (Could you really expect visitors to remember and rate all the museum's exhibits?) Experimentation? (Would you close off the exhibits one at a time and count the complaints associated with each closing?) Secondary data? (That might tell you what exhibits are most popular at other museums) The Gwalior Museum's researcher actually suggested the simple and inexpensive observation technique of keeping track of how frequently the wooden floor tile had to be replaced in front of each exhibit—indicating which exhibit drew the heaviest traffic. Of course, had the museum been in a hurry for information, another method would have been more appropriate, but the wooden floor tile approach gave museum operators a good measurement over time at a low cost.

5.3.3 Stage 3: selecting a sample

Once a researcher has determined which research design to use, the next step is to select a sample of people, organization, or whatever is of interest. The methods for selecting the sample are important for the accuracy of the study.

Though sampling is a highly developed statistical science, we all apply its basic concepts in daily life. For example, the first taste (or sample) of a bowl of vegetable may indicate that the vegetable needs salt, is too salty, or is" just right". Sampling, then, is any procedure in which a small part of the whole is used as the basis for conclusions regarding the whole.

A sample is simply a portion, or subset, of a larger population. It makes sense that a sample can provide a good representation of the whole. A well-chosen sample of lawyers in New Delhi should be representative of all New Delhi lawyers making surveying all of them unnecessary. A survey of all the members of a group is called a census. For a small group—say, a group comprising the Vice Chancellors of all universities in India-sampling is not needed. All the VCs can easily be identified and contacted. Sampling essentially requires answering these three questions:

1. Who is to be sampled? Specifying the target population, or the total group of interest, is the first aspect of sampling. The manager must make sure the population to be sampled accurately reflects the population of interest. Suppose a Maruti Service Station manager wants to analyze the service station's image among the Maruti car owners collects information about the customers from the dealer and vehicle registration office or insurance companies. Next step is to, identify who will be surveyed. It'll be all the owners of Maruti cars or those customers who gets their cars serviced at his service station or the customers who get their cars serviced at other service stations.

Lists of customers, telephone directories, membership lists, and lists of automobile registrations are a few of the many population lists from which a sample may be taken. Selecting a list from which to draw a sample is a crucial aspect of sampling. If the list is inaccurate, the sample may not be representative of the larger population of interest.

2. How big should the sample be? The traditional tongue-in-check response to this question—"big enough"—suggests the true answer. The sample must be big enough to properly portray the characteristics of the target population. In general, bigger samples are better than smaller samples. Nevertheless, if appropriate sampling techniques are used, a small proportional of the total population, will give a reliable measure of the whole. For instance, the Nielsen TV ratings survey, which appears to be highly accurate involves only a few thousands of the 103 million U.S. households. The keys here are that most families, TV viewing habits are similar and that the Nielsen families are selected with meticulous care to assure the representativeness of the sample.

Post-poll surveys conducted by different media groups often go wrong in correctly predicting the outcomes even though the surveys were spread over around 20 states 150 cities and thousands of respondents. This is because these surveys are not representative of rural population. Data is collected only from the cities and the predictions were made on the basis of urban respondent's responses.

3. How should the sample be selected? The way sampling units are selected is a major determinant of the accuracy of marketing research. There are two major sampling methods: probability sampling and non probability sampling. When the sampling procedures are such that the laws of probability influence the selection of the sample, the result is a probability sample. A simple random sample consists of individual names drawn according to chance selection procedures from a complete list of all people in a population. All these people have the same chance of being selected. The procedure is called simple because there is only one stage in the sampling process.

When sample units are selected on the basis of convenience or personal judgment (for example, if New Delhi is selected as a sample city because it appears to be representative of Indian population), the result is a non probability sample. In one type of non probability sample, a convenience sample, data are collected from the people who are most conveniently available. A professor or graduate student who administers a questionnaire to a class is using a convenience sample. It is easy and economical to collect sample data this way; but unfortunately, this type of sampling often produces unrepresentative samples. Another non probability sample, the quota sample, is often utilized by interviewers who intercept consumers at shopping malls. Within this type of sampling, people are chosen because they appear to the interviewers to be of the appropriate age, sex, race, or the like.

5.3.4 Stage 4: collecting data

Once the problem has been defined, the research techniques chosen, and the sample to be analyzed selected, the researcher must actually collect the needed data. Whatever collection method is chosen, it is the researcher's task to minimize errors in the process and errors are easy to make.

Generally, before the desired data are collected, the collection methods are pretested. A proposed questionnaire or interview script might be tried out on a small sample of respondents in an effort to assure that the instructions and questions are clear and comprehensible. The researcher may discover that the survey instrument is too long, causing respondents to lose interest, or too short, yielding inadequate information. The pretesting provides the researcher with a limited amount of data that will give an idea of what can be expected from the upcoming full-scale study. In some cases, these data will show that the study is not answering the researcher's questions. The study may then have to be redesigned. After pretesting shows the data collection method and questionnaire to be sound, the data can be collected.

5.3.5 Stage 5: analyzing the data

Once a researcher has completed what is called the fieldwork by gathering the data needed to solve the research problem, those data must be manipulated, or processed. The purpose is to place the data in a form that will answer the marketing manager's questions.

Processing requires entering the data into a computer. Data processing ordinarily begins with a job called editing, in which surveys or other data collection instruments are checked for omissions, incomplete or otherwise unusable responses, illegibility, and obvious inconsistencies. As a result of the editing process certain collection instruments may be discarded. In research reports, it is common to encounter phrase. The process may also uncover correctable errors, such as the recording of a usable response on the wrong line of a questionnaire.

Once the data collection forms have been edited, the data undergo coding. That is, meaningful categories are established so that responses can be grouped into classification usable for computer analysis. For example, for a survey focusing on response differences between men and women, a gender code, such as 1 = male and 2 = female, might be used.

After editing and coding, the researcher is ready to undertake the process of analysis. Data analysis may involve statistical analysis, qualitative analysis, or both. The type of analysis used should depend on management's information requirements, the research hypothesis, the design of the research itself, and the nature of the data collected. A review of the many statistical tools that can be used in marketing research is beyond the scope of this book. They range from simple comparisons of numbers and percentages (100 people, or 25 percent of the sample, agreed) to complex mathematical computations requiring a computer. Statistical tools such as the T-test of two means, the Chi-square test, and correlation analysis are commonly used to analyze data. It may be surprising, in light of the availability of these and many other techniques, that a great number of studies use statistics no more sophisticated than averages and percentages.

5.3.6 Stage 6: drawing conclusions and preparing a report

Remember that the purpose of marketing research is to aid managers in making effective marketing decisions. The researcher's role is to answer the question "What does this mean to marketing managers?" Therefore, the end result of the research process must be a report that usefully communicates research findings to management. Typically, management is not interested in how the findings were arrived at. Except in special cases, management is likely to want only a summary of the findings. Presenting these clearly, using graphs, charts, and other forms of artwork, is a creative challenge to the researcher and any others involved in the preparation of the final report. If the researcher does not communicate the findings so that marketing managers can understand them, the research process has been, in effect, a total waste.

5.3.7 Stage 7: following up

After the researcher submits a report to management, he or she should follow up to determine if and how management responded to the report. The researcher should ask how the report could have been improved and made more useful. This is not to say that researchers should expect that managers will always agree with a report's conclusions or pursue its suggested courses of action. Deciding such things, is, after all, the role of managers, not of researchers. Marketing management, for its part, should let researcher know how report could be improved or how future reports might be made more useful.

Part Two: Questions

1. Try to explain why marketing research is not always correct.
2. Why firms may not have a need for marketing research?

Part Three: Words and Phrases

1. intuition	直觉
2. haphazard	偶然的
3. marketing strategy	营销策略
4. rumor	谣言
5. consumer behavior	消费者行为
6. oversimplification	过度简化
7. hypothesis	假设
8. secondary data	二手数据
9. symptom	症状
10. exploratory research	探索性研究
11. meticulous	一丝不苟的
12. representativeness	代表性
13. versatile	通用的;万能的
14. plentiful	丰富的
15. quota	定额
16. inventory record	库存记录
17. manufacturer	制造商
18. Chi-square	卡方
19. scope	范围
20. sophisticated	复杂的

Part Four: Further Reading

Nielsen Holdings Company

Nielsen Holdings is a global information and measurement company that helps businesses better understand their markets. The company enables companies understand consumers and consumer behavior by measuring and monitoring what consumers watch and the brands consumers associate with on a global and local basis. The company has a presence in approximately 100 countries spread across Africa, Asia, Australia, Europe, Middle East, North America, South America, and Russia.

Nielsen Holdings was founded in August 1923 and is based in New York, United States. Whether you're eyeing markets in the next town or across continents, we understand the importance of knowing what consumers watch and buy. That's our passion and the very heart of our business.

About Nielsen: "We study consumers in more than 100 countries to give you the most complete view of trends and habits worldwide. And we're constantly evolving, not only in terms of where we measure, or who we measure, but in how our insights can help you drive profitable growth.

"Whether your business is a multinational enterprise or a single storefront, we believe innovation is the key to success, in both what you create and how you market your products and ideas. That's why we continue to develop better solutions to help you meet the needs of today's consumers, and find out where they're headed next.

"So let's put our heads together. We'll bring our insight to your business and help you grow."

Chapter 6: Market Segmentation

Part One: Text

6.1 The definition of market segmentation

We have already defined what a market is but let us look again at that definition. A market is a group of actual or potential customers for a particular product. More precisely, a market is a group of individuals or organizations that may want the good or service being offered for sale and that meet these three additional criteria:

First, they have the ability or purchasing power to buy the product being offered. Second, they have the willingness to spend money or exchange other resources to obtain the product. Third, they have the authority to make such expenditures.

Economics text books often give the impression that all consumers are alike. Economists frequently, draw no distinctions among different types of buyers, as long as they have willingness and an ability to buy. Young and old buyers, men and women, people who drink 12 beers a day and those who drink one beer on New Years Eve are all lumped together. Experience tells marketers, however, that in many cases buyers differ from one another even though they may be buying the same products. Marketers try to identify groups and subgroups within total markets—that is, they try to segment markets. Recall that market segmentation consists of dividing a heterogeneous market into a number of smaller, more homogeneous sub-markets. Almost any variable age, sex, product usage, life style, expected benefit may be used as a segmenting variable, but the logic behind the strategy is always the same.

Usually, marketers are able to cluster similar customers into specific market segments with different, and sometimes unique, demands. For example, the computer software market can be divided into two segments: the domestic market and the foreign market.

The domestic market can be segmented further into business users and home users. And the home user segment can be further divided into sophisticated personal computer user, people who hate personal computers but have to buy so their children use it for school work, people who use computers only for e-mail, and so on. The number of market segments within the total market depends largely on the strategist's ingenuity and creativity in identifying those segments.

Needless to say, a single company is unlikely to pursue all possible market segments. In fact, the idea behind market segmentation is for an organization to choose one or a few meaningful segments and concentrate its efforts on satisfying those selected parts of the market. Focusing its efforts on these targeted market segments—that is, targeting-enables the organization to allocate its marketing resources effectively. Concentrating efforts on a given market segment should result in a more precise marketing program satisfying specific market needs.

The market segment, or group of buyers, toward which an organization decides to direct its marketing plan is called the target market. The target market for shower shaver, for example, is that sub group of women who shave their legs in the shower. Because it is possible to segment markets in so many ways, target marketing opportunities abound. For example, there are "left-hand" shops specializing in products for left-handed people, tobacco shops catering to wealthy pipe smokers, and dress shops that target women who wear certain clothing sizes. In addition, numerous products bear the names or symbols of sports teams, such as the San Francisco 49ers or the Chicago Bulls, and are marketed to team fans. As you can see, the process of segmentation provides hints on how to market to the targeted segments identified.

Selection of a target market (or markets—in some cases, more than one may be selected for a product) is a three-step process, as shown in Figure 6.1. First, the total market, consisting of many different customers, is studied and broken down into its component parts that is, individual customers, families, organizations, or other units. The customers are then regrouped by the marketing strategist into market segments on the basis of one or several characteristics that segment members have in common. Then the strategist must target segments to which the organization will appeal. When that is done, the strategist has answered the question "What are our target markets?"

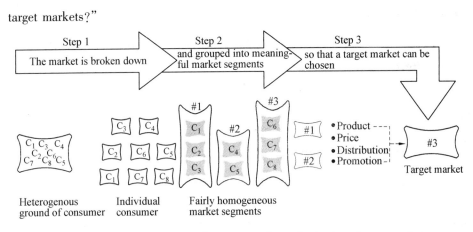

Figure 6.1 Major steps in market segmentation and selection of target markets

To sum up, the market for any product is normally made up of several segments. A "market" after all is the aggregate of consumers of a given product. And, consumers, who make a market, vary in their characteristics and buying behavior. It is thus natural that many differing segments occur within a market. Marketers usually divide the heterogeneous market for any product into segments, with relatively more homogeneous characteristics, since this helps in tapping it. And, this process of disaggregating a market into a number of sub-markets segments is known as **market segmentation**.

To put it in a nutshell, market segmentation rests on the recognition that: First, any market is made up of several sub-markets, or sub-groups of consumers, distinguished from one another by their varying needs and buying behavior, and Second, it is feasible to disaggregate the consumers into segments in such a manner that in needs, characteristics and buying behavior, the members would vary significantly among/across segments, but would be homogeneous within each segment.

6.2 Why segment the market

6.2.1 Facilitates proper choice of target market

In the first place, segmentation helps the marketer to distinguish one customer group from another within a given market and thereby enables him to decide which segment should form his target market.

6.2.2 Facilitates tapping of the market, adapting the offer to the target

Segmentation also enables the marketer to crystallize the needs of the target buyers. It also helps him to generate an accurate prediction of the likely responses from each segment of the target buyers. Moreover, when buyers are handled after careful segmentation, the responses from each segment will be homogeneous. This, in turn, will help the marketer develop marketing offers/programmes that are most suited to each group. It can achieve the specialization that is required in product, distribution, promotion and pricing for matching the particular customer group, and develop marketing offers and appeals that match the requirements of that particular group. See Exhibit 6.1.

Exhibit 6.1 Adapting offer to suit target segment

Ford modifies its models for India
Ford modified its models for the Indian target segment as shown below:
· Hgher ground clearance to make the car more compatible to the rougher road surface in India
· Stiffer rear springs to enable negotiating the ubiquitous potholes on Indian roads
· Changes in cooling requirement, with greater airflow to the rear
· Higher resistance to dust
· Compatibility of engine with the quality of fuel available in India
· Location of horn buttons on the steering wheel
As the Indian motorist uses the horn far more frequently, for cars sold in India, the horn buttons are kept on the steering wheel and not on a lever on the side as in the models sold in Europe.

The Ford Strategy. Through segmentation, car manufacturers have gained useful insights on the product features/benefits to be provided to different segments of car buyers. It will also be clear that within a given segment, the Indian requirement is often unique, giving rise to an India-specific sub-segment within any segment. Product offerings have to be tailored to suit Indian conditions, especially Indian roads. From the details provided, it will be clear that firms do appreciate this reality and they provide specific offers/models suiting the Indian segment. Exhibit 6.1 explains how Ford has gained useful insights through segmentation and adapted its offer to suit the Indian target segment. In recent years, other car makers have also identified distinct segments in the Indian car market and offered distinct models for each of them. For example, Daewoo offers eight variants of its Cielo, and Ford Mahindra offers four versions of the Ford Escort.

6.2.3 Helps divide the markets and conquer them

Through segmentation, the marketer can look at the differences among the customer groups and decide on appropriate strategic offers for each group. This is precisely why some marketing experts have described segmentation as a strategy of dividing the markets for conquering them.

6.2.4 Makes the marketing effort more efficient and economic

Segmentation also makes the marketing effort more efficient and economic. It ensures that the marketing effort is concentrated on well defined and carefully chosen segments. After all, the resources of any firm are limited and no firm can normally afford to attack and tap the entire market without any delimitation whatsoever. It would benefit the firm if the efforts were concentrated on segments that are the most productive and profitable ones.

6.2.5 Helps identify less satisfied segments and concentrate on them

Segmentation also helps the marketer assess as to what extent existing offers from competitors match the needs of different customer segments. The marketer can thus identify the relatively less satisfied segments and succeed by satisfying such segments.

6.2.6 Benefits the customer as well

Segmentation brings benefits not only to the marketer, but to the customer as well. When segmentation attains higher levels of sophistication and perfection, customers and companies can conveniently settle down with each other, as at such a stage, they can safely rely on each other's discrimination. The firm can anticipate the wants of the customers and the customers can anticipate the capabilities of the firm.

6.3 Levels and pattern of market segmentation

We begin by examining the various levels and pattern of market segmentation. Market segmentation is an effort to increase a company's precision marketing. The starting point of any segmentation discussion is mass marketing. In mass marketing, the seller engages in the mass production, mass distribution, and mass promotion of one product for all buyers. Henry Ford epitomized this marketing strategy when he offered the Model T Ford "in any color, as long as it is black". Coca-Cola also practiced mass marketing when it sold only one kind of Coke in a 6.5-ounce bottle.

The argument for mass marketing is that it creates the largest potential market, which leads to the lowest costs, which in turn can lead to lower prices or higher margins. However, many critics point to the increasing splintering of the market, which makes mass marketing more difficult. According to Regis McKenna, the proliferation of advertising media and distribution channels is making it difficult to practice "one size fits all" marketing. Some claim that mass marketing is dying. Not surprisingly, many companies are turning to micro-marketing at one of four levels: segment, niches, local areas, and individuals.

6.3.1 Segment marketing

A market segment consists of a large identifiable group within a market with similar wants, purchasing power, geographical location, buying attitudes, or buying habits. For example, an auto company may identify four broad segments: car buyers who are primarily seeking basic transportation or high performance or luxury or safety.

Segmentation is an approach midway between mass marketing and individual marketing. Each segment's buyers are assumed to be quite similar in wants and needs, yet no two buyers are really alike. Anderson and Narus urge marketers to present flexible market offerings instead of a standard offering to all members within a segment. A flexible market offering consists of two parts: a naked solution consisting of product and service elements that all segment members' value and options that some segment members' value. Each option carries an additional charge. For example, Delta Airlines offers all economy passengers a seat, food, and soft drinks. It charges extra for alcoholic beverages and earphones to those economy passengers wanting them.

Segment marketing offers several benefits over mass marketing. The company can create a more fine-tuned product or service offering and price it appropriately for the target audience. The choice of distribution channels and communication channels becomes much easier. The company also may face fewer competitors in the particular segment.

6.3.2 Niche marketing

A niche is a more narrowly defined group, typically a small market whose needs are not well served. Marketers usually identify niches by dividing a segment into sub segments or by defining a group seeking a distinctive mix of benefits. For example, the segment of heavy smokers includes those who are trying to stop smoking and those who don't care.

Whereas segments are fairly large and normally attract several competitors, niches are fairly small and normally attract only one or two. Larger companies, such as IBM, lose pieces of their market to nichers. Dalgic labeled this confrontation "guerrillas against gorillas". Some larger companies have therefore turned to niche marketing, which has required more decentralization and some changes in the way they do business. Johnson&Johnson, for example, consists of 170 affiliates (business units), many of which pursue niche markets.

The prevalence of niche—and even "microniche"—marketing can be seen in the media. Witness the proliferation of new magazines targeting specific niches, divided and subdivided along lines of ethnicity, gender, etc. For example, there is Outlook Travelers for those who love traveling; there is Inside Outside which focus on design and interior; there is Osho Times for those who believe in Osho, etc.

Niche marketers presumably understand their customers' needs so well that the customers willingly pay a premium. Ferrari gets a high price for its cars because loyal buyers feel no other automobile comes close to offering the product-service-membership benefit bundle that Ferrari does.

An attractive niche is characterized as follows: the customers in the niche have a distinct set of needs; they will pay a premium to the firm that best satisfies their needs; the niche is not likely to attract other competitors; the nicher gains certain economies through specialization; and the niche has size, profit, and growth potential. Both small and large companies can practice niche marketing.

Linneman and Stanton claim that there are riches in niches and believe that companies will have to niche or risk being nicked. Blattberg and Deighton claim that "niches too small to be served profitably today will become viable as marketing efficiency improves." The low cost of setting up shop on the internet is a key factor making it more profitable to serve even seemingly minuscule niches. Small businesses, in particular, are realizing riches from serving small niches on the World Wide Web. Fifteen percent of the commercial web sites with fewer than 10 employees take in more than $100 000, and 2 percent even ring up more than $1 million. The recipe for internet nicking success: choose a hard-to-find product that customers don't need to see and touch.

6.3.3 Local marketing

Target marketing is leading to marketing programs being tailored to the needs and wants of local customer groups (trading areas, neighborhoods, even individual stores). McDonald's offers different types of offerings in different states of India because the food habits of the people are different.

Those favoring localizing a company's marketing see national advertising as wasteful because it fails to address local needs. Those against local marketing argue that it drives up manufacturing and marketing costs by reducing economies of scale. Logistical problems become magnified when companies try to meet varying local requirements. A brand's overall image might be diluted if the product and message differ in different localities.

6.3.4 Individual marketing

The ultimate level of segmentation leads to "segments of one" "customized marketing", or "one-to-one marketing". For centuries, consumers were served as individuals: The tailor made the suit and the cobbler designed shoes for the individual. Much business-to-business marketing today is customized, in that a manufacturer will customize the offer, logistics, communications, and financial terms for each major account. New technologies—computers, databases, robotic production, e-mail, and fax-permit companies to return to customized marketing, or what is called "mass customization". Mass customization is the ability to prepare on a mass basis individually designed products and communications to meet each customer's requirements.

According to Arnold Ostle, chief designer for Mazda, "Customers will want to express their individuality with the products they buy." The opportunities offered by these technologies promise to turn marketing from "a broadcast medium to a dialogue medium", where the customer participates actively in the design of the product and offer.

Today customers are taking more individual initiative in determining what and how to buy. They log onto the internet; look up information and evaluations of product or service offers; dialogue with suppliers, users, and product critics; and make up their own minds about the best offer.

Marketers will still influence the process but in new ways. They will need to set up toll-free phone numbers and e-mail addresses to enable buyers to reach them with questions, suggestions, and complaints. They will involve customers more in the product-specification process. They will sponsor an internet home page that provides full information about the company's products, guarantees, and locations.

Just as mass production was the organizing principle of the last century, mass customization is becoming the organizing principle for the twenty-first century. Two trends are converging to make this so. One is the predominance of the customer and the importance of true customer service. Consumers are demanding not only quality products but also products that meet their individual needs. Marketing expert Regis McKenna says, "Choice has become a higher value than brand in America." Yet, it would be prohibitively expensive, if not downright impossible, to offers customers so many choices if it weren't for another trend: the emergence of new technologies.

Computer-controlled factory equipment and industrial robots can now quickly read just assembly lines. Bar-code scanners make it possible to track parts and products. Data warehouses can store trillions of bytes of customer information. Most important of all, the internet ties it all together and makes it easy for a company to interact with customers, learn about their preferences, and respond. Joseph Pine, author of Mass Customization says: "Anything you can digitize, you can customize."

Consumer goods marketers aren't the only ones riding these trends. Business-to-business marketers are also finding that they can provide customers with tailor-made goods and services as cheaply, and in the same amount of time, as it used to take to make standardized ones. Particularly for small companies, mass customization provides a way to stand out against larger competitors. For both consumer marketers and business marketers, relationship marketing is an important ingredient of mass-customization programs. Unlike mass production, which eliminates the need for human interaction, mass customization has made relationships with customers more important than ever.

6.4 Patterns of market segmentation

Market segments can be built up in segments. Suppose ice cream buyers they value sweetness and creaminess as two product attributes. Three different patterns can emerge:

6.4.1 Homogeneous preferences

Shows a market where all the consumers have roughly the same preference. The market shows no natural segments. We would predict that existing brands would be similar and cluster around the middle of the scale in both sweetness and creaminess.

6.4.2 Diffused preferences

At the other extreme, consumer preferences may be scattered throughout the space, indicating that consumers vary greatly in their preferences. The first brand to enter the market is likely to position in the center to appeal to the most people. A brand in the center minimizes the sum of total consumer dissatisfaction. A second competitor could locate next to the first brand and fight for market share. Or it could locate in a corner to attract a customer group that was not satisfied with the center brand. If several brands are in the market, they are likely to position throughout the space and show real differences to match consumer-preference differences.

6.4.3 Clustered preferences

The market might reveal distinct preference clusters, called natural market segments. The first firm in this market has three options. It might position in the center, hoping to appeal to all groups. It might position in the largest market segment (concentrated marketing). It might develop several brands, each positioned in a different segment. If the first firm developed only one brand, competitors would enter and introduce brands in the other segments.

Part Two: Questions

1. Fuji film and Kodak film are both using high quality market positioning. Which does the positioning strategy belong to?
2. For the consumer goods market, what is the main factor of market segmentation basing on?
3. What level of detail will be needed in the segmentation analysis?

Part Three: Words and Phrases

1. market segmentation   市场分割
2. criteria   标准
3. marketing positioning   市场定位
4. digitize   数字化
5. crystallise   结晶
6. clustered preferences   聚集偏好
7. individual marketing   个性化营销
8. sub-markets   细分市场
9. variant   变异
10. target audience   目标受众
11. premium   溢价
12. customized marketing   定制营销
13. homogeneous   均匀
14. according to   根据
15. niche marketing   利基营销
16. fine-tuned   微调
17. consumer-preference   消费者偏好
18. diffused preferences   扩散偏好
19. predominance   优势
20. mass production   大规模生产

Part Four: Further Reading

How to Choose Your Target Market

When starting a business, first choose your target market. When I first decided I wanted to go into business, the first question that popped into my mind was the thought, "what should I sell?" I know that this is often the case with many people—not just me.

However, a better question to ask at first is actually, "which market should I target?" To succeed in business, you need both a good target market, and a good product which that market wants. It is much easier (and cheaper) to find a good target market than to develop a product. So, it is best to first find a good target market, then to develop a product for that market. If you do it the other way around, there is a danger that after you have spent all that effort in developing your product, that there will be no market for it!

So, as a general rule, it is much better to choose who your target market will be first. How do you find a good target market for your products? A good first step is to ask yourself what you enjoy doing. In my case, I enjoy doing lots of things. For example, I like to play tennis. In addition, I am interested in the skills needed in entrepreneurship, in order to be self-sufficient. And finally, I enjoy investing in the stock market.

All these things have associated target markets. For example, since I enjoy tennis, I could try to target tennis players. Or, I could target people who are also interested in being self-sufficient. And finally, I could target stock market investors.

Another approach is to think of the problems you have which you have found solutions for. In this case, your target market could be those people who have had the same problems. For example, in the past, I had problems with credit card debt, however now I am much disciplined and no longer have a problem with this. At this stage, as an example, I could choose other people with credit card debt as a possible target market.

It is good, I think, for you to have something in common with your target market. It is much more difficult to try to work at a business where you have nothing in common with your customers. So, in fact, it is best if you fit somehow into your own target market. This will help you keep up your enthusiasm in your business—a very necessary ingredient if you are going to succeed.

So, you should now choose one or more target markets to look at. As an example, I'm going to pick two target markets to consider. The first one will be stock market investors. The second one I will look at is those with credit card debt.

What is the size of your target market?

After you have chosen one or more target markets to consider, think about the size of those target markets. Is the target market large enough to sustain a business which will provide products or services to them? A target market has to be of at least a minimum size to be viable.

In my example, the two possible target markets I have chosen—stock market investors, and those with credit card debt problems—are both very large target markets. In fact, they might be too large, and it might be wise to find a niche within those target markets. Therefore, I might then focus on a particular type of stock market investors, such as stock market investors who like a particular approach to investing (such as fundamental analysis, Warren Buffett-style).

Can this target market afford to purchase products?

My first example target market can clearly afford to purchase products which could be expensive. Stock market investors usually have to have a minimum amount of wealth in order to make profitable investments.

However, my second example—those who have problems with credit card debt—are probably not going to have enough money to be able to purchase an expensive product from me. Because of the lack of money of this target market, it is best to abandon those who have problems with credit card debt as a target market for a business. Without a target market which has money, a business could soon go bankrupt, and of course you don't want that to happen!

Therefore, in the end, I'm left with just one possibility—the stock market investors, and possibly the specific niche of those who like fundamental analysis. This would be a good target market I could direct my business towards.

Now you can think about your product or service. After you have chosen your target market, then you can begin to think about what products or services you will provide to this target market. However, remember that first you should choose a good target market!

Chapter 7: New Product Development

Part One: Text

7.1 Introduction

The need to create customer-relevant business processes is a recurrent theme in marketing evidenced in the underlying themes of previous chapters—particularly those dealing with the nature of marketing, competitiveness and strategies. Today's successful firms learn and relearn how to deal with the dynamics of consumers, competitors and technologies, all of which require companies to review and reconstitute the products and services they offer to the market. This, in turn, requires the development of new products and services to replace current ones, a notion inherent in the discussion of Levitt's (1960) "Marketing Myopia". A recent report into Best New Product Practice in the UK showed that, across a broad range of industry sectors, the average number of new products launched in the previous 5 years was 22, accounting for an average 36 percent of sales and 37 percent of profits (Tzokas, 2000). The most recent PDMA Best Practice Survey noted an average number of 38.5 new products in the previous 5 years, contributing to 32.4 percent of sales and 30.6 percent of profits (Griffin, 1997).

This chapter is concerned with what is required to bring new products and services to market, often encompassed by the framework known as the new product development (NPD) process. Of the many factors associated with successful NPD, processes and structures which are customer-focused recur (Cooper, 1979; Maidique and Zirger, 1984; Craig and Hart, 1992). A customer focus may be manifested in NPD in numerous ways, spawning much research into the nature of new product activates: their nature, their sequence and their organization (Mahajan and Wind, 1992; Griffin,1997). In this chapter, the activities, their sequence and organization required to develop new products are discussed in the light of an extensive body of research into what distinguishes successful from unsuccessful new products. The chapter starts with an overview of the commonly used NPD process model before going on to a general discussion of the usefulness of models in the NPD context. It then develops an integrating model of NPD and, finally, issues identified in current research regarding organizational structures for NPD are considered.

7.2 The process of developing new product

Considering some well-known successful innovations of the past 20 years, one might be tempted to think that they are all good ideas, the Walkman, laser printers, Automatic Teller Machines, mobile phones. And so they are, but does that mean that they could not have failed? What were the basic ideas? The Walkman: portable, personal audio entertainment. The laser printer: fast, accurate, flexible, high-quality reproduction.

Automatic Teller Machines are 24-hour cash availability from machines. As ideas, these might have been transformed into products in numerous ways, perhaps less successfully than the products we now find so familiar and convenient.

Imagine the alternative forms for personal audio entertainment, a bulkier headset which contains the tape-playing mechanism and earphones, a small hand-held player, complete with carrying handle, attached to earphones via a cord; a "backpack" style player with earphones. All of these ideas would have delivered to the idea of portable, personal audio entertainment, but which if any of these would have enjoyed the same success as the Walkman? And the automatic Teller Machines. These might have been developed as stand-alone units, much like bottle banks, requiring the identification of ideal locations, planning permission and consumer confidence to enter them. Would they have been as widespread as the hole-in-the-wall? Finally, the mobile phone: these might have developed with any number of constraining factors, including price, reach, size, weight and functionality.

Think of another "good idea"—the light-weight, low-pollution, low-cost, easily-parked town car. Now imagine one realization of the idea: three-wheeled, battery-run (with 80 km worth of charge only), and, for the British weather, an optional roof. This realization is, of course, the widely-quoted failure, the C5. Yet the idea remains a good one.

The issue at stake here is that good ideas do not automatically translate into workable, appealing products. The idea has to be given a physical reality which performs the function of the idea, which potential customers find an attractive alternative for which they are prepared to pay the asking price. This task requires NPD to be managed actively, working through a set of activities which ensure that the eventual product is makable, affordable, reliable and attractive to customers.

The activities carried out during the process of developing new products are well summarized in various NPD models. These are templates or maps which can be used to describe and guide those activities required to bring a new product from an idea or opportunity, through to a successful market launch NPD models take numerous forms.

One of the most recognized NPD models is that developed by the consultants, Booz Allen Hamilton (BAH, 1982) and this process continues to be associated with successful outcomes (Griffin, 1997; Tzokas, 2000). This model is shown in Figure 7.1.

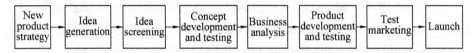

Figure 7.1　The Booz Allen Hamilton model of new product development

This model has been reformulated and shaped over several decades, with the influential derivative from Cooper and Kleinschmidt (1990) known as the "Stage-Gate" process (Figure 7.2). In the US, *the Best Practice Study* (1997) showed that 60 percent of firms used some form of Stage-Gate process, while the study in the UK by Tzokas (2000) reported only 8 percent of firms not having some specified form of process.

This and other developments of the BAH model are considered later in the chapter; below is a brief description of the tasks necessary to complete the development and launch of anew product. Each of the stages is described below in turn.

Chapter 7: New Product Development

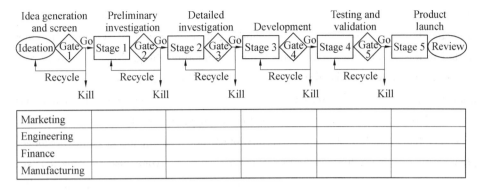

Figure 7.2 The "Stage-Gate" process

7.3 The stages of new product development process

7.3.1 New product strategy

A specific new product strategy explicitly places NPD at the heart of an organization's priorities, sets out the competitive requirements of the company's new products and is effectively the first "stage" of the development process. It comprises an explicit view of where a new programme of development sits in relation to the technologies that are employed by the company and the markets which these technologies will serve. In addition, this view must be communicated throughout the organization and the extent to which this happens is very much the responsibility of top management. In fact, much research attention has focused on the role of top management in the eventual success of NPD. While Maidique and Zirger (1984) found new product successes to be characterized by a high level of top management support, Cooperand Kleinschmidt (1987) found less proof of top management influence, discovering that many new product failures often have as much top management support. More recently, Dough and Hardy (1996) found that although lip-service was given to the importance of innovation, it often takes a backseat compared to other initiatives such as cost-cutting and downsizing, especially where there is less of a history of success in developing new products. And yet, one of the most important roles which top management have to fill is that of incorporating NPD as a meaningful component of an organization's strategy and culture.

In some cases it is necessary for the firm to change its philosophy on NPD, in turn causing a change in the whole culture. Nike's NPD process has changed dramatically over the last 15 years. Previously, they believed that every new product started in the lab and the product was the most important thing. Now, they believe it is the consumer who leads innovation and the specific reason for innovation comes from the marketplace. The reason for this change is the fierce competition that has developed in recent years within the athletic shoe industry, so that product innovation no longer led to sustained competitive advantage and manufacturers could no longer presume that if Mike Jordan chooses a certain shoe everyone else in America will follow. More emphasis was then put on marketing research and targeting smaller groups of individual customers, with the emphasis changing from push to pull NPD. The distinction between technology push and market pull is covered a little later in this chapter; however, it is worth noting that the initial change in philosophy from push to pull has been reinforced by the practice of using there tail setting to encourage "genuine product innovations instead of inappropriate line extensions".

While NPD is central to long-term success for companies, it is both expensive and risky, and a majority of "new" products and service are not entirely "new". The new product strategy specifies how innovative the firm intends to be in its NPD and how many new product projects should be resourced at any onetime. The seminal work of Booz Allen Hamilton in 1968 and in 1982 revealed the importance of this specification. In their 1968 study, an average of 58 new product ideas was required to produce one successful new product. By 1982, a new study showed this ratio had been reduced to seven to one. The reason forwarded for this change was the addition of a preliminary stage: the development of an explicit, new product strategy that identified the strategic business requirements new products should satisfy. Effective benchmarks were set up so that ideas and concepts were generated to meet strategic objectives. Seventy-seven percent of the companies studied had initiated this procedure with remarkable success. Reporting "from experience", Riek (2001) emphasizes clear planning for NPD, including the development of stages and the criteria for each stage being thought out at the initial planning stages of the development programme.

When ideas were generated in line with strategic objectives, an extremely effective "elimination" of ideas, which in the past cluttered and protracted the NPD process, occurred. Although written in the early 1980s, the lessons to be learned from the work of BAH are still relevant. For example, research by Griffin (1997) showed that "Best Practice" firms (those which were above average in the relative success of their NPD programmes, in the top third for NPD in their industry and above average in their financial success for NPD) derive their NPD activities through explicit attention to strategy, thereby becoming more efficient as they require, on average, only 3.5 ideas for one success. The less proficient firms in NPD terms need 8.4 ideas on average to produce one success, "because they carefully consider strategy first, they only initiate projects which are more closely aligned to strategy and thus have a much higher probability of success". In a similar study carried out almost UK firms, Tzokas (2000) found that more top-performing firms include strategy development for NPD, which delineates the target market, determines market need and the attractiveness of the product or service for the target market.

A consultant with PRTM, Mike Anthony, describes a company manning 22 projects, when it had capacity for only nine, and typically would only turn out three new products which would make money. Clearly an agenda strategy for cutting down on the effort going into 22 projects would give rise to the opportunity to increase the resources channeled into the remaining projects (Industry Week, 1996). Setting a clear strategy for NPD also sets up the key criteria against which all projects can be managed through to the market launch. New product strategy, which has also been called the "product innovation charter", and "new product protocol" (Crawford, 1984; Cooper, 1993), has been shown to enhance the success rates of the eventual market launch (Hultink, et al., 1997, 2000).

While it is often argued that NPD should be guided by a new product strategy, it is important that the strategy is not so prescriptive as to restrict, or stifle, the creativity necessary for NPD. In addition to stating the level of newness, a new product strategy should encompass the balance between technology and marketing, the level and nature of new product advantage, and the desired levels of synergy and risk acceptance.

Once the general direction for NPD has been set, the process of developing new ideas, discussed below, can become more focused.

7.3.2 Idea generation

This is a misleading term because, in many companies, ideas do not have to be "generated". They do, however, need to be managed. This involves identifying sources of ideas and developing means by which these sources can be activated to bring new ideas for products and services to the fore. The aim of this stage in the process is to develop a bank of ideas that fall within the parameters set by "new product strategy". Sources of new product ideas exist both within and outside the firm. Inside the company, technical departments such as research and development, design and engineering work on developing applications and technologies which will be translated into new product ideas. Equally, commercial functions such as sales and marketing will be exposed to ideas from customers and competitors. Otherwise, many company employees may have useful ideas: service mechanics, customer relations, manufacturing and warehouse employees are continually exposed to "product problems" which can be translated into new product ideas. Outside the company, competitors, customers, distributors, inventors and universities are fertile repositories of information from which new product ideas come. Both sources, however, may have to be organized in such a way as to extract ideas. In short, the sources have to be activated. A myriad of techniques may be used to activate sources of new ideas, including brainstorming, morphological analysis, perceptual mapping and scenario planning.

7.3.3 Screen

The next stage process involves in the product development and initial assessment of the extent of demand for the ideas generated and of the capability the company has to make the product. At this, the first of several evaluative stages, only a rough assessment can be made of an idea, which will not yet be expressed in terms of design, materials, features or price. Internal company opinion will be canvassed from R&D, sales, marketing, finance and production to assess whether the idea has potential, is practical, would fit a market demand, could be produced by existing plants, and to estimate the payback period. The net result of this stage is a body of ideas which are acceptable for further development. Checklists and forms have been devised to facilitate this process, requiring managers to make "guestimates" regarding potential market size, probable competition, and likely product costs, prices and revenues. However, as at this stage of the process managers are still dealing with ideas, it is unrealistic to imagine that these "guestimates" can be accurate. The "newer" the new product, the more guesswork there will be in these screening checks. It is not until the idea is developed into a concept (see below) that more accurate data on market potential and make ability can be assembled.

7.3.4 Concept development and testing

Once screened, an idea is turned into a more clearly specified concept, and testing this concept begins for its fit with company capability and its fulfillment of customer expectations. Developing the concept from the idea requires that a decision be made on the content and form of the idea. This, however, is easier said than done; the process of turning a new product idea into a fully worked out new product concept is not simply one of semantic labeling. Montoya Weiss and O'Driscoll (2000) explain that "an idea is defined as the initial, most embryonic form of new product or service idea typically a one-line description accompanied by a high-level technical diagram. A concept, on the other hand, is defined as a form, technology plus a clear statement of customer benefit". They go on to describe a formalized process implemented at Nortek, the large US tele-communications equipment manufacturer, which was developed to assist the transition of idea to concept. The project name for the development of this process was "Galileo", as the intention was to develop a mechanism (process), which, like the telescope, could aid the identification of "stars". The process is shown in Figure 7.3.

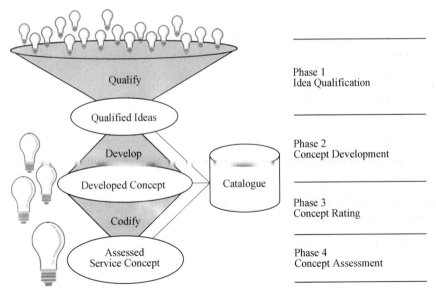

Figure 7.3 The Galileo process

Internally, the development team needs to know which varieties are most compatible with the current production plant, which require plant acquisition, which require new supplies, and this needs to be matched externally, in relation to which versions are more attractive to customers. The latter involves direct customer research to identify the appeal of the product concept, or alternative concepts to the customer. Concept testing is worth spending time and effort on, collecting sufficient data to provide adequate information upon which the full business analysis will be made.

7.3.5 Business analysis

At this stage, the major "go"/"no-go" decision will be made. The company needs to be sure that the venture is potentially worthwhile, as expenditure will increase dramatically after this stage. The analysis is based on the fullest information available to the company thus far. It encompasses:

First, a market analysis detailed potential total market, estimated market share within specific time horizon, competing products, likely price, break-even volume, identification of early adopters and specific market segments.

Second, explicit statement of technical aspects costs, production implications, supplier management and further R&D.

Third, explanation of how the project fits with corporate objectives.

The sources of information both internal and external, for this stage are market or technical research carried out thus far. The output of this stage will be a development plan with budget and an initial marketing plan.

7.3.6 Product development and testing

This is the stage where prototypes are physically made. Several tasks are related to this development. First, the finished product will be assessed regarding its level of functional performance. This is sometimes known as "alpha testing". Until now, the product has only existed in theoretical form or mock-up. It is only when component parts are brought together in a functional form that the validity of the theoretical product can be definitively established. Second, it is the first physical step in the manufacturing chain. It is not until the prototype is developed that alterations to the specific anon or to manufacturing configurations can be designed and put into place. Third, the product has to be tested with potential customers to assess the overall impression of the test product.

The topic of concept testing has been much aided by the development of the internet, for a number of reasons. The cost of "building" and "testing" prototypes virtually is, of course, a fraction of that required by physical prototypes. It means that the market research costs are lower, or that more concepts can be tested by potential customers than is the case with physical products, resulting in a final design which is more attuned to the voice of the customer. In addition, more end customers can be sampled more efficiently via the internet, although the risk of population deterioration is increased, as is the likelihood of bias, since not all potential customers selected will be willing to "test" the product virtually. A paper by Dahanand Srinivasan (2000) reported that "virtual parallel prototyping and testing on the internet provides a close match to the results generated in person using costlier physical prototypes".

Some amenable categories to customer product are testing than more others. Capital equipment, for example, is difficult to have assessed by potential customers in the same way as a chocolate bar can be taste-tested, or a dishwasher evaluated by an in-house trial. One evolving technique in industrial marketing, however, is called "beta testing", practised informally by many industrial product developers. The Best Practices research showed that beta site testing was used to a significantly greater degree by the better performing companies (Griffin, 1997).

7.3.7 Test marketing

The penultimate phase in the development cycle, test marketing, consists of small-scale tests with customers. Until now, the idea, the concept and the product have been "tested" or "evaluated" in a somewhat artificial context. Although several of these evaluations may well have compared the new product to competitive offerings, other elements of the marketing mix have not been tested, nor the likely marketing reaction by competitors. At this stage the appeal of the product is tested a midst the mix of activities comprising the market launch: salesmanship, advertising, sales promotion, distributor incentives and public relations.

Test marketing is not always feasible, or desirable. Management must decide whether the industrial costs of test marketing can be justified by the additional information that will be gathered. Furthermore, not all products are suitable for a small-scale test launch: passenger cars, for example, have market testing completed before the launch, while other products, once launched on a small scale, cannot be withdrawn, as with personal insurance. Finally, the delay involved in getting a new product to market may be advantageous to the competition, which can use the opportunity to be "first-to-market". Competitors may also wait until a company's test market results are known and use the information to help their own launch, or can distort the test results using their own tactics. Problems such as these have encouraged the development and use of computer-based market simulation models, which use basic models of consumer buying as inputs. Information on consumer awareness, trial and repeat purchases, collected via limited surveys or store data, is used to predict adoption of the new product. That said, there is a discernible trend towards market research tools over the whole process which emphasize in-depth understanding of customer needs rather than quantitative prediction and forecasting. Moreover, this more qualitative understanding is pursued through research methods which privilege continuous, longitudinal dialogue with fewer customers as opposed to snapshot, one-off feedback surveys(Griffin, 1997; Tzokas, 2000).

Part Two: Questions

1. How to increase consumption of the current product?

2. Why must a company choose a launch strategy consistent with product positioning?

Part Three: Words and Phrases

1. accurate　　　　　　准确的
2. innovation　　　　　创新
3. bulky　　　　　　　笨重的
4. template　　　　　　模板
5. preliminary investigation　初步调查
6. derivative　　　　　衍生物
7. elimination　　　　　消除
8. presume　　　　　　假定
9. validation　　　　　批准
10. myriad　　　　　　无数
11. aligned　　　　　　对齐
12. downsizing　　　　缩减
13. delineate　　　　　划定

14. fertile　　　　　　多产的
15. embryonic　　　　胚胎的
16. prototype　　　　　原型
17. validity　　　　　　有效性
18. configuration　　　配置
19. distort　　　　　　扭转
20. adoption　　　　　采用

Part Four: Further Reading

Branded Environment

In architecture and interior design, branded environments extend the experience of an organization's brand, or distinguishing characteristics as expressed in names, symbols and designs, to the design of interior or exterior physical settings. It uses space as a physical embodiment of the brand to create a "brandspace". This is achieved through "architecture, interiors, lighting, graphics, landscape" in spaces such as retail stores, showrooms, trade-fair booths and office environments.

Components of a branded environment can include finish materials, environmental graphics, way-finding devices and signage and identity systems. Creators of branded environments leverage the effect of the physical structure and organization of space to help deliver their clients' identity attributes, personality and key messages.

The creation of branded environments grew out of a movement within the practice of interior design in the 1990s that recognized that brand equity, or the perceived value in the identifying brand characteristics of an organization, could be applied to three-dimensional environments.

The practice of designing branded environments is often a research-driven effort that includes a multi-disciplinary team of strategic consultants, brand development experts, marketing and communications consultants, interior designers, architects, environmental graphic designers, and client brand managers. While particularly effective for retail, museum and exhibit design, branded environments can support the success of many organizational types, from corporate to institutional and educational. The designed environment can reflect or express the attributes of a community or the competitive advantages of a company's product or service.

Benefits of a branded environment can include improved brand position and communication, better customer recognition, differentiation from competitors and higher perceived value from investors. Internally, benefits may include higher employee satisfaction and retention, increased productivity, and better understanding of an organization's mission, vision and values.

The main aspects of branded environments in retail include merchandising, signage, and interior design. Merchandising involves arranging products in a way that makes customers most want to buy them. Signage in retail gives the customer orientation, information and an understanding of the brand identity and values. Interior design creates a physical and sensory relationship with the customer that can communicate the brand message. The brand message needs to be considered in the environmental design; otherwise the message will not be clear.

Chapter 8: Managing the Marketing Mix

Part One: Text

8.1 Introduction

Managing the marketing mix is the central task of marketing professionals. The marketing mix is the set of marketing tools often summarized as the "Four Ps": the product, its price, promotion and place that the firm uses to achieve its objectives in its target market (McCarthy, 2001). The key elements in the marketing mix are shown in Figure 8.1. The design of the marketing mix normally forms the core of all marketing courses and the textbooks that support them.

The central assumption is that if marketing professionals make and implement the right decisions about the features of the product, its price, and how it will be promoted and distributed, then the business will be successful. Unfortunately, marketers have ignored the tautological nature of this view. What is the "right" decision when it comes to making these choices concerning the marketing mix? Most marketing professionals would answer that the right marketing mix is the one that maximizes customer satisfaction and results in the highest sales or market share. But a moment's reflection reveals the fallacy of this approach. Customer satisfaction and sales can always be increased by offering more product features, lower prices than competition, higher promotional budgets and the immediate availability of the product, of outstanding customer service and support.

But inadequate margins and excessive investment requirements would make this strategy a quick route to bankruptcy. Some writers have tried to get around this problem by stating that the objective is to devise a marketing mix that provides superior customer satisfaction at a profit to the company.

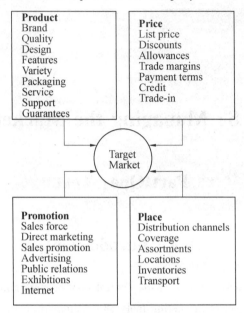

Figure 8.1 The marketing mix

But profit is an ambiguous goal. Are managers to aim at short-or long-term profits? Should they seek to maximize profits or achieve some satisfying goal? Each alternative would lead to radically different recommendations for marketing mix decisions. It is fair to conclude that most of the writing on marketing has described the marketing mix but not provided a rational framework for managing it.

In line with the new concept of value-based management, we define the objective of marketing as the development and implementation of a marketing mix that maximizes shareholder value. This definition has two advantages. First, it aligns marketing decision-making to the goals of the board and top management. The board is not interested in sales or market share per se, but rather with marketing strategies that will enhance the company's value. Corporate value is determined by the discounted sum of all future free cash flows. Second, shareholder value provides situational and unambiguous criteria for determining the marketing mix. The "right" marketing mix is the one that maximizes shareholder value.

This chapter focuses on marketing mix decisions for private sector firms whose major objective is creating value for shareholders. In non profit and public sector organizations, the objective is not shareholder value maximization but attracting enough funds to perform their social tasks.

The chapter explains the logic of this new approach to the marketing mix and illustrates its application to typical decisions about product development, pricing, promotion and distribution.

8.2 The traditional approach to the marketing mix

Marketing professionals have normally been taught a four-step approach to marketing mix decisions.

Step 1 is to define the product's (or service's) strategic objective. This emerges from an analysis of its strengths, weaknesses, opportunity and threats. Marketers have found the strategic matrices developed by consultants such as the Boston Consulting Group and McKinsey to be useful. Typically, a strategic matrix has market growth or market attractiveness as one dimension and competitive advantage as the other. A product in a highly attractive market with a strong competitive advantage would normally have a sits strategic objective rapid sales growth. A product in a poor market with no competitive advantage would be targeted for divesting.

Step 2 is a detailed analysis of the target market to assess the nature of the opportunity. What is its size and potential? How strong is the competition and how is it likely to evolve in the future.

Step 3 is research into the needs of prospective customers. What is it that customers actually want? Today, this goes beyond merely asking customers what they are looking for, but creatively seeking to discover needs that customers cannot articulate because they are unaware of the possibilities offered by new technologies and the changing environment (Hamel and Prahalad, 1991). To most marketing professionals the marketing mix is designed to meet these customer needs and wants. Each element of the mix is designed to meet a customer need. Lauterborn (1990) articulated this with the concept of the Four Cs. Consumers have certain needs, which can be grouped into Four Cs—a customer solution, cost, convenience and communication. According to this popular view, the function of the Four Ps is to match each of these Cs.

Four Cs	Four Ps
Customer solution	Product
Customer cost	Price
Communication	Promotion
Cnvenience	Place

An effective marketing mix is the one which offers a product that solves the customer's problem that is of low cost to the customer, that effectively communicates the benefits, and that can be purchased with the utmost convenience.

The problem with this "marketing" view of the marketing mix is that it ignores whether the mix makes economic sense for the company. While it maximizes value for customers it can easily minimize value for shareholders. For example, the product that gives the best customer solution is likely to be one individually tailored to a specific customer, incorporating all the features of value to that customer. But for the company, this would require a very broad product line with high manufacturing costs and substantial investment requirements. Unfortunately, what customers also want is low cost, which in most situations will mean offering them low prices. Similarly, the unconstrained pursuit of convenience and communication of the brand's benefits also involves higher costs and investment. The formula of low prices, high operating costs and high investment in promotion and distribution is not one that builds successful businesses.

A striking example of the problems of the marketing-led approach to the marketing mix has been the collapse of the Japanese economic miracle (Porter, et al., 2000). Until the early 1980s, the Japanese were held as the paragons of successful marketing (e.g., Ohmae, 1985; Hamel and Prahalad, 1994). Japanese companies such as Nissan, Matsushita, Mitsubishi, Komatsu and Canon appeared set to dominate their markets. Their formulas were similar: an overwhelming focus on investing in market share, and a marketing mix based on fully-featured products, low prices, aggressive promotion and an extensive network of dealers.

The strategy did lead to gains in market shares as consumers appreciated the superior value that Japanese companies were offering. But the profit margins and return on investment earned by these companies were very poor. For a time, the support of the Japanese banks disguised their inadequate economic performance.

The dot.com "bust" of 2000 illustrated the same sort of weaknesses. These start-ups made market share their sole priority. Products and services were given away free or below cost. Huge sums were spent on advertising and promotion in the belief that if they achieved a dominant market position in the "new economy", everything else would fall into place. The result was large number of visitors to their sites, but the companies generated no profit and eventually they ran out of cash. In 2002, Yahoo counted its global users in millions, but it worked out the average spend per head amounted to less than a cup of coffee annually. It was hardly surprising that, despite its dominant market share and brand leadership, the value of the company collapsed by 90 percent.

Successful businesses understand that building brands that satisfy consumers is necessary but not sufficient. Without generating an economic return to shareholders, a marketing mix is not sustainable.

8.3 The accounting approach to the marketing mix

Faced with poor returns, some companies, especially in the UK, adopted an accounting approach to marketing. The marketing mix was seen not as an instrument for gaining and retaining customers, but rather as a tool for directly increasing the return on investment. Return on investment can be increased in four ways: increasing sales, raising prices, reducing costs or cutting investment. The marketing mix is the central determinant of each of these levers.

For example, cutting back on the number of product variants offered to customers will reduce costs and investment. Raising prices will usually increase profitability in the short term because higher margins will offset the volume loss. Cutting advertising and promotional budgets will also boost short-term profits. Finally, savings on distribution and service will normally have positive effects on profitability, even though customers may suffer some inconvenience.

As illustrated in Figure 8.2, the accounting approach leads to a completely opposite marketing mix to the marketing approach. While the marketing focus, which puts the customer first, normally leads to broader product ranges, lower prices and more spending on promotion and distribution, the accounting one leads to the opposite pressures. The cost of the marketing approach is lower profitability and cash flow, the cost of the accounting approach is the longer-term loss of market share resulting from the lack of customer focus.

Marketers need to be aware that there are other important problems in considering profits as the objective of the business.

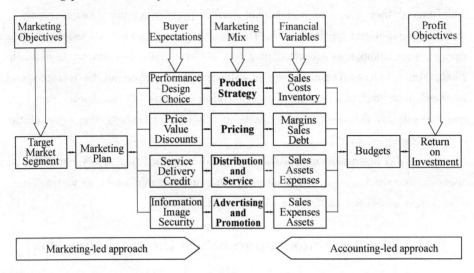

Figure 8.2　Alternative approaches to the marketing mix

8.4　Value-based marketing

A value-based approach to the marketing mix reconciles the marketing and accounting approaches in an optimal manner. The key principle is the optimum marketing mix is that which maximizes shareholder value. The concept of value-based management that the job of the board and its senior executives is to maximize shareholder value has become almost universally accepted in major businesses. As a recent Business Week (2000) study concluded, "the fundamental task of today's CEO is simply-city itself: get the stock price up period. Most companies, even those with a strong marketing orientation, now have the goal enshrined in their mission statements".

Value-based marketing is based on the belief that management should evaluate marketing mix options in the same way that shareholders do. Shareholders assess companies on their potential to create shareholder value. The company's share price reflects investors' evaluations of how much value management's current strategy will create. We need to review how investors estimate value and evaluate value-creating strategies.

The concept of value is founded on four financial principles. First, cash flow is the basis of value—it is the amount left over for shareholders after all the bills have been paid. Without the expectation of free cash flow passing into investors' hands, an asset cannot have value. Most of the dot. com companies founded in the 1990s collapsed because investors could not see how free cash flow was going to be created. The amount being spent looked to permanently exceed the revenues coming in. Next, cash flow has a time value: money today is worth more than money coming in the future. This is because investors can earn a return on cash they get today. Typically, ￥1 000 received in 10 years time is "worth" only about ￥385 today, where r is the discount rate; here r is taken to be 10 percent. Third, the opportunity cost of capital is the return investors could obtain if they invested elsewhere in companies of similar risk. Essentially this means that investors will find risky marketing strategies appealing only if the expected rewards are greater. Finally, the net present value concept brings these principles together. It shows that the value of an asset is the total of all the future free cash flows that asset generates after discounting these future sums by the appropriate opportunity cost of capital. The task of marketing and managers generally is to put in place strategies that maximize the net present value of the business. The optimal marketing mix is that combination of product, price, promotion and distribution that maximizes the net present value.

To calculate the value of an asset, or to assess whether a strategy is likely to create value, management has to forecast the future cash flows that result from their decisions, i. e. , net present value(NPV), see Formula(8.1).

$$NPV = \sum_{i}^{\infty} \frac{CF_i}{(1+r)^i} \qquad (8.1)$$

Where CF is free cash flow and r is the discount rate or opportunity cost of capital for shareholders. Clearly, analysts or investors cannot forecast cash flow decades ahead. Instead, the time period is split between a feasible forecast period, typically of 5 ~ 7 years, and a continuing value representing the value of the business at the end of the forecast period (for a comprehensive discussion, see Brearley and Myers, 1999). For a high performing business the forecast period can be called the differential advantage period. It is the number of years the business expects to maintain a market advantage over competitors allowing it to earn super-normal profits (i. e. , above the cost of capital). However, for virtually all companies, competition, the changing environment and new technologies mean that eventually profitability erodes. It is relatively rare for this differential advantage period to exceed 6 or 7 years

(Rappaport and Mauboussin, 2001). After that, companies are fortunate to earn normal profits.

In summary, we can rewrite the value of a company as Formula(8.2).

NPV = Present value of cash flow during differential advantage period+   (8.2)
Present value of cash flow after differential advantage period

There are a number of ways of calculating the latter term representing the continuing value of the business at the end of the forecast period (Copeland, et al., 2001). The most common one is the perpetuity method that assumes the business just maintains are turn on investment equal to its cost of capital. This is calculated by dividing the company's net operating profit after tax (*NOPAT*) by the cost of capital, see Formula(8.3).

$$Continuing\ value = \frac{NOPAT}{r} \quad (8.3)$$

8.5 The marketing mix and shareholder value

Value-based management is of great importance to marketing because it clarifies the central role of marketing in determining the value of the business. The marketing mix is the key driver of the share price. To understand this we need to look at the determinants of share-holder value. The value of the business and its share price are determined by the discounted sum of future cash flows examining this equation, we see that there are six ways of creating shareholder value.

8.5.1 Higher prices

Higher prices increase the operating profit margin and cash flow, so long as these are not offset by disproportionate losses involume. Here, in particular, one sees the advantage of value analysis over short-term profitability criteria for evaluating pricing. In the short term, raising prices commonly increases profits because many consumers do not immediately switch. Over the longer term, however, competitive position is often lost, leading to deterioration in cash flow and especially in the continuing value of the business.

The only sure way of achieving price developing products that offer superior value. This may be in terms functional benefits (e.g., Intel soft) or through offering brands with Micro added psychological values (e.g., Coca-Cola, Nike). If premium

Chapter 8: Managing the Marketing Mix

brands can be created, the value effects are very substantial. If sales volume is unchanged, the 5 percent price increase creates ¥33 million additional value, i.e., almost six times more than 5 percent annual volume growth. This is, of course, because a price increase normally incurs no additional operating costs or long-term capital requirement, so that the revenue increase falls straight through into additional free cash flow.

8.5.2 Lower costs

Cutting costs, as long as it does not lead to offsetting declines in customer patronage, increases cash flow and the value of the business. Variable costs can be reduced by better sourcing, fixed costs by taking out overheads, and the development of more sales and marketing channels. There is much evidence that companies with a strong customer franchise need to spend less on marketing and promotion (e.g., Reichheld, 1996).

8.5.3 Reducing investment requirements

Though this varies across businesses, typically every ¥1 million of added sales may demand ¥500 000 of additional working and fixed capital (Rappaport and Mauboussin, 2001). Clearly, cutting investment requirements can have a major impact on the free cash flow generated and consequently the share price. Again, there is increasing recognition that effective customer relationships enhance cash flow by reducing the level of working and fixed investments.

8.5.4 Accelerating cash flows

The right marketing mix can accelerate cash flows. This is important because money has a time value: money today is worth more than money tomorrow. If the cost of capital is 10 percent, ¥1 million in 5 years time is worth only ¥621 000, and in 10 years, ¥1 million is only worth ¥385 000. The faster acquisition of profitable market share and the consequent cash flows are important means of adding share-holder value.

Many marketing activities are geared to accelerating cash flows, even though marketers never conceptualize their strategies in these financial terms. For example, there is substantial evidence that when consumers have strong, positive attitudes to a brand they are quicker to respond to new products appearing under the brand umbrella. Again, marketers have studied the product life cycle and the characteristics of early adopters with the aim of developing promotional strategies to accelerate the launch and penetration of new products (Robertson, 1993).

8.5.5　Reducing business risk

The third factor determining the value of the business is the opportunity cost of capital used to discount future cash flows. This discount rate depends upon market interest rates plus the special risks attached to the specific business unit. The risk attached to a business is determined by the volatility and vulnerability of its cash flows compared to the market average (Brearley and Myers, 1999). Investors expect a higher return to justify investment in risky businesses. Because investors discount risky cash flows with a higher cost of capital, their value is reduced.

Again, there is evidence that an important function of marketing assets is to reduce the risk attached to future cash flows. Strong brands operate by building layers of value that make them less vulnerable to competition. This is a key reason why leading investors rate companies with strong brand portfolios at a premium in their industries (Buffet, 1994). Reich held (1996) and others have also demonstrated the dramatic effects on the company's net present value of increasing customer loyalty. A major focus of marketing today is on increasing loyalty; shareholder value analysis provides a powerful mechanism for demonstrating the financial contribution of these activities.

8.5.6　Extending the differential advantage period

Shareholder value is made up of two components: the present value of cash flows during the planning period and the present value of the company at the end of the planning period. Not surprisingly, since a company potentially has an infinite life, the continuing value normally greatly exceeds the value of the cash flows over the planning period.

8.6　Making marketing mix decision

This section re-examines the four main elements of the marketing mix-product, price, promotion and distribution from a value-based perspective.

8.6.1 Building valuable brands

Today, marketing professionals prefer to talk about brands rather than products. This reflects the recognition that consumers do not buy just physical attributes, but also the psychological associations associated with a supplier's offers. The concept of the brand also emphasizes that the whole presentation of the offer-design, features, variety, packaging, service and support have all to be integrated around a common identity.

8.6.2 Brands, intangible assets and the firm

In today's firm, it is intangible rather than tangible assets that create value. For many firms, brands are their most important assets, even though these brands rarely appear in published balance sheets. The role of brands and intangible assets can be seen in the resource-based theory of the firm (Grant,2000). Starting from the top of Figure 8.3, the objective of business strategy is to create shareholder value, as measured by rising share prices or dividends. The key to creating shareholder value in competitive markets possesses a differential advantage—giving customers superior value through offers or relationships that are either higher in quality or lower in cost. Achieving this differential advantage, in turn, depends upon the effectiveness of the firm's business processes. As shown, the core business processes can be grouped into three: first, the brand development process, which enables a firm to create innovative solutions to customers' problems; second, the supply chain management process, which acquires inputs and efficiently transforms them into desirable brands; and third the customer relationship management process, which identifies customers, understands their needs, builds relationships and shapes consumer perceptions of the organization and its brands.

These core business processes are the drivers of the firm's differential advantage and its ability to create shareholder value. However, these processes themselves are founded on the firm's core capabilities, which derive from the resources or assets it possesses. A firm cannot build superior business processes unless it has access to the right resources and the ability to co-ordinate them effectively. In the past, tan-Bible assets—the firm's factories, raw materials and financial resources were seen as its key strength. But today it is the intangibles that investors view most highly its technological skills, the quality of the staff, the business culture and, of course, the strength of its brands. In 2002, tangible assets accounted for less than 20 percent of the value of the world's top companies. Finally, maintaining an up-to-date resource base, upon which everything else is founded, depends upon continued investment.

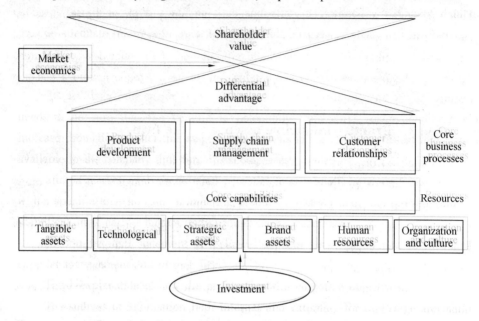

Figure 8.3　Brands within the resource-based theory of the firm

8.6.3　How brands enhance business processes

Brands create value by leveraging the firm's business processes—its new product brand development, its supply chain, and especially in building long-term relationships with its customers. An effective brand (B) can be considered as consisting of three components: a good product (P), strong differentiation (D) and added values (AV), see Formula(8.4).

$$B = P \times D \times AV \tag{8.4}$$

Building a successful brand starts with developing an effective product or service. Unfortunately, today, with the speed with which technology travels, it is increasingly difficult to build brands, and certainly to maintain them, on the basis of demonstrable, superior functional benefits. Comparably priced washing powders, cars, computers or auditing firms are usually much alike in the performance they deliver. Consequently, firms must find other ways to differentiate themselves, to create awareness and recall among customers. Hence they turn to design, colors, logos, packaging, advertising and additional services.

But while differentiation creates recognition it does not necessarily create preference. Wool Worth's, the Post Office, British Rail and the NHS are well-known brands but they are scarcely admired. To create preference a brand also has to possess positive added values. Added values give customers confidence in the choices they make. Choice today is difficult for customers because of the myriad of competitors seeking patronage, the barrage of communications, and the rapid changes in social mores and technology. Brands aim to simplify the choice process by confirming the functional or emotional associations of the brand. Increasingly, it is the emotional or experience associations that a successful brand promises that creates the consumer value.

The above discussion has focused on brands as leveraging the customer relationship business process. But there is much evidence that strong brand names also facilitate the new product development process. New products launched under a strong brand name are more likely to be trusted by consumers and to achieve faster market penetration. Strong brands also contribute to more efficient supply chains. Suppliers are more confident in forging partnerships with established brand names and making the investments to maintain these associations.

8.6.4 Valuing brands

Brands require investment in communications and other resources if they are to achieve recognition and the added values that generate customer preference. But creating customer preference is not enough; brands also have to create value for investors. Managers need to assess whether the brand investment pays off.

As with any other asset, brands create shareholder value if they positively affect the four levers of value—increasing the level of cash flow, accelerating cash flow, extending the differential period, and reducing risk. There is considerable research that brands do have these positive effects.

8.6.5 Optimizing price decisions

In many ways price is the most important element of the marketing mix. Price is the only element of the mix that directly produces revenge; all the others produce costs. In addition, small changes in price have bigger effects on both sales and shareholder value than advertising or other marketing mix changes.

8.6.6 Pricing and customer value

Most companies seek to set prices on the basis of various forms of cost plus, but this can lead to prices that are too high or too low. What customers are willing to pay depends upon the value to them of the supplier's offer; they do not care what it costs to produce. If customers perceive competitors as making similar offers, their price will determine the upper limit. However, if the company can differentiate its offer and add benefits, then it should determine how customers value these new features in setting its price.

8.6.7 Customized pricing

Customers always differ greatly in the value they perceive in a particular product or service. If a company charges a uniform price to all customers, it loses two sources of income: one is the revenue lost from customers who find the price too high and do not purchase; the other is the additional income they could have earned from customers who would have been willing to pay more. A key to effective pricing is customizing pricing to minimize these losses.

8.6.8 Distribution strategies

Today, innovation is becoming one of the most significant ways in distribution. The triggers have been the desire of consumers for greater convenience, global competition forcing companies to search for new ways to cut costs and capital employed, and facilitating technologies, notably information technology and the internet. New distribution strategies are offering consumers greater benefits in terms of convenience, speed, accessibility and lower costs that are offering pioneering companies opportunities to leapfrog competitors. Besides market advantages, these companies can often significantly reduce their operating costs and investment.

Part Two: Questions

1. Target segments in which company can profitably generate greatest customer value. Why not segment with best profits?

2. What is the difference between a strength and an opportunity in a SWOT analysis?

Part Three: Words and Phrases

1. tautological		赘述的
2. inadequate		不足的
3. maximize		最大化
4. bankruptcy		破产
5. guarantee		担保
6. margin		利润
7. shareholder		股东
8. budget		预算
9. cash flow		现金流
10. reconcile		调和
11. leverage		杠杆
12. investment		投资
13. intangible		无形
14. penetration		渗透
15. accelerate		加速
16. distribution strategy		分销策略
17. leapfrog		跨越
18. supply chain		供应链
19. asset		资产
20. resource		资源

Part Four: Further Reading

Brand Strategy

1. Building a profitable and sustainable brand

Your brand is one of your business's most valuable assets. It represents everything your business stands for and what your customers can expect when they choose your business.

In today's complex marketing environment it is important to make sure brands stand out, be unique and be able to sustain a believable and winning brand position in the minds of the customer.

Customers expect brands to deliver more they want: Clarity on what value a brand gives them, a brand to be easy to research, to be able to make better and faster buying decisions and to access after sales support and service.

A clear brand strategy and strong brand position incorporates a company's business strategy, purpose, and product positioning into a distinctive promise that informs and articulates what you stand for, what you do, who you serve, and what your customers and employees can expect when they choose your business.

A successful brand will deliver brand benefits that customers' value at every touch-point, be unique and, most importantly, enable companies to achieve long-term growth through brand loyalty and referral.

2. How we can help you with your brand strategy

Sustainable Marketing Services builds, delivers and manages strategy-led, reliable and results-focused marketing, public relations, digital and brand assets to help our clients achieve sustainable long-term growth.

We can help companies identify a unique brand position, and through a clear brand strategy strengthen the awareness and reputation of your brand, increase customer loyalty and referral, increase lead generation and sales and achieve growth.

3. Our brand strategy and positioning service includes

Customer, industry and market research and feedback; Brand position audit and review; Brand positioning workshop and recommendations; Brand positioning strategy recommendations; Brand story development; Brand internalization workshop; Brand assets review and recommendations (Following the recommendations on brand position, strategy and assets review, we are able to execute and manage an end-to-end brand development or brand revitalization).

4. Testimonial

"Originally known as Capalaba Surgery we were relocating to Alexandra Hills. We wanted to create an authentic brand that would bring our vision for our business to life. In addition, we wanted to make sure that our image conveyed our brand story in a professional, consistent way through a visual story and key messages. Sustainable Marketing Services helped us discover our natural brand story. They helped us get an understanding of what makes us unique and made recommendations on how to bring this story to life across everything from the design of our surgery with feature walls and furnishings right through to business cards, appointment cards and magnets. They even organized a feature wall and signage for us. We worked together to develop a new company name.

"We are delighted with our new brand, our team loves the design, and we believe our patients will feel more welcome and comfortable when they come to see us. Some of our patients have already said that they love the name and the logo is very soft and friendly. We feel that Sustainable Marketing Services' step-by-step system made the whole rebranding experience less daunting for us, given that we have no marketing backgrounds. They helped us understand our patient base and where we would like to take the business in the future.

"We found the team at Sustainable Marketing Services wonderful to work with and they always kept us abreast of where we were in the process. We found the personalized service was fantastic and allowed us the freedom to work one-on-one with the person creating our vision." Kieren Parton, One Life Medical.

Chapter 9: Pricing

Part One: Text

9.1 Introduction

Pricing is an issue about which academics and practitioners have been at each others' throats for a very long time. While nobody knows exactly when the "war" was started or by whom for that matter—Dean's (1947) description of company pricing policies as "the last stronghold of medievalism in modern management" was probably one of the earliest attacks in the literature about the way companies think about and go about making pricing decisions. Over the next 50 years or so, several academics followed in Dean's footsteps by criticizing practitioner approaches to pricing as lacking in rationality and professionalism, failing to understand the proper role of costs, and bypassing profit opportunities as a result of applying routinized pricing formula. The following quote encapsulates the essence of the criticism: many managers do not understand how to price, and are insecure about the adequacy of their current pricing methods. As a result, they rely on over-simplistic rules of thumb and place an exaggerated emphasis on costs.

For their part, practitioners have responded by largely ignoring what academia has to say about pricing. While an enormous literature on pricing has developed over the past half century (for relevant reviews, see Diamantopoulos, 1991, 1995; Diamantopoulos and Mathews, 1995), there have been no radical changes in the actual pricing practices of firms; indeed, "the pricing literature has produced few insights or approaches that would stimulate most businessmen to change their methods of setting prices" (Monroe, 1979). For example, a comparison of the adoption of cost-plus pricing methods over a 50-year period colludes that "in spite of the fact that the intervening years have seen countless references to the fact that cost-plus pricing pay sufficiency attention to environmental dynamics, it remains the predominant price-setting methodology" (Seymour, 1989). Practice-boners have also been quick to criticize academics as being unable to really understand what pricing is all about.

Thus, the field of pricing is characterized by a paradox. On the one hand, "price theory is one of the most highly developed fields in economics and marketing science" (Simon, 1989). On the other hand, "there is hardly another business subject area that has had so little reverberation in practice as has price theory" (Diller, 1991). Several reasons seem to underlie this paradox.

First, A lot of academic work on pricing has been focusing on pricing models of varioussorts (for relevant reviews, see Monroe and DellaBitta, 1978; Monroe and Mazudmar, 1988; Nagle, 1984; Rao, 1984, 1993). While these models are characterized by a high degree and enable the derivation of "optimal" prices, pricing strategies, discount structures, etc. , they ' do not provide operational rules for management to follow (Monroe and DellaBitta, 1978). Moreover, such models are typically very "heavy" mathematically and thus not particularly appetizing for most business executives. Last but certainly not least, a lot of price modeling has been concerned with " mathematical elegance, often at the expense of realism " (Diamantopoulos and Mathews, 1995) and has ignored the fact that "pricing in reality follows a much more complex pattern which does not lend itself so readily to mathematical generalization and diagrammatic simplification" (Lieber-man, 1969). Taken together, these shortcomings go a long way towards explaining "the minimal contributions of models in the pricing area" (Jeuland and Dolan, 1982). This is disappointing, not least because "if there is any element in the marketing mix that would seem amenable to rational decision making, it is pricing" (Urbany, 2000).

Second, the priorities of managers and their search interests of academics in the pricing field have not always (or even mostly) coincided. As Bonoma, et al. (1988) observe: "it is not that academics cannot solve managerial pricing problems or that they have no interest in solving them. Rather, it seems that academic researchers have not known. or do not focus on, the key pricing concerns of managers in order to conduct rigorous pricing research. " To the extent that the issues deemed important by managers have not been adequately addressed by researchers, it is not surprising that "pricing theory and pricing research have won little recognition in practice" (Simon, 1982). On the positive side, the gap may be closing, as indicated by the increasingly managerial orientation of several pricing texts published in the past few years (e. g., Montgomery, 1988; Seymour, 1989; Morrisand Morris, 1990; Monroe, 1990; Nagle and Holden, 1995; Dolan and Simon, 1996).

Third, pricing has always been a "difficult" area to study empirically, because of confidentiality reasons. As Bain (1949) observed half a century ago, "the reluctance of businessmen to confide to economists their methods of price calculation and the character of their associations with rival firms... has been a serious barrier to close investigation of price policy as seen by the price maker". In this context, the participation rates of firm in empirical pricing surveys have often been disappointing (Diamantopoulos, 1991), lending credibility to the view that "it has not been the tradition of management to be 'friendly' to the needs of academic researchers in the area of pricing" (Monroe and Mazudmar, 1988). While the adoption of process-oriented methodologies which rely on close co-operation with managers (e. g., Howard and Morgenroth, 1968; Capon, 1975; Farley, 1980; Bonoma, 1988; Woodside, 1992; Diamantopoulos and Mathews, 1995) may overcome the shortcomings of survey-based approaches, gaining initial access to firms is likely to remain a key obstacle in the empirical study of pricing practices.

Fourth, in the past, many of the recommendations arising from academic research on pricing have been difficult to implement by firms because of information processing capability limitations. It is all very nice to suggest that comprehensive price analyses should be under taken involving estimation of price response functions, assessment of competitive reactions, and calculations of marginal costs (to name but a few) before prices are set. It is quite another thing to actually do this effectively if you do not have access to the relevant information and/or lack the capability to analysis whatever information you might be able to get hold of. In fact, there is evidence suggesting that firms knowingly operate sub-optimal pricing systems because they are convenient and inexpensive (Seymour, 1989) or because they are consistent with previous practice and thus easier to defend (Krishna, 2000). However, recent developments in information technology in terms of better and cheaper applications software, decision support systems and web-based platforms should enhance the capability of firms to engage in more sophisticated analyses of pricing parameters. Even such basic applications as spreadsheets can make the life of a price decision maker much easier (see, for example, Laric, 1989). The point is that pricing approaches/systems, formerly seen as being "esoteric" "slow" or "expensive" (or all three), are increasingly becoming much more manageable and within the reach of most firms; and enhance the capability of firms to engage in more sophisticated analyses of pricing parameters. Even such basic applications as spreadsheets can make the life of a price decision maker much easier (see, for example, Laric, 1989).

All for profit organizations and many non profit organizations set prices on their goods or services. Whether the price is called rent (for an apartment), tuition (for education), fare (for travel), or interest (for borrowed money), the concept is the same.

Throughout most of history, prices were set by negotiation between buyers and sellers. Setting one price for all buyers arose with the development of large-scale retailing at the end of the nineteenth century, when Woolworth's and other stores followed a "strictly one-price policy" because they carried so many items and had so many employees.

Now, 100 years later, technology is taking us back to an era of negotiated pricing. The internet, corporate networks, and wireless setups are linking people, machines, and companies around the globe, connecting sellers and buyers as never before. Web sites like Compare. Net and Price Scan. com allow buyers to compare products and prices quickly and easily. On-line auction sites like eBay. com and On sale. com make it easy for buyers and sellers to negotiate prices on thousands of items. At the same time, new technologies are allowing sellers to collect detailed data about customers' buying habits, preferences—even spending limits—so they can tailor their products and prices.

In the entire marketing mix, price is the one element that produces revenue, the others produce costs. Price is also one of the most flexible elements: It can be changed quickly, unlike product features and channel commitments. Although price competition is a major problem facing companies, many do not handle pricing well. The most common mistakes are these: Pricing is too cost-oriented; price is not revised often enough to capitalize on market changes; price is set independent of the rest of the marketing mix rather than as an intrinsic element of market-positioning strategy; and price is not varied enough for different product items, market segments, and purchase occasions.

9.2　Setting the price

A firm must set a price for the first time when it develops a new product, introduces its regular product into a new distribution channel or geographical area, and enters bids on new contract work. Price is also a key element used to support a product's quality positioning, Because a firm, in developing its strategy, must decide where to position its product on price and quality, there can be competition between price-quality segments.

In setting a product's price, marketers follow a six-step procedure: selecting the pricing objective; determining demand; estimating costs; analyzing competitors' costs, prices, and offers; selecting a pricing method; selecting the final price (see Figure 9.1).

	High Price		Low Price
High Quality	Premium	High Value	Super Value
	Over Charging	Mid Value	Good Value
Low Quality	Rip-off	False Economy	Economy

Figure 9.1　Nine Price-Quality Strategies

Step 1: Selecting the pricing objective

A company can pursue any of five major objectives through pricing:

1. Survival. This is a short-term objective that is appropriate only for companies that are plagued with overcapacity, intense competition, or changing consumer wants. As long as prices cover variable costs and some fixed costs, the company will be able to remain in business.

2. Maximum current profit. To maximize current profits, companies estimate the demand and costs associated with alternative prices and then choose the price that produces maximum current profit, cash flow, or return on investment. However, by emphasizing current profits, the company may sacrifice long-run performance by ignoring the effects of other marketing-mix variables, competitors' reactions, and legal restraints on price.

3. Maximum market share. Firms such as Texas Instruments choose this

objective because they believe that higher sales volume will lead to lower unit costs and higher long-run profit. With this market-penetration pricing, the firms set the lowest price, assuming the market is price sensitive. This is appropriate when (1) the market is highly price sensitive, so a low price stimulates market growth; (2) production and distribution costs fall with accumulated production experience; and (3) a low price discourages competition.

4. Maximum market skimming. Many companies favor setting high prices to "skim" the market. This objective makes sense under the following conditions: (1) A sufficient number of buyers have a high current demand; (2) the unit costs of producing a small volume are not so high that they cancel the advantage of charging what the traffic will bear; (3) the high initial price does not attract more competitors to the market; and (4) the high price communicates the image of a superior product.

5. Product-quality leadership. Companies such as Maytag that aim to be product-quality leaders will offer premium products at premium prices. Because they offer top quality plus innovative features that deliver wanted benefits, these firms can charge more. Maytag can charge $800 for its European-style washers—double what most other washers cost—because, as its ads point out, the appliances use less water and electricity and prolong the life of clothing by being less abrasive. Here, Maytag's strategy is to encourage buyers to trade up to new models before their existing appliances wear out.

Non profit and public organizations may adopt other pricing objectives. A university aims for partial cost recovery, knowing that it must rely on private gifts and public grants to cover the remaining costs, while a non profit theater company prices its productions to fill the maximum number of seats. As another example, a social services agency may set prices geared to the varying incomes of clients.

Step 2: Determining demand

Each price will lead to a different level of demand and, therefore, will have a different impact on a company's marketing objectives. The relationship between alternative prices and the resulting current demand is captured in a demand curve. Normally, demand and price are inversely related: The higher the price, the lower the demand. In the case of prestige goods, however, the demand curve sometimes slopes upward because some consumers take the higher price to signify a better product. Still, if the price is too high, the level of demand may fall.

Price sensitivity. The demand curve shows the market's probable purchase quantity at alternative prices, summing the reactions of many individuals who have different price sensitivities. The first step in estimating demand is to understand what affects price sensitivity.

A number of forces, such as deregulation and instant price comparisons that are available over the internet, have turned products into commodities in the eyes of consumers and increased their price sensitivity. More than ever, companies need to understand the price sensitivity of their target market and the trade-offs that people are willing to make between price and product characteristics.

Vermont-based Green Mountain. com for example, is working hard to differentiate its energy products. Through extensive marketing research, the energy firm uncovered a large market of prospects who not only were concerned with the environment, but also were willing to pay more to protect it. Because Green Mountain. com is a "green" power provider—a large percentage of its power is hydroelectric—customers can help ease the environmental burden by purchasing its power. This differentiation helps the firm compete against "cheaper" brands that focus on price-sensitive consumers.

Estimating demand curves. Companies can use one of three basic methods to estimate their demand curves. The first involves statistically analyzing past prices, quantities sold, and other factors to estimate their relationships. However, building a model and fitting the data with the proper techniques calls for considerable skill.

The second approach is to conduct price experiments, as when Bennett and Wilkinson systematically varied the prices of several products sold in a discount store and observed the results. An alternative here is to charge different prices in similar territories to see how sales are affected.

The third approach is to ask buyers to state how many units they would buy at different proposed prices. One problem with this method is that buyers might understate their purchase intentions at higher prices to discourage the company from setting higher prices.

In measuring the price-demand relationship, the marketer must control for various factors that will influence demand, such as competitive response. Also, if the company changes other marketing-mix factors besides price, the effect of the price change itself will be hard to isolate.

Price elasticity of demand. Marketers need to know how responsive, or elastic, demand would be to a change in price. If demand hardly changes with a small change in price, we say the demand is inelastic. If demand changes considerably, demand is elastic. Demand is likely to be less elastic when (1) there are few or no substitutes or competitors; (2) buyers do not readily notice the higher price; (3) buyers are slow to change their buying habits and search for lower prices; and (4) buyers think the higher prices are justified by quality differences, normal inflation, and so on. If demand is elastic, sellers will consider lowering the price to produce more total revenue. This makes sense as long as the costs of producing and selling more units do not increase disproportionately.

Price elasticity depends on the magnitude and direction of the contemplated price change. It may be negligible with a small price change and substantial with a large price change; it may differ for a price cut versus a price increase. Finally, long-run price elasticity may differ from short-run elasticity. Buyers may continue to buy from their current supplier after a price increase because they do not notice the increase, or the increase is small, or they are distracted by other concerns, or they find that choosing a new supplier takes time. But they may eventually switch suppliers. The distinction between short-run and long-run elasticity means that sellers will not know the total effect of a price change until time passes.

Step 3: Estimating costs

While demand sets a ceiling on the price the company can charge for its product, costs set the floor. Every company should charge a price that covers its cost of producing, distributing, and selling the product and provides a fair return for its effort and risk.

Types of costs and levels of production. A company's costs take two forms—fixed and variable. Fixed costs (also known as over-head) are costs that do not vary with production or sales revenue, such as payments for rent, heat, interest, salaries, and other bills that must be paid regardless of output.

In contrast, variable costs vary directly with the level of production. For example, each calculator produced by Texas Instruments (TI) involves a cost of plastic, micro-processing chips, packaging, and the like. These costs tend to be constant per unit produced, but they are called variable because their total varies with the number of units produced.

Total costs consist of the sum of the fixed and variable costs for any given level of production. Average cost is the cost per unit at that level of production; it is equal to total costs divided by production. Management wants to charge a price that will at least cover the total production costs at a given level of production.

To price intelligently, management needs to know how its costs vary with different levels of production. A firm's cost per unit is high if only a few units are produced every day, but as production increases, fixed costs are spread over a higher level of production results in each unit, bringing the average cost down. At some point, however, higher production will lead to higher average cost because the plant becomes inefficient (due to problems such as machines breaking down more often). By calculating costs for different-sized plants, a company can identify the optimal plant size and production level to achieve economies of scale and bring down the average cost.

Accumulated production. Suppose TI runs a plant that produces 3 000 calculators per day. As TI gains experience producing calculators, its methods improve. Workers learn shortcuts, materials flow more smoothly, and procurement costs fall. The result, as Figure 9.2 shows, is that average cost falls with accumulated production experience. Thus, the average cost of producing the first 100 000 hand calculators is $10 per calculator. When the company has produced the first 200 000 calculators, the average cost has fallen to $9. After its accumulated production experience doubles again to 400 000, the average cost is $8. This decline in the average cost with accumulated production experience is called the experience curve or learning curve.

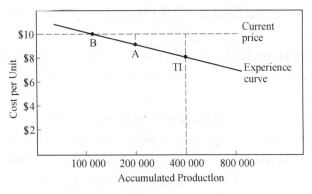

Figure 9.2　The experience curve

Now suppose TI competes against two other firms (A and B) in this industry. TI is the lowest-cost producer at $8, having produced 400 000 units in the past. If all three firms sell the calculator for $10, TI makes $2 profit per unit, A makes $1 per unit, and B breaks even. The smart move for TI would be to lower its price to

$9 to drive B out of the market; even A will consider leaving. Then TI will pick up the business that would have gone to B (and possibly A). Furthermore, price-sensitive customers will enter the market at the lower price. As production increases beyond 400 000 units, TI's costs will drop even more, restoring its profits even at a price of $9. TI has used this aggressive pricing strategy repeatedly to gain market share and drive others out of the industry.

Experience-curve pricing is risky because aggressive pricing may give the product a cheap image. This strategy also assumes that the competitors are weak and not willing to fight. Finally, the strategy may lead the firm into building more plants to meet demand while a competitor innovates a lower-cost technology and enjoys lower costs, leaving the leader stuck with old technology.

Differentiated marketing offers. Today's companies try to adapt their offers and terms to different buyers. Thus, a manufacturer will negotiate different terms with different retail chains, meaning the costs and profits will differ with each chain. To estimate the real profitability of dealing with different retailers, the manufacturer needs to use activity-based cost (ABC) accounting instead of standard cost accounting.

ABC accounting tries to identify the real costs associated with serving different customers. Both the variable costs and the overhead costs must be tagged back to each customer. Companies that fail to measure their costs correctly are not measuring their profit correctly, and they are likely to misallocate their marketing effort. Identifying the true costs arising in a customer relationship also enables a company to explain its charges better to the customer.

Target costing. We have seen that costs change with production scale and experience. They can also change as a result of a concentrated effort by the company's designers, engineers, and purchasing agents to reduce them. Many Japanese firms use a method called target costing. First, they use market research to establish a new product's desired functions, and then they determine the price at which the product will sell given its appeal and competitors' prices. They deduct the desired profit margin from this price, and this leaves the target cost they must achieve.

Next, the firms examine each cost element—design, engineering, manufacturing, sales—and break them down into further components, looking for ways to re-engineer components, eliminate functions, and bring down supplier costs.

The objective is to bring the final cost projections into the target cost range. If they cannot succeed, they may decide against developing the product because it could not sell for the target price and make the target profit. When they can succeed, profits are likely to follow.

Step 4: Analyzing competitors' costs, prices, and offers

Within the range of possible prices determined by market demand and company costs, the firm must take into account its competitors' costs, prices, and possible price reactions. If the firm's offer is similar to a major competitor's offer, then the firm will have to price close to the competitor or lose sales. If the firm's offer is inferior, it will not be able to charge more than the competitor charges. If the firm's offer is superior, it can charge more than the competitor-remembering, however, that competitors might change their prices in response at any time.

Step 5: Selecting a pricing method

The Three Cs—the customers' demand schedule, the cost function, and competitors' prices—are major considerations in setting price (see Figure 9.3). First, costs set a floor to the price. Second, competitors' prices and the prices of substitutes provide an orienting point. Third, customers' assessment of unique product features establishes the ceiling price. Companies must therefore select a pricing method that includes one or more of these considerations. We will examine five price-setting methods: markup pricing, perceived-value pricing, value pricing, going-rate pricing, and sealed-bid pricing.

1. Markup pricing. The most elementary pricing method is to add a standard markup to the product's cost. Construction companies do this when they submit job bids by estimating the total project cost and adding a standard markup for profit. Similarly, lawyers and accountants typically price by adding a standard markup on their time and costs.

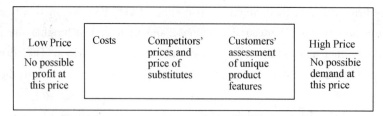

Figure 9.3   The Three Cs Model for price setting

2. Perceived-value pricing. An increasing number of companies base price on

customers' perceived value. They see the buyers' perceptions of value, not the seller's cost, as the key to pricing. Then they use the other marketing-mix elements, such as advertising, to build up perceived value in buyers' minds.

For example, when DuPont developed a new synthetic fiber for carpets, it demonstrated to carpet manufacturers that they could afford to pay DuPont as much as $1.40 per pound for the new fiber and still make their target profit. DuPont calls the $1.40 the value-in-use price. But pricing the new material at $1.40 per pound would leave the carpet manufacturers indifferent. So DuPont set the price lower than $1.40 to induce carpet manufacturers to adopt the new fiber. In this situation, DuPont used its manufacturing cost only to judge whether there was enough profit to go ahead with the new product.

The key to perceived-value pricing is to determine the market's perception of the offer's value accurately. Sellers with an inflated view of their offer's value will over-price their product, while sellers with an underestimated view will charge less than they could. Market research is therefore needed to establish the market's perception of value as a guide to effective pricing.

3. Value pricing. Value pricing is a method in which the company charges a fairly low price for a high-quality offering. Value pricing says that the price should represent a high-value offer to consumers. This is a major trend in the computer industry, which has shifted from charging top dollar for cutting-edge computers to offering basic computers at lower prices. For instance, Monorail Computer started selling PCs in 1996 for as little as $999 to woo price-sensitive buyers. Compaq and others quickly followed suit. More recently, Machines began selling its PCs for less than $500 without a monitor, targeting the 55 percent of computer less households with annual incomes of $25 000 to $30 000. Value pricing is not a matter of simply setting lower prices on one's products compared to those of competitors. It is a matter of re-engineering the company's operations to become a low-cost producer without sacrificing quality, and lowering prices significantly to attract a large number of value-conscious customers. An important type of value pricing is everyday low pricing (EDLP), which takes place at the retail level.

Retailers such as Wal-Mart and Amazon.com use EDLP pricing, posting a constant, everyday low price with few or no temporary price discounts. These constant prices eliminate week-to-week price uncertainty and can be contrasted to the "high-low" pricing of promotion-oriented competitors. In high-low pricing, the retailer charges higher prices on an everyday basis but then runs frequent promotions in which prices are temporarily lowered below the EDLP level. Retailers adopt EDLP for a number of reasons, the most important of which is that constant sales and promotions are costly and erode consumer confidence in the credibility of everyday prices. Consumers also have less time and patience for such time-honored traditions as watching for specials and clipping coupons. Yet promotions are an excellent way to create excitement and draw shoppers. For this reason, EDLP is not a guarantee of success. As supermarkets face heightened competition from store rivals and alternative channels, many are drawing shoppers using a combination of high-low and EDLP strategies, with increased advertising and promotions.

4. Going-rate pricing. In going-rate pricing, the firm bases its price largely on competitors' prices. The firm might charge the same, more, or less than its major competitor(s) charges. In oligopolistic industries that sell a commodity such as steel, paper, or fertilizer, firms normally charge the same price. The smaller firms "follow the leader", changing their prices when the market leader's prices change rather than when their own demand or costs change. Some firms may charge a slight premium or slight discount, but they typically preserve the amount of difference. When costs are difficult to measure or competitive response is uncertain, firms feel that the going price represents a good solution, since it seems to reflect the industry's collective wisdom as to the price that will yield a fair return and not jeopardize industrial harmony.

5. Sealed-bid pricing. Competitive-oriented pricing is common when firms submit sealed bids for jobs. In bidding, each firm bases its price on expectations of how competitors will price rather than on a rigid relationship to the firm's own costs or demand. Sealed-bid pricing involves two opposite pulls. The firm wants to win the contract—which means submitting the lowest price—yet it cannot set its price below cost. To solve this dilemma, the company would estimate the profit and the probability of winning with each price bid. By multiplying the profit by the probability of winning the bid on the basis of that price, the company can calculate the expected profit for each bid. For a firm that makes many bids, this method is a way of playing the odds to achieve maximum profits in the long run. However, firms that bid only occasionally or that badly want to win certain contracts will not find it advantageous to use the expected-profit criterion.

Step 6: Selecting the final price

The previous pricing methods narrow the range from which the company selects its final price. In selecting that price, the company must consider additional factors: psychological pricing, the influence of other marketing-mix elements on price, company pricing policies, and the impact of price on other parties.

Psychological pricing. Many consumers use price as an indicator of quality. Image pricing is especially effective with ego-sensitive products such as perfumes and expensive cars. A $100 bottle of perfume might contain $10 worth of scent, but gift givers pay $100 to communicate their high regard for the receiver. Similarly, price and quality perceptions of cars interact: Higher-priced cars are perceived to possess high quality; higher-quality cars are likewise perceived to be higher priced than they actually are. In general, when information about true quality is unavailable, price acts as a signal of quality.

When looking at a particular product, buyers carry in their minds a reference price formed by noticing current prices, past prices, or the buying context. Sellers often manipulate these reference prices. For example, a seller can situate its product among expensive products to imply that it belongs in the same class. Reference-price thinking is also created by stating a high manufacturer's suggested price, by indicating that the product was priced much higher originally, or by pointing to a rival's high price.

Often sellers set prices that end in an odd number, believing that customers who see a television priced at $299 instead of $300 will perceive the price as being in the $200 range rather than the $300 range. Another explanation is that odd endings convey the notion of a discount or bargain, which is why both torus.com and etoys.com set prices ending in 99. But if a company wants a high-price image instead of a low-price image, it should avoid the odd-ending tactic.

9.3 The influence of other marketing-mix elements

The final price must take into account the brand's quality and advertising relative to competition. When Farris and Reibstein examined the relationships among relative price, relative quality, and relative advertising for 227 consumer businesses, they found that brands with average relative quality but high relative advertising budgets were able to charge premium prices. Consumers apparently were willing to pay higher prices for known products than for unknown products. They also found that brands with high relative quality and high relative advertising obtained the highest prices, while brands with low quality and advertising charged the lowest prices. Finally, the positive relationship between high prices and high advertising held most strongly in the later stages of the product life cycle for market leaders. 18 Smart marketers therefore ensure that their prices fit with other marketing-mix elements.

9.3.1 Company pricing policies

The price must be consistent with company pricing policies. To accomplish this, many firms set up a pricing department to develop policies and establish or approve decisions. The aim is to ensure that the salespeople quote prices that are reasonable to customers and profitable to the company.

9.3.2 Impact of price on other parties

Management must also consider the reactions of other parties to the contemplated price. How will distributors and dealers feel about it? Will the sales force be willing to sell at that price? How will competitors react? Will suppliers raise their prices when they see the company's price? Will the government intervene and prevent this price from being charged?

In the last case, marketers need to know the laws regulating pricing. U.S. legislation outlaws price-fixing, so sellers must set prices without talking to competitors. Many federal, state, and local laws also protect consumers against deceptive pricing practices. For example, it is illegal for a company to set artificially high "regular" prices, then announce a "sale" at prices close to previous everyday prices.

9.3.3 Adapting the price

Companies usually do not set a single price, but rather a pricing structure that reflects variations in geographical demand and costs, market-segment requirements, purchase timing, order levels, delivery frequency, guarantees, service contracts, and other factors. As a result of discounts, allowances, and promotional support, a company rarely realizes the same profit from each unit of a product that it sells. Here we will examine several price-adaptation strategies: geographical pricing, price discounts and allowances, promotional pricing, discriminatory pricing, and product-mix pricing.

Part Two: Questions

1. How to maintain or even raise prices without losing market share?
2. Price reduction offered by the seller to trade channel members who perform certain functions. Please list some relevant examples.

Part Three: Words and Phrases

1. medieval   中世纪的
2. professionalism   专业主义
3. encapsulate   封装
4. methodology   方法论
5. elegance   优雅
6. reverberation   反响
7. paradox   悖论
8. calculation   计算
9. recommendation   推荐
10. esoteric   秘传的
11. pricing parameter   定价参数
12. avoidance   回避
13. decomposition   分解
14. sales revenue   销售收入
15. sales volume   销量
16. post-purchase   购后
17. magnitude   大小
18. geographic location   地理位置
19. marginal value   边际价值
20. transaction   交易

Part Four: Further Reading

This is I in a Millet employees micro channel in the circle of friends to quote a sentence from the Lei Jun in the beginning of the company's internal communication and corresponding images is red rice phone price to ￥699, screen writing greatly "bloody battle in the end" four words. Because it is inside the Millet, the details by media attention degree rather than January 3, officially announced the mobile version of red rice price of 100 yuan—at the time seems full of Millet against Huawei gunsmoke taste.

After a lapse of more than a month, set comprehensive onslaught tone of Millet and attack, the flag under the "canonical" Millet 2S price 400 yuan, from 1 699 yuan directly down to 1 299 yuan, fell to 20%; and after the price of M 2S accept open to buy, do not need pre about. Millet also announced that the series 2 (2 Millet, Millet, Millet 2a) products since October 2012 officially on sale since, so far has sold 15 million units.

Interestingly, the price of Millet 2S on the eve of the Meizu MX2 coincidence has just announced the price of 100 yuan, down from 1 699 yuan to 1 599 yuan.

Meizu will probably have a suppressed sadness. First is the Meizu MX2 prices brought about by the "bonus", 100 yuan against $400, Millet was greater dividends offset invisible; the second is following the Yellow chapter since the comeback, the media has been doubt Meizu a year shipment volume does not exceed a maximum of 300 million units, now Millet second generation single series products 16 months to sell Meizu annual sales of about 5 times and whether the series now has not Millet flagship model.

Turn over the comments on the micro-blog, Meizu's sympathy, and even some people who call for a price war with those who do not engage in subversion of Millet. But it is clear that the strength of the business community to speak, from Huawei glory did not follow the price of red rice 699 yuan price we see, from the Meizu MX2 no positive follow-up Millet 2S 1 299 yuan pricing we have seen.

But I digress, Millet follow-up Meizu price 400 yuan "overly aggressive rhetoric emotion", not mature business thinking. As difficult to imagine apple go to respond to China's domestic manufacturers carried lengthy statement should catch up with Apple's speech, massing Millet has with the Meizu opened the few and hard to imagine it will for such an adversary established emergency command room, then "emergency cut" product prices. But I do not want to spend more ink to speculate on both sides of the decision-making environment, I would like to explore why Millet dare to cut prices 400 yuan—no matter what is the motive?

Or the "rich emotion" perspective, you can put the behaviors are regarded as Millet Lei Jun and at the beginning of the year to put forward "the bitter end" slogan consistent. Now the "coping" Meizu price behavior is the "bitter end" of the second bomb. The first bomb is just getting in the January TD version of the red rice from 799 yuan to 699 yuan. That time, lying gun is released last December Huawei glory, the latter starting price is only 1 yuan lower than the original price of red rice mobile version. Two different is that Huawei did not follow up the Millet new pricing strategy, and Meizu coping style is out of refurbished machines "re edition MX2" to hold 1 299 wherever he goes.

Millet two refiners have deliberately to seize the initiative, but from the point of view of the volume and price of courage, Millet really twice "striking". Indeed, the word "volume". In the huge brand potential user groups and coerced clamping, the kinetic energy of Millet also had the onslaught of extra bonus. In fact, this is the traditional terminal manufacturers previously overlooked and difficult to understand key, from product to experience, to the depth of interaction with the user's overall brand operation before, the traditional single price of thinking in terms of volume, strength and courage and other dimensions are fully behind. In short, the product that the media, the truth in the competitors are finally aware and try to master, Millet has saved enough to lead the lead.

However, the implementation of the established slogan is not enough to explain why the courage to cut the price of Millet, and more than 20%. I think the fundamental reason lies in the cost control, coupled with the phrase "Lei often hung in the mouth of the cost pricing". As we know, Millet 2 have been launched 16 months (to officially listed for sale for), Millet 2S has also been launched fast a year, according to Moore's Law (the industry generally believe that Moore's Law applies in the mobile phone sector), BOM cost of the Millet 2 series of products have benefitted from Moore's Law; and because the Millet marketing ability is outstanding, the face of suppliers also has a stronger bargaining power.

In fact, Moore's Law has been the role of the existence of the new starting period of time, all of the phone should be reduced. But before mobile phone manufacturers rarely price promotions, they are calculated to the profit of these revenues. Of course, there are strong brands, such as the heyday of the 2005 Nokia, Apple's Jobs era, in the upcoming role of Moore's Law, the product directly to stop sales. Millet phone to release two new machines a year fast rhythm, more deeply feel the role of Moore's Law. For example, about half a year later than the 2S Millet 2, soon the price has dropped from 1999 yuan to 1 699 yuan, and even the configuration is also improved.

Cost change at the same time, the strategy is driven by the cost of Millet principle of cost pricing. Millet 2S 2 lower than 300 yuan, Millet 2S one year after the price of 400 yuan, the price policy and Moore's Law to the cost of the direction of the trend is positive. Coupled with the Millet cost pricing strategy, these changes are very direct.

Chapter 10: Distribution Channel Management

Part One: Text

10.1 Introduction

A channel of distribution may be referred to by other names, and terms vary from industry to industry. But whether channel, trade channel, or some other variant of the term is used, the functions performed remain the same. The term channel of distribution has its origins in the French word for canal, suggesting a path that goods take as they flow from producers to consumers. In this sense, a channel of distribution is defined by the organizations or individuals along the route from producer to consumer. Because the beginning and ending points of the route must be included, both producer and consumer are always members of a channel of distribution. However, there may be intermediate stops along the way. Several marketing institutions have developed to facilitate the flow of the physical product or the transfer of ownership (title) to the product from the producer to the consumer. Organizations that serve as marketing intermediaries (middlemen) specializing in distribution rather than production are external to the producing organization. When these intermediaries join with a manufacturer in a loose coalition aimed at exploiting joint opportunities, a channel of distribution is formed. A channel of distribution, then, consists of producer, consumer and any intermediary organizations that are aligned to provide a means of transferring ownership (title) or possession of a product from producer to consumer. The channel of distribution can also be seen as a system of inter dependent relationships among a set of organizations—a system that facilitates the exchange process.

All discussions of distribution channels assume that the product in question has taken on its final form. The channel of distribution for an automobile begins with a finished automobile. It does not include the paths of raw materials (such as steel) or component parts (such as tires) to the automobile manufacturer, which is an industrial user in these other channels. It should be emphasized that the channel's purpose in moving products to people is more than a simple matter of transportation. The channel of distribution must accomplish the task of transferring the title to the product as well as facilitating the physical movement of the goods to their ultimate destination. Although title transfer and the exchange of physical possession (transportation) generally follow the same channel of distribution, they do not necessarily need to follow the same path.

All but the shortest of channels include one or more intermediaries-individuals or organizations specializing in distribution rather than production (In the past, intermediaries were called middlemen). A distinction may be made between merchant intermediaries, which take title to the product, and agent intermediaries, which do not take title to the product. Although agent intermediaries never own the goods, they perform a number of marketing functions, such as selling, that facilitate further transactions in the exchange process.

Most intermediaries are independent organizations tied to the producers they deal with only by mutual agreement; they are not owned by the producers. Some intermediaries are owned by producers, such as the company-owned sales branches and sales offices that sell NCR point-of-sale systems. However, these company-owned sales branches and offices are clearly separate from the production facilities operated by the company. In service marketing, it sometimes appears that there is no channel of distribution. When a beautician delivers a product, such as a haircut or make-up advice, he or she deals directly with the customer. But even in these shortest of distribution channels, involving no intermediaries, marketing functions are being performed. The required activities are simply performed by the provider of the service (or, in a self-service environment, by the ultimate consumer). When identifiable intermediaries are present, the channel members form a coalition intended to act on joint opportunities in the marketplace. Each channel member, from producer to retailer, must be rewarded or see some opportunity for continued participation in the channel. Ultimately, for the channel to work properly, the consumer, who is not an institutional member of the channel but is the final link in

Chapter 10: Distribution Channel Management

the process, must also perceive a likely reward. Thus, the large merchandise selection and low retail prices offered by a target store must be seen as compensation for driving an extra mile or two to the store. The coalition between channel members may be a loose one resulting from negotiation or a formal set of contractual arrangements identifying each party's role in the distribution process. The conventional channel of distribution is characterized by loosely aligned, relatively autonomous marketing organizations that have developed a system to carry out a trade relationship. In contrast, formal vertical marketing systems are more tightly organized system in which the channel members are either owned by a manufacturer or a distributor, linked by contracts or other legal agreements such as franchises, to informally managed and coordinated as an integrated system through strategic alliances.

Not included in the channel of distribution are transportation companies, financial institutions, and other functional specialists selling services that assist the flow of products. They are collaborators, playing a specialized role by providing a limited facilitating service to channel members.

10.2 How intermediaries fit into distribution channels

In the previous section we outlined a conventional channel of distribution consisting of a manufacturer, a wholesaler, a retailer, and the ultimate consumer. Not all channels include all of these marketing institutions. In some cases, a unit of product may pass directly from manufacturer to consumer. In others it may be handled by not just one but two or more wholesalers. To show why these many variations exist, we will examine the role of intermediaries in marketing channels.

Consider this conventional channel of distribution: Manufacturer → Retailer → Ultimate consumer. It is possible, as shown here, to have a channel of distribution that does not include a separate wholesaler. A manufacturer can choose to sell directly to retailers, in effect eliminating the wholesaler. However, the marketing functions performed by the wholesaler must then be shifted to one of the other parties in the channel, the retailer or the manufacturer. For instance, with the wholesaler out of the picture, the manufacturer may have to create a sales force to call on the numerous retailers. If the manufacturer assumes some or all of the marketing functions, they are said to have been shifted backward in the channel. If the retailer assumes them, they are said to have been shifted forward in the channel. For example, the manufacturer may decide to perform the function of breaking bulk by sending comparatively small orders to individual retail customers. On the other hand, the retailer may be willing to accept truckload of a product, store large quantities of it, and perform the activity of breaking down these larger quantities into smaller quantities.

In any case, the functions performed by the eliminated wholesaler do not disappear; they are simply shifted to another channel member. The channel member that assumes these functions expects to be compensated in some way. The retailer may expect lower prices and higher margins for the extra work performed. The manufacturer may expect larger purchase orders, more aggressive retail promotion, or more control over the distribution process.

The key to setting the structure of a channel of distribution is to determine how the necessary marketing functions can be carried out most efficiently and effectively. Certain variables, such as price, the complexity of the product, and the number of customers to be served, can serve as guides to the appropriate channel structure. However, the functions to be performed should be the primary consideration in marketing manager's distribution plans. Let us consider some of the major functions performed by intermediaries: physical distribution, communication, and facilitating functions.

10.3　Physical distribution functions

Physical distribution functions include breaking bulk, accumulating bulk, creating assortments, reducing transactions, and transporting and storing.

10.3.1　Breaking bulk

With few exceptions, intermediaries perform a bulk-breaking function. The bulk-breaking function consists of buying in relatively large quantities, such as truckloads, and then selling in smaller quantities, passing the lesser amounts of merchandise on to retailers, organizational buyers, wholesalers, and other customers. By accumulating large quantities of goods and then breaking them into smaller amounts suitable for many buyers, intermediaries can reduce the cost of distribution for both manufacturers and consumers. Consumers do not buy and store great amounts of merchandise, which would increase their storage costs and the risks of spoilage, fire and theft. Manufacturers are spare the necessity of dividing their outputs into the small order sizes retailers or consumers might prefer. Bulk breaking is sometimes termed "resolution of economic discrepancies", because manufacturers, as a rule, turn out amounts of merchandise that are vast compared with the quantity that an individual buyer might be able to purchase. Breaking bulk resolves this discrepancy.

10.3.2 Accumulating bulk

In the majority of cases, it is the task of the intermediary to break bulk. However, an intermediary may also create bulk, buying units of the same product from many small producers and offering the larger amount to those who prefer to purchase in large quantities. These intermediaries are performing bulk-accumulating function. An intermediary performing this function is called surprisingly, an assembler. The classic examples of assemblers are in agriculture and fishing businesses. A maker of tomato sauce, such as Maggie, would probably not want to have to deal with many small farms. Assemblers gather large quantities of apples or tuna or other products attractive to large buyers as shown in Figure 10.1. Contrast the operation of assemblers with that of bulk-breaking intermediaries.

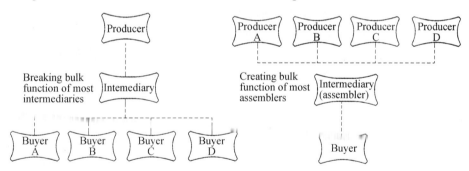

Figure 10.1 The bulk-breaking and bulk-acoumulating functions

After accumulating bulk, marketers of agricultural products and raw materials typically perform a sorting function, which involves identifying differences in quality and breaking down the product into grade or size categories. For example, eggs are sorted into jumbo grade AA, large grade AA, and so on.

10.3.3 Creating assortments

Another function that intermediaries perform is the creation of assortments of merchandise that would otherwise not be available. This assorting function resolves the economic discrepancy resulting from the factory operator's natural inclination to produce a large quantity of a single product or a line of similar products and the consumer's desire to select from a wide variety of choices. Wholesalers that purchase many different products from different manufacturers can offer retailers a greater assortment of items than an individual manufacturer is able to provide.

Consider how magazine publishers and retailers use intermediaries to solve a very big assorting problem. There are hundreds of magazine titles available from Indian publishers. No newsstand operator or other retailer carries anything like that number; a series of intermediaries is used to sort these many titles into appropriate groupings for individual stores. National wholesalers, move the hundreds of titles to hundreds of local wholesalers. Their reward for fulfilling this huge task is about 6 percent of the magazines' retail prices, out of which they must pay all expenses involved. The local distributors continue the task of breaking bulk, moving the magazines to countless supermarkets, new stands, and other retail spots. But there is more to the local wholesaler's task than simply breaking bulk and making delivery. The local wholesaler must select, from among the hundreds of available titles, the ones that are appropriate for the individual retailers' operations. Then, this assortment of titles must be assembled in the proper numbers for each retailer. The local wholesaler is paid about 20 percent of the cover prices. Complicated as this sounds, the system is so efficient that, less than 36 hours after a new Business Today is printed, it has arrived at all the retail establishments that carry the business magazine. Although the influence of wholesalers has declined in certain industries, it is obvious why wholesalers remain very important in the magazine distribution business.

10.3.4 Reducing transactions

There is one underlying reason why intermediaries can economically accumulate bulk and create assortments. The presence of intermediaries in the distribution system actually reduces the number of transactions necessary to accomplish the exchanges that keep the economy moving and consumers satisfied. As Figure 10.2 indicates, even if only four suppliers of grocery items attempt to transact business with just four retail buying headquarters, the number of interrelationships necessary is far greater than the number needed once an intermediary, such as a wholesaler, is added to the system. Channel intermediaries, in their dual roles as buying agents for their customers and selling agents for the manufacturers with which they deal, simplify the necessary transaction process considerably (Of course, channels of distribution can become too long. Such channels are common in Japan). Intermediaries not only reduce the number of transactions but also reduce the geographic distances that buyers and sellers must travel to complete exchanges and spare manufacturers the trouble of locating and contacting individual potential customers. These are some of the ways wholesalers and retailers can reduce costs. If manufacturers and consumers had to perform all these activities themselves, they would have to bear the costs involved.

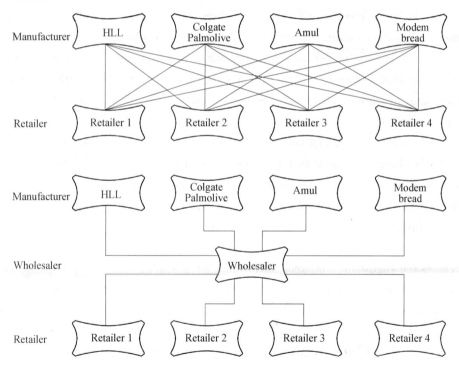

Figure 10.2　Reduction of transactions by an intermediary

10.3.5　Transporting and storing

Intermediaries, in most cases, perform or manage two other marketing functions: transporting and storing. Merchandise must be physically moved from points of production to points of consumption. This process often involves storing, or holding, the product at various spots along the way. Intermediaries of all types, including retailers, frequently store goods until they are demanded by customers further along in the channel of distribution.

Consider Haldiram namkeen—a very popular namkeen in the Rohtak market. If each person who wanted to buy (Haldiram namkeen) had to travel from Rohtak to the Haldiram namkeen manufacturing unit at New Delhi to make a purchase, those hundreds of thousands of customers—or Haldiram's employees, if the company chose to make home deliveries—would travel an incredible total distance. Wholesalers and retailers provide storage in the Rohtak market and enable Haldiram to send relatively few truckloads of namkeen to that city, greatly reducing the total distance traveled. It is clear that transportation and storage functions are necessary to satisfy the Rohtak area's demand for Haldiram namkeen. Although this example may seem far-fetched, it illustrates that one of the most important functions of intermediaries is to provide regional and local storage. The local Haldiram wholesaler, the neighborhood sweet shop, and the corner retailer all carry an inventory, and thus each performs the storage function.

We should mention that some types of intermediaries do not take possession of the goods whose distribution they facilitate. In such cases, the intermediary does not actually transport or store the merchandise. Instead, the intermediary coordinates transportation and storage or contributes in some other way to the creation of time and place utility.

Thus, you should think of transportation and storage in a broad sense that includes the contribution of wholesalers that, for example, arrange for shipment of goods from a producer-owned place of storage to an organizational buyer's place of business.

10.4 Communication and transaction functions

Intermediaries perform a communication function, which includes buying, selling, and other activities involving gathering or disseminating information. The ultimate purpose of the communication link between the manufacturer and the retailer or between the wholesaler and the retailer is to transfer ownership—that is, to complete a transaction that results in an exchange of title. Wholesalers and retailers may perform an important promotional function for manufacturers when they provide product information and price quotes. Most frequently, this communication is carried out by a sales force. However, intermediaries also use advertising and such sales promotion tools as retail displays. In other words, intermediaries perform a selling function for the manufacturer, often providing a sales force or other promotional efforts that they can supply more efficiently than the manufacturer can. The wholesaler provides a buying function for retailers, organizational users, and other customers. A wholesaler's contact with numerous manufacturers allows it to evaluate the quality of a wide assortment of goods from competing manufacturers. Thus, retailers and other customers are freed of the burden of evaluating every manufacturer's product assortments. This allows them more time to specialize in the retailing and merchandising of products.

Intermediaries further serve as channels of communication by informing buyers how products are to be sold, used, repaired, or guaranteed. They can even explain new product developments (In fact, retailers should pass along more of this information to their customers; unfortunately many retail salespeople are not trained to provide information of this sort). Because intermediaries typically deal with a number of manufacturers or other suppliers of goods, they are in a unique position to serve as conduits of information.

Intermediaries, being "in the middle", are well placed not only to pass information from producers to other channel members but also to collect information from channel members or retail shoppers and return it to producers. For example, suppose a retailer receives serious consumer complaints about a product or some product-related matter such as repair service. The retailer should pass this information backward in the channel to the wholesaler, who can bring the matter to the attention of the producer. Should is the key word here. Too often, whether because of apathy or the fear of somehow being blamed for a problem, intermediaries fail to perform this potentially valuable service. Marketers at all levels should encourage communication throughout channels of distribution, because the satisfaction of all channel members and consumers is at stake.

10.5　Facilitating functions

The transportation and storage functions of channel intermediaries are their most obvious contributions to the operation of the marketing system. However, intermediaries perform additional, so-called facilitating functions, which are not quite so apparent to observers of a channel in operation. Because the tasks of a channel intermediary can be so varied, it is nearly impossible to list all the facilitating functions a channel member might perform. However, three major categories of facilitating functions should be mentioned specifically: providing extra services, offering credit, and taking risks.

10.5.1　Extra services

Channel member, particularly intermediaries, can and do provide a range of extra services that increase the efficiency and effectiveness of the channel; intermediaries thus perform a service function. For many products, the availability of a post-sale repair service is an absolute necessity. Office photocopiers, for examples, always seem to need either routine maintenance or minor or major overhauls. Wholesalers and retailers of such machines usually offer repair services on either a contract or an emergency basis. They also carry necessary supplies like paper. Other products—such as personal computers and cellular phones—are not so prone to breakdowns, yet buyers like to know that repair service is available should it ever be needed. Technical support is critical for many internet and software companies. Honoring manufacturers' guarantees can be another responsibility of intermediaries.

10.5.2　Credit services

Most intermediaries perform a credit function by offering credit service of one kind or another. Although some wholesalers and retailers operate exclusively on a cash-and-carry basis, promising to pass related savings on to the customers, they make up a relatively small proportion of the millions of intermediaries operating in India.

Some credit services provided by channel members may not be immediately obvious. A retailer that accepts Master Card or Visa provides a credit service that in fact, costs the retailer a percent of the sales fee, which it must pay to the credit card company. Many small/medium retailers offer their own credit plans, which involve a more clear-cut provision of service than accepting "outside" card. Wholesalers and other non-retailer channel members may provide credit in a number of ways. Although a supplier may have a credit system so unique that buyer pays particular notice, supplier credit systems are generally so widespread throughout a trade that buyers scarcely see the credit system as a true service intermediaries in many fields routinely offer 30, 60 or more days to pay for merchandise ordered. Often, the days do not start "counting" until the goods are delivered to the buyer's place of business. In effect, such a service permits the buyer to make some money on a product before having to pay for it.

10.5.3 Risk taking

In almost everything they do, channel intermediaries perform a risk-taking function. When purchasing a product from a manufacturer or supplier of any type, intermediaries run the risk of getting stuck with an item that has fallen out of favor with the buying public because of a shift in fashion or the death of a fad. It is also possible for a product to spoil while it is in storage or lost through fire or some other disaster. Intermediaries bear these risks in addition to market risk.

Intermediaries run obvious risks in offering credit to the individuals and organizations to which they sell. They take legal risks in that intermediaries, not manufacturers, can be held responsible for problems caused by faulty products or misleading claims. When intermediaries, for whatever reason, seek to avoid the service of risk taking, the distribution system becomes less effective. In hard economic times, for example, retailers and wholesalers are tempted to engage in "hand to mouth" buying, ordering small quantities of products and attempting to sell them before placing yet another small order. Such behavior defeats the whole purpose of the marketing channel by eliminating the "buy in large quantities, sell in smaller quantities" premise on which most channels are based. Table 10.1 summarizes the basic functions that channel intermediaries perform.

Table 10.1 What a channel intermediary does for its suppliers and its customers

MARKETING FUNCTION	PERFORMED FOR SUPPLIERS	PERFORMED FOR CUSTOMERS
Physical distribution functions	Breaking bulk Accumulating bulk Creating assortments Transporation Storage	Sorting products into desired quantities Assorting items into desired variety Delivery(transportation) Storage
Communication functions	Promotion, especially selling and communication of product information Gathering customer information	Buying based on interpretations of customer needs Dissemination of information
Facilitating functions	Financing customer purchase Providing management services Taking risks	Credit financing Repair services Technical support

10.5.4 Typical channels of distribution

We have already suggested that not all channels of distribution are alike. In fact, the variety of distribution channels is extensive indeed. That is because marketers are constantly seeking new ways to perform the distribution function. Both manufacturers and intermediaries have developed all sorts of variations on the basic theme of distribution. Each variation was developed in an effort to perform the distribution function better and thereby attract business.

Channels may be distinguished by the number of intermediaries they include; the more intermediaries, the longer the channel. Some organizations choose to sell their products directly to the consumer or organizational user; others use long channels that include numbers of wholesalers, agents, and retailers to reach buyers.

10.5.5 Channel-design decisions

A new firm typically starts as a local operation selling in a limited market. It usually uses existing intermediaries. The number of intermediaries in any local market is apt to be limited; a few manufacturers' sales agents, a few wholesalers, several established retailers, a few trucking companies, and a few warehouses.

Deciding on the best channels might not be a problem. The problem might be to convince the available intermediaries to handle the firm's line. If the firm is successful, it might branch into new markets. It might have to use different channels in different markets. In smaller markets, the firm might sell directly to retailers; in larger markets, it might sell through distributors. In rural areas, it might work with general-goods merchants; in urban areas, with limited-line merchants. In one part of the country, it might grant exclusive franchises; in another, it might sell through all outlets willing to handle the merchandise. In one country it might use international sales agents; in another, it might partner with a local firm. In short the channel system evolves in response to local opportunities and conditions.

10.6 Channel-management decisions

After a company has chosen a channel alternative, it must select, train, motivate, and evaluate the individual intermediaries. Then, because neither the marketing environment nor the product life cycle remains static, the company must be ready to modify these channel arrangements over time.

10.6.1 Selecting channel members

During the selection process, producers should determine what characteristics distinguish the better intermediaries. They will want to evaluate number of years in business, other lines carried, growth and profit record, solvency, cooperativeness, and reputation. If the intermediaries are sales agents, producers will want to evaluate the number and character of other lines carried and the size and quality of the sales force.

If the intermediaries are store or internet retailers that want exclusive distribution, the producer will want to evaluate locations, brand strength, future growth potential, and type of clientele.

Selection of channel participants is actually a two-way process: Just as producers select their channel members, the intermediaries also select their producer partners. Yet producers vary in their ability to attract qualified intermediaries. Toyota was able to attract many new dealers when it first introduced its Lexus line, but Polaroid initially had to sell through mass-merchandising outlets when photographic-equipment stores would not carry its cameras.

Selection can be a lengthy process. Consider the experience of Japan's Epson Corporation. A leading manufacturer of computer printers, Epson decided to add computers to its product line but chose to recruit new distributors rather than sell through its existing distributors. The firm hired a recruiting firm to find candidates who (1) had distribution experience with major appliances, (2) were willing and able to set up their own distributorships, (3) would accept Epson's financial arrangements, and (4) would handle only Epson equipment, although they could stock other companies' software. After the recruiting firm went to great effort to find qualified candidates, Epson terminated its existing distributors and began selling through the new channel members. Despite this time-consuming, detailed selection process, Epson never succeeded as a computer manufacturer.

10.6.2 Training channel members

Companies need to plan and implement careful training program for their distributors and dealers because the intermediaries will be viewed as the company by end users. Microsoft, for example, requires third-party service engineers who work with its software applications to complete a number of courses and take certification exams. Those who pass are formally recognized as Microsoft Certified Professionals, and they can use this designation to promote business.

As another example, Ford Motor Company beams training programs and technical information via its satellite-based Ford Star Network to more than 6 000 dealer sites. Service engineers at each dealership sit at a conference table and view a monitor on which an instructor explains procedures such as repairing on board electronics and then answers questions. Such training initiatives keep employees updated on the latest product specifications and service requirements.

10.6.3 Motivating channel members

The most successful firms view their channel members in the same way they view their end users. This means determining their intermediaries' needs and then tailoring the channel positioning to provide superior value to these intermediaries. To improve intermediaries' performance, the company should provide training, market research, and other capability-building programs. And the company must constantly reinforce that its intermediaries are partners in the joint effort to satisfy customers.

More sophisticated companies go beyond merely gaining intermediaries' cooperation and instead try to forge a long-term partnership with distributors. The manufacturer communicates clearly what it wants from its distributors in the way of market coverage, inventory levels, marketing development, account solicitation, technical advice and services, and marketing information. The manufacturer then seeks distributor agreement with these policies and may introduce a compensation plan or other rewards for adhering to the policies. For example, Dayco Corporation, a maker of engineered plastics and rubber products, strengthens channel partnerships by running an annual week-long retreat with 20 distributors' executives and 20 Dayco executives.

Still, too many manufacturers think of their distributors and dealers as customers rather than as working partners. Up to now, we have treated manufacturers and distributors as separate organizations. But many manufacturers are distributors of related products made by other manufacturers, and some distributors also own or contract for the manufacture of in-house brands. JC Penney sells national brands of jeans by manufacturers such as Levi Strauss in addition to a line of jeans under the Original Arizona Jeans company private label. This situation, which is common in the jeans industry and in many others, complicates the process of selecting and motivating channel members.

10.6.4 Evaluating channel members

Producers must periodically evaluate intermediaries' performance against such standards as sales-quota attainment, average inventory levels, customer delivery time, treatment of damaged and lost goods, and cooperation in promotional and training programs.

A producer will occasionally discover that it is paying too much to particular intermediaries for what they are actually doing. As one example, a manufacturer that was compensating a distributor for holding inventories found that the inventories were actually held in a public warehouse at the manufacturer's expense. Producers should therefore set up functional discounts in which they pay specified amounts for the trade channel's performance of each agreed-upon service. Under performers need to be counseled, retrained, re-motivated, or terminated.

10.6.5 Modifying channel arrangements

Channel arrangements must be reviewed periodically and modified when distribution is not working as planned, consumer buying patterns change, the market expands, new competition arises, innovative distribution channels emerge, or the product moves into later stages in the product life cycle.

Rarely will a marketing channel remain effective over the entire product life cycle. Early buyers might be willing to pay for high value-added channels, but later buyers will switch to lower-cost channels. This was the pattern for many products, including small office copiers, which were first sold by manufacturers' direct sales forces, later through office-equipment dealers, still later through mass merchandisers, and now by mail-order firms and internet marketers.

Miland Lele developed the grid in Figure 10.3 to show how marketing channels have changed for PCs and designer apparel at different stages in the product life cycle. As the grid indicates, new products in the introductory stage of the life cycle enter the market through specialist channels that attract early adopters. As interest grows, higher-volume channels appear (dedicated chains, department stores), offering some services, but not as many as the previous channels. In the maturity stage, where grow this slowing, some competitors move their product into lower-cost channels (mass merchandisers). In decline, even lower-cost channels emerge (mail-order, discount websites, off-price discounters).

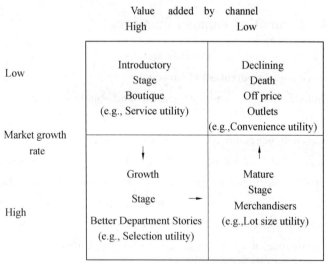

Figure 10.3 Channel value added and market growth rate

Adding or dropping an individual channel member requires an incremental analysis to determine what the firm's profits would look like with and without this intermediary. Sometimes a producer considers dropping all intermediaries whose sales are below a certain amount. For example, Navistar noted at one time that 5 percent of its dealers sold fewer than three or four trucks a year. It cost the company more to service these dealers than their sales were worth. But dropping these dealers could have system-wide repercussions. The unit costs of producing trucks would be higher because the overhead would be spread over fewer trucks, some employees and equipment would be idled, some business in these markets would go to competitors, and other dealers might become insecure. All of these factors have to be taken into account when changing channel arrangements. The most difficult decision involves revising the overall channel strategy.

Distribution channels can become outmoded over time, as a gap arises between the existing distribution system and the ideal system that would satisfy target customers' (and producers') requirements. Examples abound: Avon's door-to-door system for selling cosmetics had to be modified as more women entered the workforce, and IBM's exclusive reliance on a field sales force had to be modified with the introduction of low-priced personal computers. Dell Computer started out selling PCs by mail to consumers and businesses, briefly added retail stores as part of an expansion strategy, then cut out store distribution in favor of the internet (www.dell.com), a direct channel where customers could more easily order customized PCs.

10.7 Channel dynamics

In the ever-changing marketing environment, distribution channels do not stand still. New wholesaling and retailing institutions emerge, and new channel systems evolve. We look next at the recent growth of vertical, horizontal, and multi-channel marketing systems and see how these systems cooperate, conflict, and compete.

10.7.1 Horizontal marketing systems

Another channel development is the horizontal marketing system, in which two or more unrelated companies put together resources or programs to exploit an emerging marketing opportunity. Each company lacks the capital, know-how, production, or marketing resources to venture alone, or it is afraid of the risk. The companies might work with each other on a temporary or permanent basis or create a joint venture company.

Adler calls this symbiotic marketing. Consider the long-standing agreement between Sara Lee Intimates and Wal-Mart, which has enabled the partners to grow their business from an initial $134 million account to a $1 billion partnership over 10 years. Both firms have merchandise, operations, MIS, and marketing managers devoted solely to this agreement. They meet regularly to iron out problems and make plans, requiring the sharing of marketing information, inventory levels, sales history, price changes, and other proprietary information.

10.7.2　Multichannel marketing systems

In the past, many companies sold to a single market through a single channel. Today, with the proliferation of customer segments and channel possibilities, more companies have adopted multichannel marketing. Multichannel marketing occurs when a single firm uses two or more marketing channels to reach one or more customer segments.

As one example, the Parker-Hannif in Corporation (PHC) sells pneumatic drills to the lumber, fishing, and aircraft industries. Instead of selling through one industrial distributor, PHC has established three separate channels—forestry equipment distributors, marine distributors, and industrial distributors. There appears to be little conflict because each type of distributor sells to a separate target segment.

By adding more channels, companies can gain three important benefits. The first is increased market coverage—companies often add a channel to reach a customer segment that its current channels cannot reach. The second is lower channel cost—companies may add a new channel to lower the cost of selling to an existing customer group (selling by phone rather than personally visiting small customers). The third is more customized selling—companies may add a channel whose selling features fit customer requirements better (adding a technical sales force to sell more complex equipment).

However, new channels typically introduce conflict and control problems. First, different channels may end up competing for the same customers. Second, as the new channels become more independent, the company may have difficulty maintaining cooperation among all of the members. Consider the dilemma faced by insurance firms that sell home, auto, and life insurance policies through agents. On the one hand, shopping for insurance via websites such as Quote smith. com and ibex. com can save customers both time and money while giving insurers access to more prospects. On the other hand, using internet intermediaries could potentially alienate the 1.8 million U. S. insurance agents who now sell the bulk of the policies and make their living from commissions that can range as high as 20 percent. While Geico and other insurers that sell directly to customers are moving quickly to open internet channels, firms with established agent networks are moving more cautiously. Their dilemma is summed up by a spokesperson for the St. Paul Companies, who says: "We must work to build business on-line in a way that does not disenfranchise our agents and brokers."

10.7.3 Conflict, cooperation, and competition

No matter how well channels are designed and managed, there will be some conflict, if for no other reason than the interests of independent business entities do not always coincide. Here we examine three questions: What types of conflict arise in channels? What causes channel conflict? What can be done to resolve conflict situations?

10.7.4 Types of conflict and competition

Vertical channel conflict means conflict between different levels within the same channel. As one example, General Motors has come into conflict with its dealers in trying to enforce policies on service, pricing, and advertising. As another example, Coca-Cola came into conflict with its bottlers who agreed also to bottle Dr. Pepper.

Vertical channel conflict is currently raging in consumer packaged goods, where power has shifted from producers to retailers. Even as manufacturers continue to pump out thousands of new products, retailers seeking maximum productivity from their limited shelf space are able to collect slotting fees from manufacturers for stocking new products, display fees to cover space costs, fines for late deliveries and incomplete orders, and exit fees to cover the cost of returning goods to producers. Trying to regain power from retailers, manufacturers are expanding into alternative channels, putting more emphasis on market-leading brands, and developing stronger links with important retailers through value-added distribution systems and programs that benefit all members of the channel.

Horizontal channel conflict involves conflict between members at the same level within the channel. Horizontal channel conflict erupted, for instance, when some

Pizza Inn franchisees complained about other Pizza Inn franchisees cheating on ingredients, maintaining poor service, and hurting the overall Pizza Inn image.

Multichannel conflict exists when the manufacturer has established two or more channels that sell to the same market. For instance, when Goodyear began selling its tires through Sears, Wal-Mart, and Discount Tire, the move angered its independent dealers. Goodyear eventually placated them by offering exclusive tire models that would not be sold in other retail outlets.

10.7.5 Causes of channel conflict

Why does channel conflict erupt? One major cause is goal incompatibility. For example, the manufacturer may want to achieve rapid market penetration through a low-price policy. The dealers, in contrast, may prefer to work with high margins for short-run profitability. Sometimes conflict arises from unclear roles and rights. This is what happened when IBM started selling PCs to large accounts through its own sales force while its licensed dealers were also trying to sell to large accounts. Territory bound-arise and credit for sales often produce conflict in such situations.

By adding new channels, a company faces the possibility of channel conflict, as the earlier insurance example indicated. Conflict can also stem from differences inperception, as when the producer is optimistic about the short-term economic outlook and wants dealers to carry more inventory, while its dealers are more pessimistic about future prospects.

At times, conflict can arise because of the intermediaries' great dependence on the manufacturer. The fortunes of exclusive dealers, such as auto dealers, are intimately affected by the manufacturer's product and pricing decisions. This creates a high potential for conflict.

10.7.6 Managing channel conflict

Some channel conflict can be constructive and can lead to more dynamic adaptation in a changing environment. Too much conflict can be dysfunctional, however, so the challenge is not to eliminate conflict but to manage it better.

Part Two: Questions

1. According to the wheel of retailing, when a new retail form appears, how

would you characterize its image?

2. What are the targeted consumers want from the channel?

Part Three: Words and Phrases

1. channel management	渠道管理
2. negotiation	谈判
3. Colgate-Palmolive	高露洁
4. facilitating function	辅助功能
5. assortment	分类
6. raw material	原材料
7. point-of-sale	销售点
8. intermediary	中间商,中介机构
9. wholesaler	批发商
10. merchandise	商品
11. price quote	价格报价
12. photocopier	复印机
13. warehouse	仓库
14. agent	代理
15. effectiveness	有效性
16. extensive	广泛的
17. retailer	零售商
18. distributor	经销商
19. provision	条款,规定
20. summarize	总结

Part Four: Further Reading

Marketing Strategies for Personal Selling

Personal selling is a strategy that salespeople use to convince customers to purchase a product. The salesperson uses a personalized approach, tailored to meet the individual needs of the customer, to demonstrate the ways that the product will benefit him. The customer is given the opportunity to ask questions, and the salesperson addresses any concerns he has about the product.

Ask questions. When trying to sell a product to a customer, you need to know why he is interested in the product or service. Find out if he is currently a customer of one of your competitors. If so, ask why he is unsatisfied with its products or services, making him consider switching to yours. Inquire as to who the key decision-makers in his company are and see if he has a timeline for making a final decision on the product. Gathering this type of information from him will help you to know what he's looking to gain from your company, so you are better able to meet his needs with your sales pitch.

Address Concerns. Ask the customer to share any concerns he has about your product or service with you. If you are able to address these issues, you can increase your chances of easing his mind and convincing him to bring his business to your company. It is always better to know any potential concerns that a client has with your company, so you have a chance to diffuse them. Sometimes the customer just needs a little more information about your product or service to feel comfortable making a decision.

Related Reading: Theories of Selling

Ask for the sale. Your job is not done after you have finished your sales presentation. It is important to ask the customer for the sale. You can directly ask if he has decided to buy your product or service, or you can do it in an indirect manner such as asking when he would like to start receiving the services or how many of the specific product he would like to order. This will help you to know where you stand with the customer. If he hesitates, ask what's holding him back from the sale. If you are able to address his concerns, you are more likely to get the sale.

Follow-up. A good salesperson always follows up with both prospects and clients after making a presentation. If a prospective customer is still unsure of the benefits of your product or service, this is another chance to address his concerns. If he has already decided to purchase your product or service, it's important to check in and make sure he is satisfied with it.

Chapter 11: Promotion Mix

Part One: Text

11.1 Introduction

Broadly speaking, promotion means to push forward or to advance an idea to gain its acceptance and approval. Promotion is any communicative activity whose main object is to move forwards a product, service or idea in a chain of distribution. It is an effort by a marketer to inform and persuade buyers to accept, use, recommend, and repurchase the idea, good or service which is being promoted. Thus, promotion is a form of communication with an additional element of persuasion. The promotional activities always attempt to affect knowledge, attitudes preferences, and behavior of recipients, i.e., buyers.

In any exchange activity, communication is absolutely necessary. A company may have the best product, package, etc. but still people may not buy the product if they haven't heard of it. The marketer must communicate to his prospective buyers and provide them with adequate information in a persuasive language. People must know that the right product is available at the right place and at the right price. This is the job of promotion in marketing.

Thus promotion is the process of marketing communication involving information, persuasion and influence. Promotion has three specific purposes. First, it communicates marketing information to consumers, users, and prospects; Second, besides just communication, promotion persuades and convinces the buyers; Third, promotional efforts act as powerful tools of communication. Providing the cutting edge to its entire marketing programmed. Thus promotion is a form of non-price competition.

Promotion is thus responsible for awakening and stimulating demand, capture demand from rivals and maintaining demand for products even against keen competition.

11.2 Every company can choose from the following tools of promotion, popularly known as the promotion-mix variables: advertising, sales promotion, personal selling, public relations

11.2.1 Advertising

Advertising is perhaps the most important tool of promotion that companies use to direct persuasive communications to target buyers and publics. Advertising is defined by the American Management Association as "any paid form of non-personal presentation and promotion of ideas, goods or services by an identified sponsor". Advertising through various media like magazines, newspapers, radio, television, outdoor displays, etc., has many purposes: "long-term build-up the organization's corporate image (institutional advertising), or long-term build-up of a particular brand (brand advertising), information dissemination about a sale, service or event (classified advertising), announcement of a special sale (sale or promotional advertising) and advocacy of a particular cause advocacy advertising."

Organizations obtain their advertising in different ways. In small companies, advertising is handled by someone in the sales or marketing department who works with an advertising agency. Large companies on other hand, set up their own advertising departments, whose work is to develop the total budget, approve advertising agency ads campaigns, dealer displays, etc.

In developing an advertising programmed, marketing managers must always start with the identification of the target market and buyer motives then proceed to make the five major decisions in developing advertising programmed, known as the five Ms:

First, What are the advertising objectives (Mission); Second, How much can be spent (Money); Third, What message should be sent (Message); Fourth, What media should be used (Media); Fifth, How should the results be evaluated (Measurement).

The first step in developing an advertising programme is to set the advertising objectives. These objectives must flow from prior decisions on the target market, market positioning and marketing mix. The objectives can be classified on the basis of the aim which can be either to (a) inform the target about the product features, performance, service available, a price change or new uses, etc. (called informative advertising) or (b) to persuade the prospect to may be remain brand loyal, or switch brands, or to purchase now, etc. (called persuasive advertising) or (c) to remind the buyer or the prospect about the product or its features, price whereto buy it from, etc. (called reminder advertising). The choice of the advertising objectives should be based on a thorough analysis of reached its current marketing situation, e. g. , if the product has maturity stage in its product-life cycle, and the company is the market leader, and if the brand usage is low, the proper objective should be to stimulate more brand usage(as in the case of Colgate toothpaste or surf). On the other hand, if the product is new and at the introduction stage of the PLC and the company is not a market leader but its brand is superior to the leader, (as in the case of captain cook salt) then the proper objective may be to convince the prospects about the brands superiority.

After determining the objectives, the company can proceed to establish advertising budget for each product. Every company would like to end the amount required to achieve the sales goal. But how should its decide how much to spend on advertising. There are several methods from which a company can choose from while deciding on how much to spend:

First, What all-you-can-afford method.

Many companies set the promotion budget at what they think the company can afford. However, this method completely ignores the role of promotion as an investment and the immediate impact of promotion on sales volume. It leads to an uncertain annual promotion budget.

Second, Competitive parity method.

Some companies set their promotion budget to achieve parity with their competitors. Two arguments have been advanced for this method. One is that the competitors' expenditures represents the collective wisdom of the industry and second is that maintaining a competitive parity helps prevent promotion wars.

Third, Objective-task method.

This method calls upon marketers to develop their promotion budgets by defining their specific communication objectives, determining the tasks that must performed to achieve these objectives, and estimating the costs performing these tasks. The sum of these costs is the proposed promotion budget. This method has the advantage of requiring management to spell out its assumptions about the relationship between the amount spent, exposure levels, trial rates and regular usage.

Fourth, Percentage of sales method.

Many companies set their promotion expenditure at a specified percentage of sales (either current or anticipated). A number of advantages is claimed for the percentage of sales method. First, it means that promotion expenditures would vary with what the company can "afford". Second, it encourages management to think in terms of the relationship between promotion cost, selling price and profit per unit. Third, it encourages competitive stability to the extent that competing firms spend approximately the same percentage of their sales on promotion.

Many studies on "sales effect of advertising expenditures" neglect the message creativity. One study found that the effect the creativity factor in a campaign is more important than the amount money spent. Only after gaining attention can a commercial help to increase the brand's sales.

Advertisers go through the following steps to develop a creative strategy message generation, message evaluation and selection and message execution.

First, Message Generation: In principle, the product's message (theme, appeal) should be decided as part of developing the product concept; expresses the major benefit that the brand offers. Creative people use several methods to generate possible advertising appeals. Many creative people proceed inductively by talking to consumers, dealers, experts and competitors. Consumers are the major source of good ideas. Their feelings about the strength and shortcomings of existing brands provide important clues to creative strategy.

Second, Message Evaluation and Selection: The advertiser needs to evaluate the alternative messages. A good ad normally focuses on one central selling proposition without trying to give too much product information which dilutes the ad's impact. Messages should be rated on desirability, exclusiveness and believability. The message must first say something a desirable or interesting about the product. The message must also something exclusive or distinctive that does not apply to every brand the product category. Finally, the message must be believable.

Third, Message Execution: The impact of the message "depends not only upon what is said" but also on "how it is said". Some ads aim for rational positioning (designed to appeal to the rational mind), e. g., Surf-washes clothes whitest, whereas other advertisements aim for emotional positioning, which appeal to the emotions of love, tenderness, care, etc. The choice of headlines, copy and so on, can make a difference to the ad's impact. The advertiser usually prepares a copy strategy statement describing the objective, content, support and tone of the desired ad. Creative people must find a style, tone, words, and format for executing the message. All of these elements must deliver a cohesive image and message. Since few people read the body copy, the picture and headline must summarize the selling proposition.

A number of researchers of print advertisements report that the picture, headline, and copy are important in this order. The reader first notices the picture and hence it must be strong enough to draw attention. Then the headline must be effective in propelling the person to read the copy which itself must be well composed. Even then, a really outstanding ad will be noted by less than 50% of the exposed audience, about 30% of the exposed audience might recall the headline's main point, about 25% might remember the advertiser's name and less than 10% will have read most of the body copy.

Deciding on the media. The advertiser's next task is to choose advertising media to carry the advertising message. The steps are deciding on desired reach, frequency and impact, choosing among major media types, selecting specific media vehicles, and deciding on media timing.

Evaluating advertising effectiveness. Good planning and control of advertising depends critically on measures of advertising effectiveness. Most advertisers try to measure the communication effect of an ad that is its potential effect on awareness knowledge or preference. They would like to measure the sales-effect but often find it is too difficult to measure. Yet both can be researched.

11.2.2 Sales promotion

"Sales Promotion is a direct and immediate inducement that adds an extra value to the product so that it prompts the dealers, distributors or the ultimate consumers to buy the product."

According to the American Marketing Association, "Sales promotion means to give short term incentives to encourage purchase or sale of a product or service. Sales promotion includes those activities that supplement both personal selling and advertising, and co-ordinate them and help to make them effective, such as display, shows and expositions demonstrations and other non-recurrent selling efforts in the ordinary routine". Sales promotion helps in solving the short-term problems of the marketing manager, the impact of these methods are not very lasting durable and the results of these efforts are not lasting as those advertising and personal selling. Sales promotion is more of a catalyst and a supporting communication effort to advertising and personal selling.

Objectives of sales promotion. Sales promotions, as a tool of communication and promotion, fulfills the following objectives:

Sales promotion helps in introducing new products.

It also helps in overcoming any unique competitive situation.

It is useful for unloading the accumulated inventory or stock of the goods in the market.

It can be used for overcoming the seasonal slumps in sales.

Sales promotion helps in getting new accounts, i. e., clients or customers.

It helps in retrieving the lost accounts.

It acts as a support and supplement to the advertising effort.

It also acts as a support and supplement to the salesman's efforts.

It aims at persuading salesmen to sell the full line of the products and not just concentrate on a few products.

It helps in persuading the dealer to buy more stock from the company, i. e., to increase the size of the order.

Its objective is to create a stronger and quicker response from the consumers.

It also helps to boost dropping sales of any product of the company.

Sales promotion techniques.

Communication: sales promotion attracts the attention of the consumer and gives him such information that he is led to the product or service.

Incentive: they give some incentive, concession, inducement contribution that gives added value to the consumer.

Invitation: they give a distinct invitation to the consumer to enter into a transaction with the dealer or the company.

11.2.3 Personal selling

It is essential to communicate, persuade and motivate the target customers in order to make the product and price known and acceptable to the target consumers. For this, personal selling is adopted as an effective tool. The company's sales persons who may be referred to as the salesmen or sales representatives or sales executives, who are on its payroll, communicate with the target consumers, so as to make an order of sale and motivate them to positively respond to it and finally to clinch the deal. According to the American Marketing Association, "Personal selling can be defined as an oral presentation, in conversation with one or more prospective purchasers, for the purpose of making ales".

According to F. E. Webster, Jr., "Personal selling is a highly distinctive form of promotion. Like other forms of promotion, personal selling is basically a method of communication, but unlike others it is a two-way, rather than unidirectional communication. It involves not only the individual but social behavior. Each of the persons in face-to-face contact, salesman and prospect influences the other. The outcome of each sales situation depends heavily upon the success that both the parties experience in communicating with each other and reaching a common understanding of needs and goals. The main task involved personal selling is to match specific products with specific consumers as to secure transfer of ownership".

According to K. B. Hass, Personal selling basically consists of the interpretation of product and service features in terms of benefits and advantages to the buyer and of persuading the buyers to buy the right kind and quantity of the product.

Objectives of personal selling. Personal selling helps in the following major areas: To improve the sales volume of the company's different products; To ensure the proper mix of products in the total sales volume; To increase the market share of the company; To increase the profits of the company; To reduce the overall selling expenses; To gain new accounts and improve business growth; It helps in the appointment of dealers and expansion of the distribution channel; To secure channel members co-operation in stocking as well as selling the products of the company.

11.2.4 Public relations

Public relations is a very important and resourceful tool of the promotion mix. According to Kotler, "Public relations induces a variety of programmes designed to improve, maintain or protect a company of product image, through press conferences, seminars, speeches, annual reports charitable donations, etc."

The major tools in public relations are publications: annual reports brochures, articles, company magazines and news letters; events: special events like news conference, anniversary celebration of the company, sponsoring sports and cultural events; News: the companies find and create favorable news ; speeches:by company executives at trade associations, sales meetings, etc. ; identity media: companies also use such devices as company logos, stationery, business cards, uniforms, etc. , which help in identifying the company.

Public relations (PR) is another important marketing tool, which until recently, was treated as a marketing step-child. The PR department is typically located at corporate headquarters; and its staff is so busy dealing with various public-stockholders, employees,legislators' community leaders—that PR support for product marketing objective tends to be neglected.

Objectives of public relations. Social awareness can be created through the plan, regarding a product, service, person, organizer, PR promotion, etc. It helps to build credibility by communicating the message for example, in editorials of newspapers, etc. It assists in the launch of new products; It assists in repositioning of a product. It helps in building up consumer interest in a particular product category. It also helps in influencing the specific target groups. Public relations help to define products that have faced problems or complaints from the public. It helps to build the corporate image in such a way that it projects favorably on its products.

Promotion is one of the most important components of company's overall marketing mix. The methods of promotion are advertising, sales of promotion, personal selling and public relations. The purpose promotion is to inform, persuade, and remind customers. It must integrated into firm's strategic planning because effective execution requires that all elements of marketing mix—product, price, place and promotion coordinated. While deciding on the promotional mix(combination of advertising, sales promotion, personal selling and public relations), management should consider the nature of the market and product, the stage of the product's life cycle and funds available for promotion. The key to a successful promotional campaign is to carefully plan and coordinate all the components of promotion.

Part Two: Questions

1. Discuss in brief the role of promotion in marketing effort of a company. Also write a short note on public relations.

2. What is advertising? How advertising budget is decided? What are different advertising media?

Part Three: Words and Phrases

1. acceptance	验收	
2. persuasion	说服	
3. advocacy	宣传	
4. measurement	测量	
5. objective-task	目标任务	
6. maturity	成熟	
7. tenderness	柔和	
8. approximately	大约	
9. slump	下降	
10. incentive	激励	
11. exclusiveness	排他性	
12. execution	执行	
13. cohesive	衔接	
14. inducement	诱因	
15. clinch	成交	
16. association	协会	
17. public relation	公共关系	
18. combination	组合	
19. campaign	运动	
20. coordinate	协调,坐标	

Part Four: Further Reading

What is Promotion in Marketing Mix?

The marketing mix is one of the most essential pieces of marketing information that a business owner needs to understand. The marketing mix is a term that deals with the individual components of a comprehensive marketing plan. Promotion is one of the four main components of this mix, and it is essential to complete the sales process.

Promoted by Communication

The promotion component of the marketing mix is all about communication with the customer. If a business cannot effectively communicate its message to the public, it will not close sales. This aspect of marketing involves actually advertising to the consumers and selling them the product. With this component of the marketing mix, you have to look at how you are getting the word out about your products and services. Every company uses promotion a little bit differently, but the ultimate goal is still the same.

Advertising

One of the most essential components of promotion is advertising. Most businesses use some type of advertising to bring in new customers. This is a direct form of communication in which a business has to pay for the right to gain access to consumers. Advertising can take place in a number of different ways such as radio ads, TV ads, newspaper ads and online ads. The company has to allocate a specific amount of money to advertising to ensure enough customers are coming in.

Personal Selling

Another critical component of promotion involves personal selling. Although not every company uses personal selling, many use this form of promotion to develop relationships with customers. Personal selling involves hiring a sales staff to work directly with the customers. By using personal sales, you can create more repeat business through positive relationships. You also can bring in extra sales through prospecting instead of having to rely solely on spending money to bring people in the door.

Public Relations

Public relations is another essential part of the promotion mix. Public relations deals with the overall general perception of the company. This can come through using news releases, news stories and other strategies to shape the perception of the company. Maintaining a good reputation in the public eye is important for most businesses, and this area of promotion deals with handling publicity. This could be done with the help of a public relations firm or handled internally.

Chapter 12: The Marketing of Services

Part One: Text

12.1 Introduction

Is the marketing of services fundamentally different to the marketing of goods? Or is services marketing just a special case of general marketing theory? This chapter discusses the distinctive characteristics of services and the extent to which these call for a revision to the general principles of marketing. While many of the general principles can be applied to services, there are areas where a new set of tools needs to be developed. Of particular importance are: the effects of service intangibility on buyers' decision-making processes; the effects of producing services "live" in the presence of the consumer; and the crucial role played by an organization's employees in the total product offer.

There is debate about the significance of services to national economies, and indeed how services should be defined. Before discussing the distinctive marketing needs of services, this chapter offers a contextual background to the service sector. By the end of the chapter, you should be able to judge the extent to which services call for a distinct set of marketing principles, rather than simple adaptation of universal principles of marketing.

12.2 The development of service economy

We have always had service industries, and indeed there are numerous biblical references to services as diverse as inn keeping, money lending and market trading.

Chapter 12: The Marketing of Services

Over time, the service sector has grown in volume and in the importance ascribed to it.

Early economists saw services as being totally unproductive, adding nothing of value to an economy. Adam Smith included the efforts of intermediaries, doctors, lawyers and the armed forces among those who were "unproductive of any value" (Smith, 1977) and this remained the dominant attitude towards services until the latter part of the nineteenth century. Economists now recognize that tan-Bible products may not exist at all without a series of services being performed in order to produce them and to make them available to consumers. So an agent distributing agricultural produce performs as valuable a task as the farmer. Without the provision of transport and intermediary services, agricultural products produced in areas of surplus would be of little value.

Services have had a major impact on national economies and many service industries have facilitated improved productivity elsewhere in the manufacturing and agricultural sectors. As an example, transport and distribution services have often had the effect of stimulating economic development at local and national levels (e.g., following the improvement of rail or road services). One reason for many developing countries' inability to fully exploit their natural resources has been the ineffectiveness of their distribution services.

It could even be argued that the economic development which occurred in England during the early part of the nineteenth century was really a services revolution rather than an "industrial revolution". Visions of new technologies involving steam power, factory systems and metal production have led to the dominant view that England's development was primarily a result of progress in the manufacturing sector. But could the industrial revolution have happened without the services sector? The period saw the development of many services whose presence was vital to economic development. Without the development of railways, goods could not have been distributed from centralized factories to geographically dispersed consumers and many people would not have been able to get to work. Investment in new factories called for a banking system that could circulate funds at a national rather than a purely local level. A service sector emerged to meet the needs of manufacturing, including intermediaries who were essential to get manufacturers' goods to increasingly dispersed markets. Today, we continue to rely on services to exploit developments in the manufacturing sector.

There is little doubt that the services sector has become a dominant force in developed economies, accounting for about three-quarters of all employment in the USA, UK, Canada and Australia. There appears to be a close correlation between the level of economic development in an economy (expressed by its GDP per capita) and the strength of its service sector. However, there is the continuing perception among some groups of people that service sector jobs are somehow second rate, often associated with low paid, unskilled and casual employment. It is difficult to generalize on this point, but different cultures at a similar level of economic development may view their service industries quite differently. In the UK and Germany, service is often associated with servitude, while in the USA being of service almost goes to the heart of the national culture.

The academic literature on marketing theory and applications has been dominated by the manufactured goods sector. This is probably not surprising, because marketing in its modern form first took root in those manufacturing sectors that faced the greatest competition from the 1930s on wards. In growing, the services sector has become more competitive and therefore taken on board the principles of marketing. Deregulation of many services and rising expectations of consumers have had a dramatic effect on marketing activities within the sector.

12.3 Services and consumer value

While marketing remained focused on tangible products, value could be assessed with respect to readily observable benchmarks; for example, the value of pure commodity materials such as heating oil, natural gas and coal could be measured by reference to the units of calorific value obtained by the buyer per unit of expenditure. Value could be objectively assessed in the sense that an external observer of a transaction would be able to deduce the existence of a similar level of value.

The introduction of a significant service element to a product offer reduces the power of tangible benchmarks to explain value. There is now a widespread literature which recognizes that services can only be defined in the minds of consumers (e.g., Holbrook, 1995; Oliver, 1999). Considerable research has therefore sought to establish the nature of expectations which consumers develop prior to consumption of a service, and which act as a reference against which service delivery is assessed (Parasuraman, et al., 1985).

With the augmentation of services, a link between quality and value becomes more difficult to establish. Quality has been defined as "conforming to requirements" (Crosby, 1984). This implies that organizations must establish customers' requirements and specifications. Once established, the quality goal of the various functions of an organization is to comply with these specifications. However, the questions remain: whose requirements and whose specifications? A second series of definitions therefore state that quality is all about fitness for use (Juran, 1982), a definition based primarily on satisfying customers' needs. If quality is defined as the extent to which a service meet customers' requirements, the problem remains of identifying just what those requirements are. Service quality is a highly abstract construct. Many analyses of service quality have attempted to distinguish between objective measures of quality and other measures which are based on the more subjective perceptions of customers. Gronroos (1984), for example, identified "technical" and "functional" quality respectively as being the two principle components of quality. While tangible products allow consumers process to "see and believe", services require "imagine and believe". In the buying for services, quality is much difficult to assess prior to purchase than case for goods.

It was noted earlier that there has been recent comment that "experience" has supplanted tangible product qualities, service and intangible relationship benefits as a means of adding differential value to a product offer. The centrality of experience to defining value was noted by Holbrook (1999), who defined consumer value as an "interactive, relativistic preference experience". There has been excited speculation that we are moving to an experience-based economy (Pine and Gilmore, 1999), in which we place increasing value in satisfying higher order needs through experiences. The proliferation of stylish coffee shops and themed restaurants provides some evidence to support this argument. However, evidence of a general movement towards value through experiences is quite patchy, as witnessed by the profitable growth of "no frills" retailers, hotels and airlines.

12.4 What is service

It can be difficult to define just what is meant by a service because most products we buy contain a mixture of goods elements and service elements. A meal in a restaurant contains a combination of goods elements (the food) and service elements (the manner in which the food is served). Even apparently "pure" goods such as timber often contain service elements, such as the service required in transporting timber from where it was produced to where a customer requires it.

Modern definitions of services focus on the fact that a service in itself produces no tangible output, although it may be instrumental in producing some tangible output. A contemporary definition is provided by Kotler, et al. (2001): in a more tongue-in-cheek manner, services have been described as "anything which cannot be dropped on your foot".

"Pure" services have a number of distinctive characteristics that differentiate them from goods and have implications for the manner in which they are marketed. These characteristics are often described as intangibility, inseparability, variability; perish ability and the inability to own a seance.

12.5 The services marketing mix

The marketing mix is the set of tools available to an organization to shape the nature of its offer to customers. The mix is not based on any theory, but on the need for marketing managers to break down their decision making into a number of identifiable and actionable headings. Goods marketers are familiar with the 4Ps of product, price, promotion and place. Early analysis by Borden (1965) of marketing mix elements was based on a study of manufacturing industry at a time when the importance of services to the economy was relatively unimportant. More recently, the 4Ps of the marketing mix have been found to be too limited in their application to services.

12.5.1 Products

A product is anything that an organization offers to potential customers, whether it is tangible or intangible. After initial hesitation, most marketing managers are now happy to talk about an intangible service as a product. Thus, bank accounts, insurance policies and holidays are frequently referred to as products, sometimes to the amusement of non-marketers, and pop stars or even politicians are referred to as a product to be marketed.

Marketing mix management must recognize a number of significant differences between goods and services. A number of authors (e.g., Kotler, 1997) have described a model comprising various levels of product definition. The model developed by Kotler starts from the "core" level (defining the basic needs which are satisfied by the product), through a "tangible" level (the tangible manifestation of the product), through to an "augmented" level (the additional services which are added to the product). While this analysis is held to be true of products in general, doubts have been expressed about whether it can be applied to the service offer. Is it possible to identify a core service representing the essence of a consumer's perceived need that requires satisfying?

If such a core service exists, can it be made available in a form that is "consumer friendly", and if so, what elements are included in this form? Finally, is there a level of service corresponding to the augmented product that allows a service provider to differentiate its service offer from that of its competitors in the same way as a car manufacturer differentiates its augmented product from that of its competitors?

Most analyses of the service offer recognize that the problems of inseparability and intangibility make application of the three generic levels of product offer less meaningful to the service offer.

12.5.2 Pricing

Within the services sector, the term price often passes under a number of names, sometimes reflecting the nature of the relationship between customer and provider in which exchanges take place. Professional services companies therefore talk about fees, while other organizations use terms such as fares, tolls, rates, charges and subscriptions. The art of successful pricing is to establish a price level which is sufficiently low that an exchange represents good value to buyers, yet is high enough to allow a service provider to achieve its financial objectives.

In principle, setting prices for services is fundamentally similar to the processes involved in respect of goods. At a strategic level, a price position needs to be established and implemented with respect to the strength of customer demand, the costs of production and the prices that competitors are charging. A number of points of difference with respect to services pricing are noted here: the effects of inseparability; the effects on pricing of cost structures; and the effects of distorted markets for services.

The inseparable nature of services makes the possibilities for price discrimination between different groups of users much greater than is usually the case with manufactured goods. Goods can easily be purchased by one person, stored and sold to another person. If price segmentation allowed one group to buy a manufactured good at a discounted price, it would be possible for this group to buy the item and sell it on to people in higher priced segments, thereby reducing the effectiveness of the segmentation exercise. This point has not been lost on entrepreneurs who buy branded perfumes cheaply in the Far Eastern "grey market" and import them to the UK, where prices are relatively high. Because services are produced at the point of consumption, it is possible to control the availability of services to different segments. Therefore, a hairdresser who offers a discounted price for the elderly segment is able to ensure that only such people are charged the lower price—the elderly person cannot go into the hairdressers to buy a haircut and sell it on to a younger segment, which would otherwise be charged the full price for the service.

12.5.3 Promotion

A well-formulated service offer, distributed through appropriate channels at a price that represents good value to potential customers, places less emphasis on the promotion element of the marketing mix. Nevertheless, few services especially those provided in competitive markets can dispense with promotion completely.

Although the principles of communication are similar for goods and services, a number of distinctive promotional needs of services can be identified, deriving from the distinguishing characteristics of services.

12.5.4 Place

Place decisions refer to the ease of access which potential customers have to a service. For services, it is more appropriate to talk about accessibility as a mix element, rather than place. The inseparability of services makes the task of passing on service benefits much more complex than is the case with manufactured goods. Inseparability implies that services are consumed at the point of production; in other words, a service cannot be produced by one person in one place and handled by other people to make it available to customers in other places. A service cannot therefore be produced where costs are lowest and sold where demand is greatest—customer accessibility must be designed into the service production system.

While services organizations often have a desire to centralize production in order to achieve economies of scale, consumers usually seek local access to services, often at a time that may not be economic for the producer to cater to. Service location decisions therefore involve a trade-off between the needs of the producer and the needs of the consumer. This is in contrast to goods manufacturers who can manufacture goods in one location where production is most economic, then ship the goods to where they are most needed.

Place decisions can involve physical location decisions (as in deciding where to place a hotel), decisions about which intermediaries to use in making a service accessible to a consumer (e. g., whether a tour operator uses travel agents or sells its holidays direct to customers) and non-location decisions which are used to make services available (e. g., the use of telephone delivery systems). For pure services, decisions about how to physically move a good are of little strategic relevance. However, most services involve movement of goods of some form. These can either be materials necessary to produce a service (such as travel brochures and fast food packaging material) or the service can have as its whole purpose the movement of goods (e. g., road haulage, plant hire).

12.5.5 People

For most services, people are a vital element of the marketing mix. It can be almost cliche to say that, for some businesses, the employees are the business—if these are taken away, the organization is left with very few assets with which it can seek to gain competitive advantage in meeting customers' needs.

Where production can be separated from consumption—as is the case with most manufactured goods—management can usually take measures to reduce the direct effects of people on the final output as received by customers. Therefore, the buyer of a car is not concerned whether a production worker dresses untidily, uses bad language at work or turns up for work late, so long as there are quality control measures which reject the results of lax behavior before they reach the customer. In service industries, everybody is what Gummesson (1999) has called a "part-time marketer" in that their actions have a much more direct effect on the output received by customers. While the importance attached to people management in improving quality within manufacturing companies is increasing (for example, through the development of quality circles), people planning assumes much greater importance within the services sector. This is especially true in those services where staff have a high level of contact with customers. For this reason, it is essential that services organizations clearly specify what is expected from personnel in their interaction with customers. To achieve the specified standard, methods of recruiting, training, motivating and rewarding staff cannot be regarded as purely personnel decisions—they are important marketing mix decisions.

12.5.6　Processes

Production processes are usually of little concern to consumers of manufactured goods, but can be of critical concern to consumers of "high contact" services, where the consumer can be seen as a co-producer of the service. A customer of a restaurant is deeply affected by the manner in which staffs serve them and the amount of waiting which is involved during the production process. Issues arise as to the boundary between the producer and consumer in terms of the allocation of production functions—for example, a restaurant might require a customer to collect their meal from a counter, or to deposit their own rubbish. With services, a clear distinction cannot be made between marketing and operations management.

Much attention encounters has gone into the study of defined by Shostack (1985) as "a period of time during which a consumer directly interacts with a service". Among the multiplicity of service encounters, some will be crucial to successful completion of the service delivery process. These are often referred to as critical incidents and have been defined by Bitner, et al. (1990) as "specific interactions between customers and service firm employees that are especially satisfying or especially dissatisfying". While their definition focuses on the role of personnel in critical incidents, they can also arise as a result of interaction with the service provider's equipment.

12.5.7　Physical evidence

The intangible nature of a service means that potential customers are unable to judge a service before it is consumed, increasing the risk inherent in a purchase decision. An important element of marketing planning is therefore to reduce this level of risk by offering tangible evidence of the promised service delivery. This evidence can take a number of forms. At its simplest, a brochure can describe and give pictures of important elements of the service product—a holiday brochure gives pictorial evidence of hotels and resorts for this purpose. The appearance of staff can give evidence about the nature of a service—a tidily dressed ticket clerk for an airline gives some evidence that the airline operation as a whole is run with care and attention. Buildings are frequently used to give evidence of service characteristics. Towards the end of the nineteenth century, UK banks outbid each other to produce grand buildings which signified stability and substance to potential investors, who had been frightened by a history of banks disappearing with their savings. Today, a clean, bright environment used in a service outlet can help reassure potential customers at the point where they make a service purchase decision. For this reason, fast food and photo processing outlets often use red and yellow color schemes to convey an image of speedy service.

Tangibility is further provided by evidence of service production methods. Some services provide many opportunities for customers to see the process of production; indeed, the whole purpose of the service may be to see the production process (e.g., a pop concert). Often, this tangible evidence can be seen before a decision to purchase a service is made, either by direct observation of a service being performed on somebody else (e.g., watching the work of a builder) or indirectly through a description of the service production process (a role played by brochures which specify and illustrate the service production process). On the other hand, some services provide very few tangible clues about the nature of the service production process. Portfolio management services are not only produced largely out of sight of the consumer, it is also difficult to specify in advance in a brochure what the service outcomes will be.

Part Two: Questions

1. Why do we need to pay special attention to the marketing of services, when they are just an aid to the production and marketing of goods?

2. What is the nature of the service act?

Part Three: Words and Phrases

1. revision   修订
2. intangibility   无形性
3. contextual   语境
4. biblical   圣经的

5. reference 参考
6. benchmark 基准
7. hesitation 犹豫
8. widespread 广泛的
9. consumption 消费
10. calorific 发热
11. patchy 片状
12. manifestation 表现
13. speculation 投机
14. essential 本质
15. boundary 边界
16. observation 观察
17. allocation 配置
18. interaction 相互作用
19. inherent 固有的
20. relevance 关联

Part Four: Further Reading

9 Principles for Great Branding by Design

We all know great design has a critical role to play in building a great brand. But how do we go about making that happen? I recently had the opportunity to speak to three top designers about that very question: Robert Brunner, founder of the design shop Ammunition and author of *Do You Matter: How Great Design Will Make People Love Your Company*; Joe Doucet, founder of Joe Doucet Studio and David Hill, vice president of design at Lenovo and author of the *Design Matters* blog.

Through these conversations, it became clear that the link between design and branding is important, and that having a top design team is to crucial to having a winning brand.

Here's what I learned:

1. Branding and design are, to a large extent, inseparable. "A brand is not your logo or ID system," says Brunner, "It's a gut feeling people have about you. When two or more people have the same feeling, you have a brand. You get that feeling via smart design, which creates the experiences people have with the brand. Everything

you do creates the brand experience, ergo design is your brand."

2. If design is the brand, stop thinking of branding and design as distinct disciplines. "It's all about integrating design and brand," says Doucet, "We need to cease thinking of them as different disciplines. The essence of the Apple brand comes through its design. Take the logo off a BMW and you still know it's a BMW."

3. Brands need to create an emotional relationship with people. "We are all emotional beings and we have emotional relationships with brands we trust," says Brunner, "Designers need to make that happen. A designer must take the values and assets of a company and transform them in a special way that connects with people emotionally."

4. Designers need to "get" the essence of the brand. "For designers to build a great brand, they have to understand it," Hill points out, "You need to understand its history, its values, and what it means to people. Can you imagine designing the latent Jeep without understanding the brand archetype of what it means for a product to be a Jeep?"

5. Design needs to be strategic from the outset. "For design to have a major impact, it's got to get involved at the strategic level," said Hill, "It can't be an after thought or superficial trappings to be put on post product creation. Samsung's brand became powerful only after they put a Chief Design Officer in place and made it a priority for the company."

6. Integrate design early in the process to drive innovation and create solutions. "Good designers approach design as an opportunity to ask questions," says Doucet, "Solution generation starts by questioning initial assumptions. Rather than ask myself 'How should I design Widget X?' I need to be asking 'Do we really need Widget X or is there a better solution to this customer problem?' So a designer needs be there at the beginning and be connected to the decision-makers. For example, at Braun, Dieter Rams sat across from the owner of the company."

7. Don't overdesign. "With the increasing emphasis on design in the world today, it's important to avoid the over-designed syndrome," says Hill, "A simple, well-thought-through, authentic design is often the best. Everything doesn't need to be redesigned; sometimes what we have in hand is better than what we seek. It's not all about being different; it's about being better. If Levi Strauss wanted me to redesign the patch on the back of their jeans, I would look in their archives for the original."

8. Use design to continually reinvent the brand. "Some folks think they know branding," says Doucet, "Figured it out long ago. 'Hi. I'm someone you'll like. You'll know it's me because I always wear a red polo shirt (pantone 185 to be exact) with blue pants and a yellow belt.' You can't think that way today. Brands need to allow themselves to constantly update, and be much more fluid. Look at Google; they morph their logo for special occasions. Constant change is a big part of who they are."

9. Use design to make a difference. "Design can make a difference in how we live," says Brunner, "Take sustainability. A lot of what is done in that area is 'making bad, better.' We're taking wasteful things and seeing how we can make them not so bad. We need to start thinking about how we can use our design tools to encourage people to change. You do that by making 'doing better' also be fun, interesting and (importantly) the path of least resistance. And you do it in an encouraging, not controlling, way. Design needs to do that in order to reach a larger audience than just the small group that is socially driven."

While these steps may require a new way of thinking about design for some, they're key steps to the path for those who want to build a great brand and make life better for those who experience them.

Chapter 13: E-Marketing

Part One : Text

13.1 Introduction

In a short period of time, e-marketing has become a facet of marketing that cannot be ignored. With some enthusiastic adopters of digital technologies such as Cisco, easy Jet and IBM now achieving the majority of their sales and customer service on-line, many organizations are examining how they can best make use of this new medium. However, the medium is perhaps best known for the spectacular "dot-com" failures such as Boo. com, Peapod, Click-mango, etc. Consequently, marketers need to carefully assess the significance of e-marketing and assimilate it, as appropriate, into all aspects of marketing from strategy and planning to marketing research, objectives setting, buyer behavior, marketing communications and the marketing mix. The key phrase here is "as appropriate". The impact of new technologies such as the internet will vary greatly according to the existing product, market, and channel structure and business model of each organization.

This chapter outlines an approach to e-marketing planning, which can be applied to all organizations. The approach is based on careful assessment of the opportunities and threats, clearly defined objectives and strategies, and selection of appropriate e-marketing tactical tools and resources to achieve these strategies.

13.2 What is e-marketing

There are now many terms with the e-prefix, and many different interpretations.

Within any organization, developing a common understanding for terms such as e-commerce, e-business and e-marketing, and how they interrelate, is important to enable development of a consistent, coherent strategy. We will now briefly review these terms and how they relate.

Electronic commerce (e-commerce) is often thought to simply refer to buying and selling using the internet; people immediately think of consumer retail purchases from companies such as Amazon. But e-commerce involves much more than electronically mediated financial transactions between organizations and customers. Most commentators now consider e-commerce to refer to all electronically mediated transactions between an organization and any third party it deals with. By this definition, all "moments of truth" involving electronically mediated requests for information and all on-line inbound and outbound marketing communications such as e-mail marketing are also part of e-commerce. Kalakota and Whinston (1997) refer to a range of different perspectives fore-commerce that highlight the type of communications involved:

First, a communications perspective—the delivery of information, products/services or payment by electronic means.

Second, a business process perspective—the application of technology towards the automation of business transactions and work flows.

Third, a service perspective—enabling cost cutting at the same time as increasing the speed and quality of service delivery.

Fourth, an on-line perspective—the buying and selling of products and information on-line.

When evaluating the impact of e-commerce on an organization, it is instructive to identify opportunities for buy-side and sell-side e-commerce transactions. Buy-side e-commerce refers to transactions to procure resources needed by an organization from its suppliers.

These business-to-business (B2B) transactions are often neglected in favor of discussion of sell-side e-commerce, which refers to transactions involved with selling products to an organization's customers through distributors as appropriate.

E-business is broader: referring to both buy-side and sell-side e-commerce and the internal use of internet technologies through an intranet to streamline business processes. Using an intranet to share ideas and market research on a new product development or marketing performance data are examples of e-business marketing applications.

E-marketing can be simply expressed as the use of electronic communications technology to achieve marketing objectives (see, for example, McDonald and Wilson, 1999). The electronic communications technology refers to:

First, the use of internet-based (TCP/IP) network technology for communications within an organization using an intranet, beyond the organization to partners such as suppliers, distributors and key account customers using password-based access to extra nets and the open internet, where information is accessible by all with internet access.

Second, the use of web servers or websites to enable informational or financial exchanges as e-commerce transactions.

Third, the use of other digital access platforms, such as interactive digital TV, wireless or mobile phones and games consoles.

Fourth, the use of electronic mail for managing enquirer (inbound e-mail) and for promotion (outbound e-mail).

Fifth, integration of the digital access platforms and e-mail with other information systems, such as customer databases and applications for customer relationship management and supply chain management.

To illustrate some of the opportunities of e-marketing, it is useful to reapply the definition of marketing from the Chartered Institute of Marketing: E-marketing can identify, anticipate and satisfy customer needs efficiently.

13.3 Participants in e-marketing

The options for digital communications between a business and its customers are summarized in Figure 13.1. The bulk of internet business both now and in the foreseeable future comes from industrial and commercial markets known as business-to-business (B2B), and not consumer markets known as business-to-consumer (B2C) markets. Most estimates suggest that B2B companies will reap 10 times more revenue than their B2C counter-parts. In 2000, Gartner estimated that world-wide B2B transactions will rise from $145 billion in 1999 to $7.3 trillion in the year 2004. These increases are driven by the desire of large organizations to reduce costs and increase supply chain efficiency. For example, in the late 1990s, General Electric made the decision to procure $1 billion worth of purchases on-line in year

1, followed by \$3 billion in year 2, followed by total procurement on-line. More recently, Cisco Systems announced that they will no longer do business with suppliers who can't take orders via the web. Ford and General Motors have combined forces through the B2B marketplace Covisint (www. covisint. net) and moved their \$300 billion and \$500 billion supply chains on-line. Already large-scale trading is occurring. It was reported in May 2001 that the largest auction ever had occurred in which participated, hands, with 1 200 different five parts total order volume over supplier changed 3 billion euros.

The other transaction types shown in Figure 13.1 are less significant in terms of revenue volumes: these are customer-to-customer interactions (C2C; best known as consumer auctions, but can also be achieved as B2C and B2B communities) and customer-to-business (C2B; novel buying models where customers approach the business on their own terms).

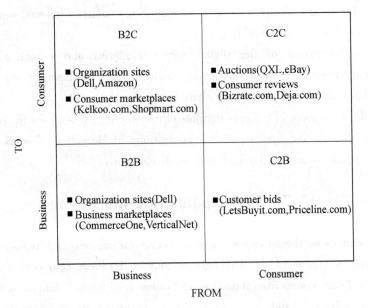

Figure 13.1   Options for on-line communications between an organization and its customers

13.4   The e-marketing plan

The e-marketing plan should be informed by, and integrate with, the objectives and strategies of the marketing plan. Plans should be integrated such that developing the e-marketing plan may give insights that result in the other plans being updated. Smith and Chaffey (2001) use the SOSTAC framework to suggest an approach to e-marketing planning, and a similar approach will be adopted here. SOSTAC stands for: Situation, Objectives and Strategy, Tactics, Action and Control. As such, it has a structure that is broadly consistent with other models of the process of strategic marketing planning as described.

13.4.1 Situation analysis

Situation analysis is the first art of thee-marketing plan. It explains "where are we now?" This includes analysis internally within the organization and, externally, of the business environment. These traditional analytical areas should also be assessed from an e-marketing perspective as follows:

First, KPIs-Key Performance Indicators which identify the business success criteria, results and performance against targets and benchmarks.

Second, SWOT analysis-identifying e-marketing specific internal Strengths, and Weaknesses, as well as external Opportunities and Threats.

Third, PEST-Political, Economic, Social and Technological variables that shapes your marketplace. Legal constraints on e-marketing are particularly significant in controlling use of customer data for direct marketing, for example, through e-mail, and the introduction of new laws should be carefully monitored.

Fourth, Customers—how many are on-line, how many prefer different platforms such as i TV and mobile or wireless? Are there new channel segments emerging?

Fifth, Competitors—who are they? What is the iron-line proposition? How successful are they on-line? Are there new on-line adversaries?

Sixth, Distributors—are new, online, intermediaries emerging while old off-line distributors are being wiped out (disinter mediation)? What are the potential channel conflicts?

13.4.2 External analysis

We will concentrate on the micro-environment of customers (demand analysis), competitors and distributors.

1. Demand analysis. For customers, market research should identify which customers are on-line; what are their profiles in terms of geo-demographics and for B2B their position in the decision-making unit. To build demand estimates, we need

to know the proportion of customers in each market and segment who:

First, have access to different channels. Figure 13.2, a curve typical for most western countries, shows that digital TV and mobile phone access are increasingly important for B2C marketing, while in B2B markets internet access is higher (Figure 13.3).

Second, are influenced by using which channel or channels? Although the proportion of e-commerce transactions for all purchases is low, the role of the internet in influencing purchase is significant for high involvement purchases such as financial services, holidays or cars. For example, it is now estimated that over half the purchasers of new cars in some western countries will research the purchase on-line, even though the proportion purchasing entirely on-line is only in single figures. Understanding the reach of a website and its role in influencing purchase is clearly important in setting e-marketing budgets.

Third, purchase using which channel or channels? The propensity to purchase on-line is dependent on different variables over which the marketer has relatively little control. However, factors which affect the propensity to purchase can be estimated for different types of products. De Kare-Silver (2000) suggests factors that should be considered include product characteristics, familiarity and confidence, and consumer attributes. Typical results from the evaluation are: groceries (27/50), mortgages (15/50) travel (31/50) and books (38/50). De Kare-Silver states that any product scoring over 20 has good potential, since the score for consumer attributes is likely to increase through time. Given this, he suggests companies will regularly need to review the score for their products. The effectiveness of this test is now demonstrated by data for on-line purchases in different product categories (Figure 13.4).

It is also important to understand the barriers and motivations that affect the use of digital media by consumers. The reasons, aspirations and expectations can then be reflected in your communications.

2. Competitor analysis. For competitors, bench marking will reveal how digital media are being exploited. For e-tailors continuous monitoring is required and services such as that of Gomez.com provide independent scorecards. Criteria include ease of use, customer confidence (e.g., availability, depth and breadth of customer service options, including phone, e-mail and branch locations), on-site resources, relationship services and overall cost. The success of different companies in and out of sector in achieving on-line sales should also be bench marked.

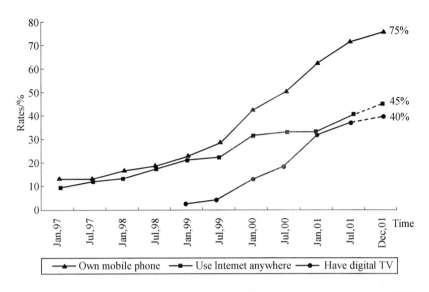

Figure 13.2 UK rates of adoption of new media with kind permission of e-MORI
Source: www.e-mori.co.uk

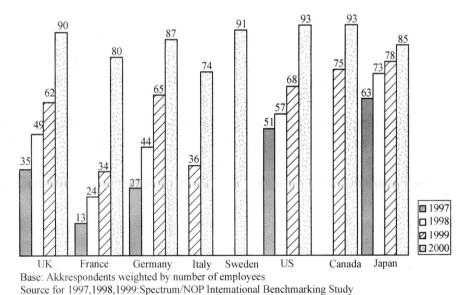

Base: Akkrespondents weighted by number of employees
Source for 1997,1998,1999:Spectrum/NOP Intemational Benchmarking Study

Figure 13.3 Proportion of organizations with internet access(2000)

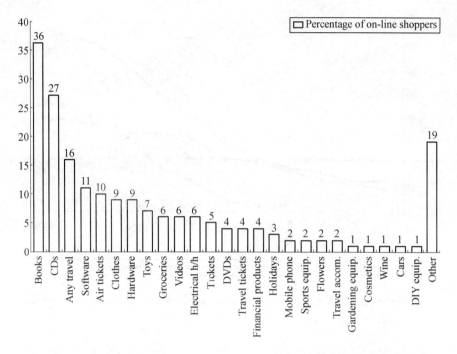

Figure 13.4　Percentage of on-line purchasers in the six months to November 2000

3. Intermediary analysis. For distributors and intermediaries, a key influence of the internet is its impact on channel structures. These marketplace phenomena should be assessed and then evaluated as part of strategy:

First, disintermediation—the removal of intermediaries such as distributors or brokers that formerly linked a company to its customers. A car manufacturer selling direct to customers rather than through a dealership is an example of this.

Second, reintermediation—the creation of new intermediaries between customers and suppliers providing services such as supplier search and product evaluation. Many new brokers offering discounted cars have had a significant impact on the car market.

Third, countermediation—the creation of a new intermediary by an established company. Here an existing player or players form a new intermediary to compete against new intermediaries.

13.4.3　Internal analysis

Internal analysis involves assessment of the current status of e-marketing implementation. Quelch and Klein (1996) developed a five-stage model referring to the development of sell-side e-commerce. For existing companies the stages are: image and product information; information collection; customer support and service; internal support and service; transactions. Considering sell-side e-commerce. (Chaffey,2003) suggest there are six choices/level for a company deciding on which marketing services to offer via an on-line presence.

Level 0. No website or presence on the web.

Level 1. Basic web presence. Company places an entry in a website listing company names such as www. yell. co. uk to make people searching the web aware of the existence of a company or its products. There is no website at this stage.

Level 2. Simple static informational website contains basic company and product information, sometimes referred to as brochure-ware.

Level 3. Simple interactive site. Users are able to search the site and make queries to retrieve information such as product availability and pricing. Queries by e-mail may also be supported.

Level 4. Interactive site supporting transactions with users. The functions offered will vary according to the company. They will usually be limited to on-line buying. Other functions might include an interactive customer service help desk which is linked into direct marketing objectives.

Level 5. Fully interactive site supporting the whole buying process. Provides relationship marketing with individual customers and facilitates the full range of marketing exchanges.

Note that such stage models of website development are most appropriate to companies whose products can be sold on-line through transcription e-commerce. Stage models also apply to a range of different types of on-line presence and business models, each with different objectives.

Four of the major different types of on-line presence are:

Transactional e-commerce site. Stage models as described above. Examples: a car manufacturer such as Vauxhall (www. buy power vauxhall. co. uk) or retailers such as Tesco (www. tesco. com).

Services-oriented relationship building website. For companies such as professional services companies, on-line transactions are inappropriate. Through time these sites will develop increasing information depth and question and answer facilities. Examples: Accenture (www. accenture. com) and Arthur Andersen

Knowledge Space (www. knowledgespace. com).

These are intended to support the off-line brand by developing an on-line experience of the brand. They are typical for low-value, high-volume. Fast Moving Consumer Goods (FMCG brands). Examples: Tango (www. tango. com), Guinness (www. guinness. com).

Portal site, service delivery and links to information services. Examples: Yahoo! (www. yahoo. com) and Vertical Net (www. verticalnet. com). Similar stage models can also be developed for all aspects of supply chain management which are necessary as part of delivering the marketing concept. Table 13.1 presents a synthesis of stage models for e-business development. Organizations can assess their position on the continuum between stages 1 and 4 for the different aspects of e-business development shown in the column on the left. When companies devise strategies and tactics they may return to the stage models to specify which level of innovation they are looking to achieve at future points in time.

Table 13.1 A stage model for e-business development

	1. Web presence	2. E-commerce	3. Integrated e-commerce	4. E-business
Services available	Brochureware or interaction with product catalogues and customer service	Transactional e-commerce on buy-side or sell-side	Buy- and sell-side integrated with ERP or legacy systems Personalization of services	Full intergration between all internal organizational processes and elements of the value network
Organizational scope	Isolated departments, e. g. , marketing department	Cross-organizational	Cross-organizational	Across the enterprise and beyond (extraprise)
Transformation	Technological infrastructure	Technology and new responsibilities identified for e-commerce	Internal business processes and company structure	Change to e-business culture, linking of business processes with partners

Table 13.1 (Continued)

	1. Web presence	2. E-commerce	3. Integrated e-commerce	4. E-business
Strategy	Limited	Sell-side e-commerce strategy, not well integrated with business strategy	E-commerce strategy integrated with business strategy using a value-chain approach	E-business strategy incorporated as part of business strategy

13.4.4 E-marketing objectives

Objectives clarify the purpose and direction of e-marketing. Smith and Chaffey (2001) suggest there are five broad benefits, reasons or objectives of e-marketing. These can be summarized as the 5Ss of e-marketing objectives. Marketers will decide whether all or only some will drive e-marketing:

Sell. Grow sales (through wider distribution to customers you can't service off-line or perhaps a wider product range than in local store, or better prices).

Serve. Add value (give customers extra benefits on-line, or product development in response to on-line dialogue).

Speak. Get closer to customers by tracking them, asking them questions, conducting on-line interviews, creating a dialogue, monitoring chat rooms, learning about them.

Save costs of service, sales transactions and administration, print and post. Can you reduce transaction costs and therefore either make on-line sales more profitable or use cost savings to enable you to cut prices, which in turn could enable you to generate greater market share?

Sizzle. Extend the brand on-line. Reinforce brand values in a totally new medium. The web scores very highly as a medium for creating brand awareness and recognition.

Specific objectives are created for each. Consider sales a typical objective might be: to grow the business with on-line sales, e.g., to generate at least 10 percent of sales on-line within six months. Or to generate an extra ￥100 000 worth of sales on-line by December.

These objectives can be further broken down, e.g., to achieve ￥100 000 of on-line sales means you have to generate 1 000 on-line customers spending on average ¥100 in the time period. If, say, your conversion rate of visitors to customers was a high 10 percent, then this means you have to generate 10 000 visitors to your site.

Specific targets for the on-line revenue contribution for different e-channels should be set for the future, for example, Fisher as shown in Figure(2001), in the *Financial Times*, reported a range of variation in on-line contribution for Sandvike Steel. At the revenue time of number of all orders were transacted over the web. Nordic countries are leading the way. Around 20 percent of all orders from Denmark are on-line and 31 percent of those from Sweden. The proportion in the US, however, is only 3 percent, since most business goes through distributors and is conducted by electronic data interchange (EDI). Over the next six months, the company hopes to raise the US figure to 40 percent and, in two years, between 40 and 50 percent of total orders are planned to come via the web.

Annika Roos, marketing manager at Sandvik Steel, specified Sandvik's objectives as follows: "by the end of December, 2001, we want a confirmation from at least 80 percent of key customers that they consider the extra net to be a major reason to deal with Sandvik. Ouraim is to have 200 key customers using the extra net at the end of June 2001."

Objectives should also be set for the percentage of customers who are reached or influenced by each channel (indirect on-line revenue contribution or brand awareness in the target market). The on-line revenue contribution should also consider cannibalization are on-line sales achieved at the expense of traditional channels? Another major on-line objective might be to consolidate relationships and increase loyalty from 50 to 75 percent among high-spending customer segments during the year.

With the increasing economic power of and pressure on business in society today, consumers and other stakeholders are increasingly demanding of businesses. The context in which organizations are operating has changed dramatically in the last decade. There is a rising tide of expectation across all sectors of society which manifests itself in many ways, from taking to the street with placards to taking to the desk with a pen and paper, to taking to the internet. Protest, silent or violent, is a factor in today's society, and one which business and marketing within the business have to take into account if they are to continue to thrive.

There is no doubt about consumer expectation for corporate responsibility and support for cause-related marketing. Over 80 percent of consumers clearly indicate that, price and quality being equal, linking with a cause would make a difference; they would switch retail outlets, change brands and have a much better perception of a company trying to make the world a better place.

Part Two: Questions

1. How can companies use e-marketing for competitive advantage?
2. What marketing opportunities do on-line channels provide?

Part Three: Words and Phrases

1.	coherent	相干
2.	procure	采购
3.	commentator	评论员
4.	monitor	监控
5.	electronic commerce	电子商务
6.	consolidate	巩固
7.	cannibalization	蚕食
8.	phenomena	现象
9.	inappropriate	不恰当的
10.	dialogue	对话
11.	generate	生成
12.	current status	现状
13.	synthesis	合成
14.	portal site	门户网站
15.	mortgage	抵押贷款
16.	propensity	倾向
17.	streamline	流线
18.	facilitate	方便
19.	framework	框架
20.	loyalty	忠诚

Part Four: Further Reading

Physical Distribution Management

Part of logistics management, physical distribution is concerned with the transporting of merchandise, raw materials, or by-products, such as hazardous waste, from the source to the customer. A manager of physical distribution must also assess and control the cost of transporting these goods and materials, as well as to determine the most efficient way to store them, which usually involves some form of warehousing. Hence, physical distribution (PD) is concerned with inventory control, as well as with packaging and handling. Customer relations, order processing, and marketing are also related activities of PD.

In essence, physical distribution management (PDM) involves controlling the movement of materials and goods from their source to their destination. It is a highly complex process, and one of the most important aspects of any business. PDM is the "other" side of marketing. While marketing creates demand, PDM's goal is to satisfy demand as quickly, capably, and cheaply as possible.

One could maintain that PD is as old as civilization. Even merchants in ancient times had to move goods and raw materials to their destination, and to engage in storage and inventory control. Until the Industrial Revolution, however, these activities were carried out inefficiently: goods usually were replenished slowly, and there were far fewer goods than in the era of mass production. If marketing was conducted at all, it was usually done at the point of purchase.

The Industrial Revolution ushered in mass production and, by the late 19th century, the beginnings of mass marketing. Goods and raw materials also were conveyed over greater distances. Nonetheless, until World War II, PD was far less important than production and marketing. Physical distribution of goods and materials also remained basically unchanged, carried out as separate, unrelated activities-transportation and handling, storage, and inventory control.

The postwar years witnessed an unprecedented explosion of consumer goods and brands, thanks to modern mass marketing, the population explosion, and the increasing sophistication of the average consumer. The sheer volume and variety of goods enormously complicated their distribution and storage. A wholesaler of breakfast cereals, for instance, no longer handled a few cereal brands, but dozens of them, and with the proliferation of supermarkets, was confronted with the problem of greater demand and continuous product turnover. The cost of distribution escalated as well, further adding to the complexity of distribution. A seminal article on physical distribution ("New Strategies to Move Goods"), appearing in a September 1966 issue of Business Week, for the first time fostered an awareness of PD as a separate category of business. This eventually generated textbooks on physical distribution management, as well as courses in business schools. For the first time, PD, as well as cost control, became central concerns of upper management.

By this time, computers had slowly entered the realm of PD, at least in the United States. It was not until the 1970s, however, that computers were fully utilized. Their effect over time was to integrate the hitherto disparate categories of PD—transportation, storage, inventory, and distribution—into closely related activities.

Currently, computerization is performing the major functions of physical distribution management, from long-range strategic planning to day-to-day logistics, inventory, and market forecasting. The best of these systems are tightly integrated with inventory and other logistics systems, and may even be linked to customers' systems, as is the case with efficient consumer response (ECR) systems. ECR systems, which some have criticized as being to narrowly focused, attempt to maximize distribution efficiency by delivering inventory on a just-in-time basis. Advanced distribution systems may employ satellite tracking and routing of trucks, electronically tagged pallets or cargo containers, and elaborate data monitoring and storage capabilities. Data collected from these activities are used to identify weak spots in the chain and benchmark improvements.

Often upstart companies, and even some large ones as well, rely on third-party distributors for at least some of their physical distribution, and hence there is an entire industry of third-party logistics services. These and other outsourcing services received a great deal of attention during the 1990s, as manufacturing companies sought to eliminate peripheral activities when they could do so at cost savings. Smaller companies, on the other hand, frequently lack the expertise or resources to perform their own distribution. Nonetheless, some distribution analysts criticize the outsourcing movement because the net cost savings may be less than anticipated and the quality of the logistics service may be hard for the manufacturer to control.

Up to now, PDM has been concerned with the movement of physical objects. In the future, however, it will have to accommodate itself to the increasing shift of the economy away from manufacturing and toward service industries. In this new realm, environmental cleanup and the disposal of waste undoubtedly will be increasingly important to PDM. The expansion of global markets is also affecting PDM, requiring enormous technical and operational refinement.

Chapter 14: International Marketing

Part One : Text

14.1 Deciding whether to go abroad

Most companies would prefer to remain domestic if their domestic market were large enough. Managers would not need to learn other languages and laws, deal with volatile currencies, face political and legal uncertainties, or redesign their products to suit different customer needs and expectations. Business would be easier and safer. Yet several factors are drawing more and more companies into the international arena:

First, Global firms offering better products or lower prices can attack the company's domestic market. The company might want to counter attack these competitors in their home markets. For example, Japanese car makers entered the American market and captured the significant part of the market.

Second, The company discovers that some foreign markets present higher profit opportunities than the domestic market. For example, India and China offers huge opportunities for "value for money" products because of their population base.

Third, The company needs a larger customer base to achieve economies of scale which is not possible in case of developed countries where population growth rate has established.

Fourth, The company wants to reduce its dependence on any one market. So that poor performance in one market did not hurt its profitability.

Fifth, The company's customers are going abroad and require international servicing because the barriers to move across the countries are fast declining.

Before making a decision to go abroad, the company must weigh several risks:

First, The company might not understand foreign customer preferences and fail to offer a competitively attractive product (Table 14.1 lists some famous blunders in this arena).

Second, The company might not understand the foreign country's business culture or know how to deal effectively with foreign nationals. Table 14.1 lists some of the many challenges.

Table 14.1 Blunders in international market

Hallmark cards failed when they were introduced in France. The French dislike syrupy sentiment and prefer writing their own cards.

Philips began to earn a profit in Japan only after it had reduced the size of its coffeemakers to fit into smaller Japanese kitchens and its shavers to fit smaller Japanese hands.

Coca-Cola had to withdraw its two-liter bottle in Spain after discovering that few Spaniards owned refrigerators with large enough compartments to accommodate it.

General Foods' Tand initially failed in France because it was positioned as a substitute for orange juice at breakfast. The French drink little orange juice and almost none at breakfast.

Kellogg's Pop-Tarts failed in Britain because the percentage of British homes with toasters was significantly lower than in the United States and the product was too sweet for British tastes.

P&G Crest toothpaste initially failed in Mexico when it used the U.S. campaign. Mexicans did not care as much for the decay-prevention benefit, nor did scientifically oriented advertising appeal to them.

General Foods squandered millions trying to introduce packaged cake mixes to Japanese consumers. The company failed to note that only 3 percent of Japanese homes were equipped with ovens. Then they promoted the idea of baking cakes in Japanese rice cookers, overlooking the fact that the Japanese use their rice cookers throughout the day to keep rice warm and ready.

S.C. Johnson's wax floor polish initially failed in Japan. The wax made the floors too slippery, and Johnson had overlooked the fact that Japanese do not wear shoes in their homes.

Because of the competing advantages and risks, companies often do not act until some event thrusts them into the international arena. Someone—a domestic exporter, a foreign importer, a foreign government—solicits the company to sell abroad. Or the company is saddled with overcapacity and must find additional markets for its goods.

14.2 Deciding which markets to enter

In deciding to go abroad, the company needs to define its international marketing objectives and policies. What proportion of foreign to total sales will it seek? Most companies start small when they venture abroad. Some plan to stay small. Others have bigger plans, believing that their foreign business will eventually be equal to or even more important than their domestic business. The company must decide whether to market in a few countries or many countries and determine how fast to expand.

Generally speaking, it makes sense to operate in fewer countries with a deeper commitment and penetration in each. Ayal and Zif have argued that a company should enter fewer countries when market entry and market control costs are high. Product and communication adaptation costs are high. Population and income size and growth are high in the initial countries chosen. Dominant foreign firms can establish high barriers to entry.

The company must also decide on the types of countries to consider. Attractiveness is influenced by the product, geography, income and population, political climate, and other factors. The seller might have a predilection for certain countries or regions. Kenichi Ohmae recommends that companies concentrate on selling in the "triad markets"—the United States, Western Europe, and the Far East because these markets account for a large percent of all international trade. Although Ohmae's position makes short-run sense, it can spell disaster for the world economy in the long run. The unmet needs of the developing world represent huge potential markets for food, clothing, shelter, consumer electronics, appliances, and other goods. Many market leaders are now rushing into Eastern Europe, China, Vietnam and India where there are many unmet needs to satisfy. Regional economic integration—trading agreements between blocs of countries—has intensified in recent years. This development means that companies are more likely to enter entire regions overseas rather than do business with one nation at a time.

14.2.1 Regional free made zones

Certain countries have formed free trade zones or economic communities-groups of nations organized to work toward common goals in the regulation of international trade. One such community is the European Union (EU). Formed in 1957, the European Union set out to create a single European market by reducing barriers to the free flow of products, services, finances, and labor among member countries and developing policies on trade with nonmember nations. Today, the European Union is using a common currency, the euro monetary system. In 1998, 11 participating countries locked their exchange rates together, as a first step in a multi year plan for a common currency (Britain, Denmark and Sweden are the holdouts, so far). The euro coins and bills that will eventually replace member countries' currencies will not be in circulation until 2002, and businesses and private citizens will not be required to switch before then. Today, the European Union represents one of the world's single largest markets. Its 15 member countries contain more than 370 million consumers and account for 20 percent of the world's exports. As more European nations seek admission to the EU in the twenty-first century, it could contain as many as 450 million people in 28 countries. European unification offers tremendous trade opportunities for U.S. and other non-European firms. However, it also poses threats. As a result of increased unification, European companies will grow bigger and more competitive. Witness the competition in the aircraft industry between Europe's Airbus consortium and the Untied States' Boeing. Perhaps an even bigger concern, however, is that lower barriers inside Europe will only create thicker outside walls. Some observers envision a "fortress Europe" that heaps favors on firms from EU countries but hinders outsiders by imposing obstacles such as stiffer import quotas, local content requirements, and other non-tariff (non tax) barriers.

Also, companies that plan to create "pan-European" marketing campaigns directed to a unified Europe should proceed with caution. Even if the European Union truly does manage to standardize its general trade regulations and implement the euro, creating an economic community will not create a homogeneous market. Companies marketing in Europe face 14 different languages, 2 000 years of historical and cultural differences, and a daunting mass of local rules.

The most successful pan-European ads are those that are highly visual and symbolic.

These ads focus on the product and consumer and are aimed at one of the two audiences that market researchers really agree are turning into Euro consumers—the young and the rich. One such ad is for TAG Heuer watches in which a swimmer races a shark, a hurdler leaps over an over sized razor blade, and a relay runner grabs a dynamite baton, all mind games that athletes everywhere use to rev up their performance. In North America, the United States and Canada phased out trade barriers in 1989. In January 1994, the North American Free Trade Agreement (NAFTA) established a free trade zone among the United States, Mexico and Canada. The agreement created a single market of 360 million people who produce and consume $6.7 trillion worth of goods and services. As it is implemented over a 15-year period, NAFTA will eliminate all trade barriers and investment restrictions among the three countries. Prior to NAFTA, tariffs on American products entering Mexico averaged 13 percent, whereas U.S. tariffs on Mexican goods averaged 6 percent. Other free trade areas are forming in Latin America and South America. For example, MERCOSUL now links Brazil, Colombia and Mexico. Chile and Mexico have formed a successful free trade zone. Venezuela, Colombia and Mexico—the "Group of Three"—are negotiating a free trade area as well. It is likely that NAFTA will eventually merge with this and other arrangements to form an all-Americas free trade zone. Although the United States has long regarded Latin America as its backyard, it is the European nations that have tapped this market's enormous potential. As Washington's efforts to extend NAFTA to Latin America have stalled, European countries have moved in with a vengeance. MERCOSUL's two-way trade with the EU in 1995 amounted to $43 billion, a total that exceeded trade with the United States by $14 billion. When Latin American countries instituted market reforms and privatized public utilities, European companies rushed in to grab up lucrative contracts for rebuilding Latin America's infrastructure. Spain's Telefonica de Espana has spent $5 billion buying phone companies in Brazil, Chile, Peru, and Argentina. European companies have moved rapidly into the private sector in Brazil, seven of the ten largest private companies are European owned, compared to two controlled by Americans. Among the notable European companies operating in Latin America are automotive giants Volkswagen and Fiat, the French supermarket chain Carrefours, and the Anglo-Dutch personal care products group Gessy-Lever.

As U.S. companies have watched Europeans make inroads in Latin America, they have pressured Washington to move more quickly on integrating Chile into NAFTA and toward Free Trade Area of the Americas. MERCOSUL doesn't represent only a huge domestic market of 220 million consumers; with its entire Pacific Coast beckoning toward Asia, MERCOSUL also stands to become an important low-cost platform for world export. Yet two groups in the United States—labor unions and environmentalists—are skeptical about the benefits of a Free Trade Area of the Americas. Union feel that NAFTA has already led to the exodus of manufacturing jobs to Mexico where wage rates are much lower. Environmentalists point out that companies unwilling to play by the strict rules of the U.S. Environmental Protection Agency relocate to Mexico, where pollution regulation has been lax.

Eighteen Pacific Rim countries, including the NAFTA member states, Japan and China, have been discussing the possible creation of a pan-Pacific free trade area under the auspices of the Asian Pacific Economic Cooperation forum (APEC). There are also active attempts at regional economic integration in the Caribbean, Southeast Asia, and parts of Africa. Yet, however much nations and regions integrate their trading policies and standards; each nation still has unique features that must be understood. A nation's readiness for different products and services and its attractiveness as a market to foreign firms depend on its economic, political-legal, and cultural environments.

14.2.2 Evaluating potential markets

Suppose a company has assembled a list of potential markets to enter. How does it choose among them? Many companies prefer to sell to neighboring countries because they understand these countries better, and they can control their costs better. It is not surprising that the United States' largest market is Canada, or that Swedish companies first sold to their Scandinavian neighbors. As growing numbers of U.S. companies expand abroad, many are deciding the best place to start is next door, in Canada. At other times, psychic proximity determines choices. Many U.S. firms prefer to sell in Canada, England, and Australia—rather than in larger markets such as Germany and France because they feel more comfortable with the language, laws and culture. In general, a company prefers to enter countries that rank high on market attractiveness; that are low in market risk; and in which the company possesses a competitive advantage.

14.3 Deciding how to enter the market

Once a company decides to target a particular country, it has to determine the best mode of entry. Its broad choices are indirect exporting, direct exporting, licensing, joint ventures and direct investment. These five market-entry strategies are shown in Figure 14.1. Each succeeding strategy involves more commitment, risk, control and profit potential.

14.3.1 Indirect export

The normal way to get involved in a foreign market is through export. Occasional

Chapter 14: International Marketing

exporting is a passive level of involvement in which the company exports from time to time, either on its own initiative or in response to unsolicited orders from abroad. Active exporting takes place when the company makes a commitment to expand its exports to a particular market. In either case, the company produces its goods in the home country and might or might not adapt them to the foreign market. Companies typically start with indirect exporting—that is, they work through independent intermediaries to export their product. There are four types of intermediaries: (1) Domestic-based export merchants buy the manufacturer's products and then sell them abroad. (2) Domestic-based export agents seek and negotiate foreign purchases and are paid a commission. Included in this group are trading companies. (3) Cooperative organizations carry on exporting activities on behalf of several producers and are partly under their administrative control. They are often used by producers of primary products such as fruits or nuts. (4) Export-management companies agree to manage a company's export activities for a fee. Indirect export has two advantages. First, it involves less investment. The firm does not have to develop an export department, an overseas sales force, or a set of foreign contacts. Second, it involves less risk. Because international-marketing intermediaries bring know-how and services to the relationship, the seller will normally make fewer mistakes.

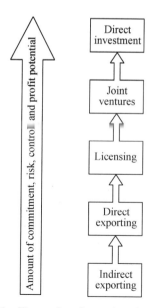

Figure 14.1 Five modes of entry into foreign markets

14.3.2 Direct exports

Companies eventually may decide to handle their own exports. The investment and risk are somewhat greater, but so is the potential return.

A company can carry on direct exporting in several ways:

First, Domestic-based export department or division: Might evolve into a self contained export department operating as a profit center.

Second, Overseas sales branch or subsidiary: The sales branch handles sales and distribution and might handle warehousing and promotion as well. It often serves as a display and customer service center.

Third, Traveling export sales representatives: Home-based sales representatives are sent abroad to find business.

Fourth, Foreign-based distributors or agents: These distributors and agents might be given exclusive rights to represent the company in that country or only limited rights.

Whether companies decide to export indirectly or directly, many companies use exporting as a way to "test the waters" before building a plant and manufacturing a product overseas. One of the best ways to initiate or extend export activities is by exhibiting at an overseas trade show. A U.S. software firm might show its product at an international software expo in Hong Kong. With the World Wide Web, it may not even be necessary to attend trade shows to show one's wares to overseas buyers and distributors. Electronic communication via the internet is extending the reach of companies, particularly small ones, to worldwide markets. The internet has become an effective means of everything from gaining free exporting information and guidelines, conducting market research and offering customers several time zones away a secure process for ordering and paying for products.

14.3.3 Licensing

Licensing is a simple way to become involved in international marketing. The licensor licenses a foreign company to use a manufacturing process, trademark, patent, trade secret, or other item of value for a fee or royalty. The licensor gains entry at little risk; the licensee gains production expertise or a well-known product or brand name. Licensing has some potential disadvantages. The licensor has less control over the licensee than if it had set up its own production and sales facilities.

Furthermore, if the licensee is very successful, the firm has given up profits; which the firm might have earned if it entered in that country on their own and if and when the contract ends, the company might find that it has created a competitor. To avoid this, the licensor usually supplies some proprietary ingredients or components needed in the product (as Coca-Cola does). But the best strategy is for the licensor to lead in innovation so that the licensee will continue to depend on the licensor.

There are several variations on a licensing arrangement. Companies such as Hyatt and Marriot sell management contracts to owners of foreign hotels to manage these businesses for a fee. The management firm may even be given the option to purchase some share in the managed company within a stated period.

Another variation is contract manufacturing, in which the firm hires local manufacturers to produce the product. Contract manufacturing has the drawback of giving the company less control over the manufacturing process and the loss of potential profits on manufacturing. However, it offers a chance to start faster, with less risk and with the opportunity to form a partnership or buy out the local manufacturer later.

Finally, a company can enter a foreign market through franchising, which is a more complete form a licensing. The franchiser offers a complete brand concept and operating system. In return, the franchisee invests in and pays certain fees to the franchiser. McDonald's KFC and Avis have entered scores of countries by franchising their retail concepts.

14.3.4 Joint ventures

Foreign investors may join with local investors to create a joint venture company in which they share ownership and control.

Forming a joint venture may be necessary or desirable for economic or political reasons. The foreign firm might lack the financial, physical, or managerial resources to undertake the venture alone. Or the foreign government might require joint ownership as a condition for entry. Even corporate giants need joint ventures to crack the toughest markets.

When it wanted to enter China's ice cream market, Unilever joined forces with Sumstar, a state-owned Chinese investment company. The venture's general manager says Sumstar's help with the formidable Chinese bureaucracy was crucial in getting a high tech ice cream plant up and running in just 12 months.

Joint ownership has certain drawbacks. The partners might disagree over investment, marketing, or other policies. One partner might want to reinvest earnings for growth, and the other partner might want to declare more dividends. The failure of the joint venture between AT&T and Olivetti was due to the companies' inability to agree on strategy. Furthermore, joint ownership can prevent a multinational company from carrying out specific manufacturing and marketing policies on a worldwide basis.

14.3.5 Direct investment

The ultimate form of foreign involvement is direct ownership of foreign-based assembly or manufacturing facilities. The foreign company can buy part or full interest in a local company or build its own facilities. If the foreign market appears large enough, foreign production facilities offer distinct advantages. First, the firm secures cost economies in the form of cheaper labor or raw materials, foreign-government investment incentives, and freight savings. Second, the firm strengthens its image in the host country because it creates jobs. Third, the firm develops a deeper relationship with government, customers, local suppliers, and distributors, enabling it to adapt its products better to the local environment. Fourth, the firm retains full control over its investment and therefore can develop manufacturing and marketing policies that serve its long-term international objectives. Fifth, the firm assures itself access to the market in case the host country starts insisting that locally purchased goods have domestic content.

The main disadvantage of direct investment is that the firm exposes a large investment to risks such as blocked or devalued currencies, worsening markets, or expropriation. The firm will find it expensive to reduce or close down its operations, because the host country might require substantial severance pay to the employees.

14.3.6 The internationalization process

Most countries lament that too few of their companies participate in foreign trade. This keep the country from earning sufficient foreign exchange to pay for needed imports. Many governments sponsor aggressive export-promotion programs to get their companies to export. These programs require a deep understanding of how companies become internationalized.

14.4 Deciding on the marketing program

International companies must decide how much to adapt their marketing strategy to local conditions. At one extreme are companies that use a globally standardized marketing mix worldwide. Standardization of the product, advertising and distribution channels promises the lowest costs. At the other extreme is an adapted marketing mix, where the producer adjusts the marketing-mix elements to each target market. Between the two extremes, many possibilities exist. Here we will examine potential adaptations that firms might make to their product, promotion, price, and distribution as they enter foreign markets.

14.4.1 Product

Keegan has distinguished five adaptation strategies of product and promotion to a foreign market (Figure 14.2).

		Product		
		Do not change product	Adapt product	Develop new product
Promotion	Do not change promotion	Straight extension	Product adaptation	Product invention
	Adapt promotion	Communication adaptation	Dual adaptation	

Figure 14.2   Five international product and promotion strategies

Straight extension means introducing the product in the foreign market without any change. Top management instructs its sales people: " Find customers for the product as it is. " However, the company should first determine whether foreign consumers use that product. Deodorant usage among men ranges from 80 percent in the United States to 55 percent in Sweden to 28 percent in Italy to 8 percent in the Philippines. In interviewing women in one country about how often they used a deodorant, a typical response was "I use it when I go dancing once a year", hardly grounds for introducing the product.

Straight extension has been successful with cameras, consumer electronics, and many machine tools. In other cases, it has been a disaster. Straight extension is tempting because it involves no additional R&D expense, manufacturing, retooling, or promotional modification. But it can be costly in the long run.

Product adaptation involves altering the product to meet local conditions or preferences. There are several levels of adaptation. A company can produce a regional version of its product, such as a Western European version. Finnish cellular phone superstar Nokia made its 1 100 series phone especially for India. Developers built in rudimentary voice recognition for Asia, where keyboards are a problem and raised the ring volume so the phone could be heard on crowded Asian streets.

Product invention consists of creating something new. It can take two forms, Backward invention is reintroducing earlier product forms that are well adapted to a foreign country's needs. Forward invention is creating a new product to meet a need in another country. There is an enormous need in less developed countries for low-cost, high-protein foods. Companies such as Quaker Oats, Swift, and Monsanto are researching these countries' nutrition needs, formulating new foods, and developing advertising campaigns to gain product trial and acceptance. In globalization's latest twist, American companies are not only inventing new products for overseas markets but also lifting products and ideas from their international operations and bringing them home. Product invention is a costly strategy, but the payoffs can be great, particularly if you can parlay a product innovation overseas into a new hit at home.

A growing part of international trade is taking place in services. The world market for services is growing at double the rate of world merchandise trade. Large firms in accounting, advertising, banking, communications, construction, insurance, law, management consulting, and retailing are pursuing global expansion. Arthur Andersen, American Express, Citicorp, Hilton, and Thomas Cook are known worldwide.

At the same time, many countries have erected entry barriers or regulations. Brazil requires all accountants to possess a professional degree from a Brazilian university. Many Western European countries want to limit the number of U.S. television programs and films shown in their countries. Many U.S. states bar foreign bank branches. At the same time, the United States is pressuring the Republic of Korea to open its markets to U.S. banks. The General Agreement of Tariffs and Trade (GATT) is pressing for more free trade in international services, but the progress is slow.

14.4.2 Promotion

Companies can run the same advertising and promotion campaigns used in the home market or change them for each local market, a process called communication adaptation. If it adapts both the product and the communication, the company engages in dual adaptation.

Consider the message. The company can change its message at four different levels. The company can use one message everywhere, varying only the language, name, and Colors. Exxon used "Put a tiger in your tank" with minor variations and gained international recognition. Colors might be changed to avoid taboos in some countries. Purple is associated with death in Burma and some Latin American nations; white is a mourning color in India; and green is associated with disease in Malaysia. Even names and headlines may have to be modified. When Clairol introduced the "Mist Stick", a curling iron, into Germany, it found that mist is slang for manure. Few Germans wanted to purchase a "manure stick". In Spain, Chevrolet's Nova translated as "it doesn't go".

The second possibility is to use the same theme globally but adapt the copy to each local market. For example, a Camay soap commercial showed a beautiful woman bathing. In Venezuela, a man was seen in the bathroom; in Italy and France, only a man's hand was seen; and in Japan, the man waited outside.

The third approach consists of developing a global pool of ads, from which each country selects the most appropriate one. Coca-cola and Goodyear use this approach. Finally, some companies allow their country managers to create country-specific ads-within guidelines, of course.

The use of media also requires international adaptation because media availability varies from country to country. Norway, Belgium, and France do not allow cigarettes and alcohol to be advertised on TV, Austria and Italy regulate TV advertising to children. Saudi Arabia does not want advertisers to use women in ads. India taxes advertising. Magazines vary in availability and effectiveness; they play a major role in Italy and a minor one in Austria. Newspapers have a national reach in the United Kingdom, but the advertiser can buy only local newspaper coverage in Spain.

Marketers must also adapt sales-promotion techniques to different markets. Greece prohibits coupons and France prohibits games of chance and limits premiums and gifts to 5 percent of product value. People in Europe and Japan tend to make inquiries via mail rather than phone—which may have ramifications for direct-mail and other sales-promotion campaigns. The result of these varying preferences and restrictions is that international companies generally assign sales promotion as a responsibility of local management.

14.4.3　Price

Multinationals face several pricing problems when selling abroad. They must deal with price escalation, transfer prices, dumping charges, and gray markets.

When companies sell their goods abroad, they face a price escalation problem. A Gucci handbag may sell for $120 in Italy and $240 in the United States. Why? Gucci has to add the cost of transportation, tariffs, importer margin, wholesaler margin, and retailer margin to its factory price. Depending on these added costs, as well as the currency-fluctuation risk; the product might have to sell for two to five times as much in another country to make the same profit for the manufacturer. Because the cost escalation varies from country to country, the question is how to set the prices in different countries.

If the company charges too high a price to a subsidiary, it may end up paying higher tariff duties, although it may pay lower income taxes in the foreign country. If the company charges too low a price to its subsidiary, it can be charged with dumping. Dumping occurs when a company charges either less than its costs or less than it charges in its home market, in order to enter or win a market. Zenith accused Japanese television manufacturers of dumping their TV sets on the U.S. market. When the U.S. Customers Bureau finds evidence of dumping, it can levy a dumping tariff on the guilty company. Various governments are watching for abuses and often force companies to charge the arm's-length price—that is, the price charged by other competitors for the same or a similar product.

Many multinational are plagued by the gray-market problem. A gray market occurs when the same product sells at different prices geographically. Dealers in the low-price country find ways to sell some of their products in higher-price countries, thus earning more.

Very often a company finds some enterprising distributors buying more than they can sell in their own country and reshipping goods to another country to take advantage of price differences. Multinationals try to prevent gray markets by policing the distributors, by raising their prices to lower-cost distributors, or by altering the product characteristics or service warranties for different countries.

In the European Union, the gray market may disappear altogether with the transition to a single currency unit. The adoption of the single currency by 11 countries will certainly reduce the amount of price differentiation. In 1998, a bottle of Gatorade, for instance, cost 3.5 European currency units (ECU) in Germany but only about 0.9 in Spain. Once consumers recognize price differentiation by country, companies will be forced to harmonize prices throughout the countries that have adopted the single currency. Companies and marketers that offer the most innovative, specialized, or necessary products or services will be least affected by price transparency.

The internet will also reduce price differentiation between countries. When companies sell their wares over the internet, price will become transparent as customers can easily find out how much products sell for in different countries. Take an on-line training course, for instance. Whereas the price of a classroom-delivered day of training can vary significantly from the United States to France to Thailand, the price of an on-line-delivered day of training would have to be similar.

Another global pricing challenge that has arisen in recent years is that countries with overcapacity, cheap currencies, and the need to export aggressively have pushed prices down and devalued their currencies. For multinational firms this poses challenges: Sluggish demand and reluctance to pay Niger prices make selling in these emerging markets difficult. Instead of lowering prices, and taking a loss, some multinationals have found more lucrative and creative means of coping.

14.4.4 Place (distribution channels)

Too many manufacturers think their job is done once the product leaves the factory. They should pay attention to how the product moves within the foreign country. They should take a whole-channel view of the problem of distributing products to final users, and ultimate user. In the first link, seller's international marketing headquarters, the export department or international division makes decisions on channels and other marketing-mix elements. The second link, channels between nations, gets the products to the borders of the foreign nation. The decisions made in this link include the types of intermediaries (agents, trading companies that will be used, the type of transportation air, sea), and the financing and risk arrangements. The third link, channels within foreign nations, gets the products from their entry point to final buyers and users.

14.5 Deciding on the marketing organization

Companies manage their international marketing activities in three ways: through export departments, international divisions, or a global organization.

14.5.1 Export department

A firm normally gets into international marketing by simply shipping out its goods. If its international sales expand, the company organize an export department consisting of a sales manager and a few assistants. As sales increase further, the export department is expanded to include various marketing services so that the company can go after business more aggressively. If the firm moves into joint ventures or direct investment, the export department will no longer be adequate to manage international operations.

14.5.2 International division

Many companies become involved in several international markets and ventures. Sooner or later they will create international divisions to handle all their international activity.

The international division is headed by a division president—who sets goals and budgets, and is responsible for the company's international growth. The international division's corporate staff consists of functional specialists who provide services to various operating units. Operating units can be organized in several ways. First, they can be geographical organizations. Reporting to the international division president might be regional vice presidents for North America, Latin America, Europe, Africa, the Middle East, and the Far East. Reporting to the regional vice president are country managers who are responsible for a sales force, sales branches, distributors, and licensees in the respective countries. Or the operating units may be world product groups, each with an international vice president responsible for world wide sales of each product group. The vice presidents may draw on corporate-staff area specialists for expertise on different geographical areas. Finally, operating units may be international subsidiaries, each headed by a president. The various subsidiary presidents report to the president of the international division.

14.5.3 Global organization

Several firms have become truly global organizations. Their top corporate management and staff plan worldwide manufacturing facilities, marketing policies, financial flows, and logistical systems. The global operating units report directly to the chief executive or executive committee, not to the head of an international division. Executives are trained in worldwide operations, not just domestic or international. Management is recruited from many countries; components and supplies are purchased where they can be obtained at the least cost; and investments are made where the anticipated returns are greatest.

These companies face several organizational complexities. For example, when pricing a company's mainframe computers to a large banking system in Germany, how much influence should be wielded by the headquarters product manager, by the company's market manager for the banking sector, and by the company's German country manager? Bartlett and Ghoshal have proposed circumstances under which different approaches work best. In their Managing Across Borders, they describe forces that favor "global integration" (e.g., capital-intensive production, homogeneous demand) versus "national responsiveness" (e.g., local standards and barriers, strong local preferences). They distinguish three organizational strategies:

First, A global strategy treats the world as a single market. This strategy is warranted when the forces for global integration are strong and the forces for national responsiveness are weak. This is true of the consumer electronics market, for example, where most buyers will accept a fairly standardized pocket radio, CD player or TV Matsushita has performed better than GE and Philips in the consumer electronics market because Matsushita operates in a more globally coordinated and standardized way.

Second, A multinational strategy treats the world as a portfolio of national opportunities. This strategy is warranted when the forces favoring national responsiveness are strong and the forces favoring global integration are weak. This is the situation in the branded packaged-goods business (food product cleaning products). Bartlett and Ghoshal cite Unilever as a better performer than Kao and P&G because Unilever grants more decision-making autonomy to its local branches.

Third, A "Global" strategy standardizes certain core elements and localizes other elements. This strategy makes sense for an industry (such as telecommunications) where each nation requires some adaptation of its equipment but the providing company can also standardize some of the core components. Bartlett and Ghoshal cite Ericsson as balancing these considerations better than NEC (too globally oriented) and ITT (too locally oriented).

Part Two: Questions

1. Explain how managing an offering may be different in international markets.

2. Why companies must conduct research before setting prices in international markets?

Part Three: Words and Phrases

1. standardize	规范
2. core component	核心部件
3. portfolio	组合
4. logistical	后勤
5. overcapacity	产能过剩
6. symbolic	符号
7. multinational firm	跨国公司
8. geographical	地理
9. lucrative	有利可图的
10. domestic	国内的
11. volatile	挥发性
12. capture	捕获
13. penetration	渗透
14. blunder	错误
15. implement	实施
16. integration-trading	整合交易
17. executive committee	执行委员会
18. global expansion	全球扩张
19. rudimentary	基本的
20. equipment	设备

Part Four: Further Reading

The term Green Marketing came into prominence in the late 1980s and early 1990s. The proceedings of this workshop resulted in one of the first books on green marketing entitled "Ecological Marketing".

The Corporate Social Responsibility (CSR) Reports started with the ice cream seller Ben & Jerry's where the financial report was supplemented by a greater view on the company's environmental impact. In 1987 a document prepared by the World Commission on Environment and Development defined sustainable development as meeting "the needs of the present without compromising the ability of future generations to meet their own need", this became known as the Brund and Report, and was another step towards widespread thinking on sustainability in everyday activity. Two tangible milestones for wave 1 of green marketing came in the form of published books, both of which were called Green Marketing. They were by Ken Peattie (1992) in the United Kingdom and by Jacquelyn Ottman (1993) in the United States of America.

According to Jacquelyn Ottman, (author of *The New Rules of Green Marketing: Strategies, Tools, and Inspiration for Sustainable Branding*) from an organizational standpoint, environmental considerations should be integrated into all aspects of marketing—new product development and communications and all points in between. The holistic nature of green also suggests that besides suppliers and retailers new stakeholders be enlisted, including educators, members of the community, regulators, and NGOs. Environmental issues should be balanced with primary customer needs.

The past decade has shown that harnessing consumer power to effect positive environmental change is far easier said than done. The so-called "green consumer" movements in the U.S. and other countries have struggled to reach critical mass and to remain in the forefront of shoppers' minds. While public opinion polls taken since the late 1980s have shown consistently that a significant percentage of consumers in the U.S. and elsewhere profess a strong willingness to favor environmentally conscious products and companies, consumers' efforts to do so in real life have remained sketchy at best. One of green marketing's challenges is the lack of standards or public consensus about what constitutes "green", according to Joel

Makower, a writer on green marketing. In essence, there is no definition of "how good is good enough" when it comes to a product or company making green marketing claims. This lack of consensus—by consumers, marketers, activists, regulators, and influential people—has slowed the growth of green products, says Makower, because companies are often reluctant to promote their green attributes, and consumers are often skeptical about claims.

  Despite these challenges, green marketing has continued to gain adherents, particularly in light of growing global concern about climate change.

References

[1] KOTLER P. Marketing management [M]. 10th Edition. Upper Saddle River: Prentice-Hall Inc., 2000.

[2] PRIDE, FERRELL. Marketing concepts and strategies [M]. New York: Houghton Mifflin Company, 1989.

[3] LEVITT T. Marketing intangible products and product intangibles[J]. Cornell Hospitality Quarterly, 1981, 22(2):37-44.

[4] DONALD F. KURATKO, RICHARD M H. Entrepreneurship—A contemporary approach[M]. Fort Worth: The Dryden press, San Diego: Harcourt Brace College Publishers.

[5] THOMAS W. ZIMMERER, NORMAN M. Entrepreneurship and new venture formation[M]. Upper Saddle River: Printice Hall, 1998.

[6] ROBERT D. HISRICH, MICHAEL P. Entrepreneurship[M]. New Delhi: McGraw Hill Publishing Company, 2001.

[7] VAN FLEET. Contemporary management [M]. Boston: Houghton Mifflin Company, 2010.

[8] MICHAEL E Porter. Competitive strategy: techniques for analyzing industries and competitors[M]. NewYork: Free Press, 1980.

[9] THOMAS V B. The marketircg edge: making strategies work[M]. New York: Free Press, 1985.

[10] FRED R David. Strategic management: concepts and cases[M]. 8th Edition. New York: South-Western, Division of Thomson Learning, 2010.

[11] FRASER P S. The Practice of Public Relations[M]. 8th Edition. 北京:清华大学出版社, 2001.

[12] COVER FIGURE. Marketing and brand strategy of the changde cigarette factory [J]. China's Foreign Trade. 2000(12):14-15.

[13] KOTLER P, KEVEN L K. Marketing management[M]. San Antonio : Pearson Education, 2008.

[14] RAISCH D W. The e-marketplace: strategies for success in B2B e-commerce [M]. 北京:北京理工大学出版社,2000.

[15] DAVID E A. Information systems project management[M]. New York: SAGE Publications,2008.

[16] MICHAEL R S. Consumer behavior[M]. 4th Edition. San Antonio : Pearson Education, 2008.

[17] LILIEN G L, KOTLER P, SRIDHAR M K. Marketing models[M]. Upper Saddle River:Prentice - Hall Inc. ,2006.

[18] KUMAR N, SCHEER L, KOTLER P. From market driven to market driving [J]. European Management Journal, 2000, 18(2): 129-142.

[19] SHAH N H, SHUKLA K T. Optimal production schedule in declining market for an imperfect production system [J]. International Journal of Machine Learning & Cybernetics, 2010, 1(1):89-99.

[20] HENKOFF R, SAMPLE A. Service is everybody's business[J]. Fortune, 1994.

[21] KOTLER P, PAUL N B. Marketing professional services[M]. Upper Saddle River:Prentice-Hall, 1984.

[22] TWEDT D W. How to plan new products, improve old ones, and create better advertising[J]. Journal of Marketing, 1969, 33(1):53-57.